TEEN GAMBLING

TEEN GAMBLING

Understanding a Growing Epidemic

Jeffrey L. Derevensky

ROWMAN & LITTLEFIELD PUBLISHERS, INC.
Lanham • Boulder • New York • Toronto • Plymouth, UK

Published by Rowman & Littlefield Publishers, Inc.
A wholly owned subsidiary of The Rowman & Littlefield Publishing Group, Inc.
4501 Forbes Boulevard, Suite 200, Lanham, Maryland 20706
www.rowman.com

10 Thornbury Road, Plymouth PL6 7PP, United Kingdom

British Library Cataloguing in Publication Information Available

Library of Congress Cataloging-in-Publication Data

Derevensky, Jeffrey L.
  Teen gambling : understanding a growing epidemic / Jeffrey Derevensky.
    p. cm.
  Summary: "In light of a growing epidemic of teen gambling, this book
provides a better understanding of the causes and extent of youth gambling
problems, assessment tools to identify teens with gambling addictions and
related issues, and strategies for the prevention and treatment of youth who
gamble"—Provided by publisher.
  ISBN 978-1-4422-0226-9 (cloth : alk. paper) — ISBN 978-1-4422-0228-3
(electronic)
  1. Teenage gamblers—Psychology. 2. Teenage gamblers—Social conditions.
3. Adolescent psychology. I. Title.
  HV6710.D47 2012
  362.2'5—dc23

                                                        2012007630

⊗™ The paper used in this publication meets the minimum requirements of
American National Standard for Information Sciences—Permanence of Paper
for Printed Library Materials, ANSI/NISO Z39.48-1992.

Printed in the United States of America

Dedicated to Lynette
my wife, companion, and friend

CONTENTS

ACKNOWLEDGMENTS

I am grateful to my many colleagues too numerous to mention who have repeatedly helped in so many ways and have dedicated themselves to the scholarly investigations and pursuits that helped form the foundation for this book. To Dr. Durand Jacobs, Dr. Henry Lesieur, Dr. Howard Shaffer, Dr. Mark Griffiths, and Dr. Harold Wynne, true pioneers in the field of gambling studies, thank you for your support and many valuable suggestions over the years. I wish to especially thank Dr. Rina Gupta, my friend and colleague, for her many years of collaborative work and profound research and clinical insights.

I would like to also thank the many staff members, graduate and post-doctoral students, and research assistants who played an essential role in helping guide our research toward establishing the determinants of problem gambling. For over two decades the entire staff at the International Centre for Youth Gambling Problems and High-Risk Behaviors at McGill University has been dedicated and has worked tirelessly in helping foster our understanding of adolescent gambling behavior. These committed professionals have provided invaluable expertise in our many research projects and the development of our award-winning prevention programs and have been instrumental in shaping our treatment initiatives. Without their help much of the centre's activities and accomplishments could not have been realized.

I am particularly grateful to my wife, Lynette, who spent many hours and weekends diligently working on editing multiple versions of this book, identifying strengths and weaknesses, and providing invaluable support. Without her support, insight, and encouragement, this book would never have been completed. To Victoria, my daughter, who also sacrificed family time during this project, I wish to extend my thanks for her support.

For over twenty years my colleagues and I have tried to dedicate our research and prevention and treatment programs toward helping individuals in need and impacting social policy. I am grateful to the many youth who not only participated in our research and clinical projects but who helped provide me with great insight into this addiction.

PREFACE

Never before in our history have we witnessed such an explosion of worldwide gambling opportunities. The national and international expansion of regulated and traditional forms of gambling as well as increased non-traditional forms of gambling are indicative of a major shift toward society's general acceptance of gambling as a legitimate form of recreation and entertainment. The perception of gambling as one of sin and vice has been transformed by the industry and our governments. Once unthinkable, governments have tempered their attitudes toward the expansion of gambling venues and the inclusion of technologically based gambling opportunities. Gambling is now considered an important source of revenue, an opportunity for increased employment, and a socially acceptable leisure activity. Today, in many jurisdictions one does not have to travel far to get to a casino, locate a convenience store where lottery products can be purchased, or find a venue in which there are electronic gambling machines. One can even access multiple forms of gambling via one's laptop, Tablet, or smart phone over the Internet.

Gambling, once thought to be strictly an adult activity, has become an increasingly popular pastime among adolescents. Whether engaged in wagering on games of personal skill, poker among friends, purchasing lottery tickets, playing electronic gambling machines, sports wagering, or participating in casino-type games, gambling's popularity among the young is on the rise. There is clear unequivocal evidence that large numbers of young people, many of whom are under the legal age to gamble at regulated revenues, remain actively involved and engaged in almost all forms of regulated and unregulated gambling activities, in spite of legal prohibitions.

During the past two decades, we have witnessed an unprecedented growth in gambling opportunities and easily accessible venues. In light of the perceived economic gains, governments once strongly opposed to gambling's expansion have succumbed to the will of the people. The glitz and glamour once only found in Las Vegas, Atlantic City, and Monaco can be found in countless states and countries. Gambling remains among the fastest growing industries in the world, with global revenues exceeding all forms of entertainment—movies, videogames, and music combined.

The rise and proliferation of gambling has not been without concomitant associated problems. While the American Psychiatric Association and the World Health Organization have both identified pathological gambling as a recognized psychiatric disorder, there is a common misconception that this disorder is relegated only to adults and not to adolescents. Yet prevalence study after prevalence study, independent of the type of instrument used for screening, points to the excessively high prevalence rates of gambling problems among adolescents and young adults. Prevalence rates among adolescents are surprisingly between two and four times that of adults, while those aged 18-25 exhibit the highest prevalence of problem gambling among the adult population.

Adolescence as a developmental stage is often fraught with a number of potentially risky behaviors, be it alcohol and substance use, drinking and driving, eating disorders, unprotected sex, or excessive videogame playing. Thus it is not unreasonable to think that youth would also be at high risk for developing gambling-related problems. In spite of the seriousness of gambling-related problems, adolescents still profess that they can stop gambling at any time and view themselves as invulnerable and invincible. The allure of gambling, the thrill and excitement, the provocative advertisements, and the adrenaline rush so often accompanying gambling propels adolescents to continue to gamble in spite of repeated losses and accompanying negative consequences. This is further compounded by parents and teachers who fail to find youth gambling problematic. Yet, despite our growing knowledge concerning youth gambling behavior, few prevention programs exist within our schools, and many treatment programs remain adult-focused.

Gambling and problem gambling among our adolescents have been masked and overshadowed by more visible problems including substance and alcohol abuse, smoking, teenage suicide, and HIV. This has led some clinicians and researchers to suggest that gambling may be a hidden or invisible addiction. Its detection is difficult—you cannot see it in their eyes, smell it on their breath, or assess problem gambling through a urine sample or blood test. Yet, all the research and clinical evidence suggest that a gambling problem can be as debilitating and problematic as any other addiction with both severe short-term and long-term negative consequences.

A gambling problem is a progressive disorder with a complex etiology. While different pathways toward problem gambling are explored in this book it is nevertheless important to note that problem gamblers do not constitute a homogeneous group but rather differ in many ways. This complexity has led us to incorporate a multifactorial biopsychosocial model in trying to explain gambling behaviors and their trajectory toward problem gambling. While there is some research suggesting it may take an adult approximately seven years from the onset of gambling to develop a serious gambling problem, our youth are doing it in greater numbers and more quickly. This disorder typically results in disrupted relationships, mental health issues, interpersonal problems, financial difficulties, and increased legal and judicial problems.

To highlight the severity of this problem, the following abridged excerpt is from a former pathological gambler who began gambling at a very early age who describes the impact on his life:

> To quote Mick and the Stones [Mick Jagger and the Rolling Stones], please allow me to introduce myself. My name is John, or Richard, or Steven, or Betty, or Patricia, Miguel or Dwayne, Pierre or Gabriella, Mohammed or Cheng-Li. Gamblers are men, women, Chinese, Jewish, white, black. You get my point.

In less than a month I will be celebrating my 35th birthday. Actually, celebrating is probably not the most accurate choice of words to use. There's no joy in Mudville today.[1] Casey flailed at a curve ball low and away. His helmet flew off his head. He managed to catch it in his hands as he corkscrewed his body into the ground and fell in a heap. Strike three. Game over. Not pretty.

Two weeks ago I moved out of the home I shared with my then girlfriend of a year and a half. I have moved into the extra bedroom of my parents' apartment. I am in debt. I am unemployed right now, not as a direct result of my gambling addiction but it certainly played a large part in it. I am angry, sad, confused, relieved, frustrated, nervous, and hopeful. For the first time in my life I can see a future, my future.

For the better part of twenty years I have been living with a secret so debilitating that it has rendered me paralyzed. Only my immediate family knew of my gambling problem, but even they didn't realize how bad it was. When I got into trouble, they thought I had stopped. Then I lied. I hid my situation from them, from my friends, from my boss, from my girlfriends, and from the woman I wanted to spend the rest of my life with. She doesn't appear to be in my future. The tears don't seem to wash away all the hurt.

When you have lived your life in darkness and despair, when you have lied to those you love more than you love yourself, when you live day after day fully aware of the magnitude of the problem and yet you are unwilling or unable or too weak to do anything about it, that's a gambling problem. —Tom

Youth gambling represents a potentially serious public policy and health issue. While the research and our understanding of adolescent gambling problems have increased dramatically over the past several decades, there is still much that is unknown. Unlike other forms of addictive behavior (e.g., alcohol or substance use), gambling activities are constantly evolving. Who would have thought ten years ago that people would be gambling in such huge numbers over the Internet or that the number of states and countries with casinos would be so prolific, that in virtually any location you can turn on the television in the evening and see some championship poker tournaments, or that massive numbers of individuals would be willing to spend $10,000 as the entrance fee for the opportunity to be the next World Champion of Poker.

This book will help place gambling within a historical context, explore our current understanding of the determinants of adolescent gambling and problem gambling, provide strategies to assess problem gambling, examine the impact of technological changes on gambling behaviors, identify strategies for the prevention of youth gambling problems, and suggest ways in which we can help adolescents suffering with a gambling problem. In an effort to help stem the growing epidemic of problem gambling, our governments need to adopt and enforce tighter regulatory controls while moving forward toward the development of more effective harm-minimization strategies and responsible policies.

Our increased understanding of the trajectory of gambling behaviors, ways to screen youth, and programs to help prevent potential gambling-related problems from emerging will ultimately help minimize the numbers of youth and adults with this disorder. I remain confident that our governments and industry leaders will develop and implement responsible policies toward youth gambling and stem this epidemic and growing tide of problem gambling.

NOTE

1. *Casey at the Bat: A Ballad of the Republic Sung in the Year 1888* is a baseball poem written in 1888 by Ernest Lawrence Thayer and initially published in the *San Francisco Examiner* on June 3, 1888. In the poem, a baseball team from the fictional town of Mudville (implied to be the home team) is losing by two runs with two outs and two players on base in their last inning. Both the team and its fans believed "if only" they could somehow get "Mighty Casey" (Mudville's star player) up to bat they would have a chance of winning.

1

GAMBLING: AN INTRODUCTION AND HISTORICAL PERSPECTIVE

The landscape of gambling has been dramatically altered during the past twenty years. Never before in our history have gambling opportunities been so easily accessible and readily available. The widespread legalization of multiple forms of gambling, on an international level, remains unprecedented. The glitz, glamour, and excitement once only found in Nevada (Las Vegas and Reno) and Atlantic City have transcended state and national borders. Multibillion dollar mega resorts abound around the globe and are continuing to be developed. State after state, country after country, see vast opportunities for increased tourism, economic growth, employment, and increased governmental revenues. Gambling, which was once legal in only certain select jurisdictions, is now omnipresent, from the corner convenience store where one can purchase lottery tickets, to enhanced horse tracks now referred to as "racinos" (combining horse tracks, electronic gambling machines, and often certain types of casino games), to electronic gambling machine parlors, casinos, and now Internet and mobile wagering (using smart phones). Gambling revenues in Macau, a small island and former Portuguese colony currently housing a strip of casinos off the coast of China and Hong Kong, have revenues that have surpassed and quadrupled those of Las Vegas, with the two destination casinos in Singapore not far behind. In North and South America, Europe, Australasia, and Asia, a burgeoning industry has emerged with few signs of abating.

Gambling remains among the fastest growing industries globally, a multibillion dollar worldwide business generating enormous revenues that play an ever increasingly important role for corporations, investors, and governments. As the world economy has suffered, legislators around the globe believe that establishing and/or increasing gambling operations will help ease their financial burdens and increase employment. Jurisdictions and countries once previously strongly opposed to gambling have succumbed to the will of the people and the lure of the potential lucrative sources of revenues. Televised poker tournaments abound with well-known celebrities endorsing and promoting Internet gambling tournaments and websites. With names like PokerStars, Party Poker, Full Tilt Poker, and Unibet, a new arena has opened for gambling. While not recession-proof, the industry has continued to grow and develop at an unbelievably rapid rate. State after state has proposals for increasing the number of gambling venues and the types of gambling permissible. Technological advances have brought multiple forms of gambling directly into the home through Internet and mobile wagering sites. Even in jurisdictions where specific forms of gambling or certain types of gambling are prohibited, vast numbers of opportunities to gamble still exist.

For most individuals, gambling for money remains an enjoyable form of entertainment and a socially acceptable recreational pastime. However, for some individuals, what begins as an enjoyable, relatively benign activity can escalate into a problem with serious social, emotional, interpersonal, physical, financial, and legal ramifications.

Since the beginning of civilization, people have been wagering on the outcome of events that are uncertain. Gambling was well known to the Babylonians, Etruscans, Romans, Greeks, and Chinese. Some famous Roman emperors—Augustus, Caligula, and Nero—were reported to be avid gamblers. Our early literature and ancient art had many examples of gambling as was evident in the writings of Homer, Chaucer, and Shakespeare.

The history of gambling includes royalty: kings and queens (not only on face cards), knights, noblemen, politicians, clergymen, pirates, and commoners alike. While some have suggested that gambling is the *Devil's* invention (Plato went as far as to suggest that a demon, Theuth, created dice), most view it as an enjoyable recreational pastime. The evolution of gambling, or "gaming" as it is often more recently referred to, has seen many twists and turns.

The mystique surrounding gambling has been accompanied by many prominent and not so prominent players. In England, King Henry VIII once lost the largest and most famous church bells, the Jesus Bells that were hanging in the tower of St. Paul's Cathedral, in a dice game. American gangsters, Bugsy Siegel, Lucky Luciano, and Meyer Lansky, were famous for turning the desert town of Las Vegas into a gambling mecca while the wealthy were frequenting Monte Carlo and developing this small state into a gambling resort for the European rich and famous. Not to be outdone, today's sports celebrities, musicians, and Hollywood entertainers have become the new "high rollers" alongside politicians and successful entrepreneurs.

Gambling's history is replete with great stories and folklore; gunfights over poker tables in the Old West, wars, organized crime families' control and infiltration of casinos, with thrilling, daring robberies and exploits, and even great disasters. There are reports that the great Chicago fire of 1871, which destroyed much of the city, may have been the result of a game of dice. While folklore has it that Mrs. O'Leary was busy milking her cow one evening and the cow accidentally kicked over the lantern which started the Chicago fire in her barn, she later testified in court that she had not been in the barn that evening at all but rather was sound asleep in her bedroom. Some seventy years later, a wealthy Chicago entrepreneur, Louis Cohn, left a bequest to Northwestern University accompanied by a document admitting that he and not Mrs. O'Leary's cow was responsible for knocking over the lantern that resulted in the devastating Chicago fire. He reportedly admitted to accidentally knocking over the lantern in a moment of great excitement while shooting dice with some friends in the barn. His only explanation: "I was winning."

Hollywood, capitalizing upon the American psyche, has produced numerous popular gambling-themed movies (e.g., *Casino,*

Twenty-One, Bugsy, Ocean's Eleven, Ocean's Twelve, Ocean's Thirteen, Rounders, and *The Hustler*), not to mention nearly all of the James Bond movies have some gambling-related theme. Seated at the baccarat table is the debonair James Bond, with his martini, stirred not shaken, and beautiful women. Television programs in North America have similarly incorporated the glamorous backdrop of Las Vegas as an added enticement. Shows like *Vegas* and *CSI-Las Vegas* use gambling resorts and casinos as a backdrop and a way of attracting viewers. Some critics have gone as far as to suggest that these television shows are really only 60-minute advertisements for gambling resorts.

Gambling has become so normalized in our society that lottery scratch tickets often are based on cartoon characters (e.g., Betty Boop, Beetle Bailey, Flintstones, Jetsons), children's games (Monopoly, Twister, Battleship, Scrabble, Clue, Yahtzee), successful television shows (*Deal or No Deal),* and movies (*Indiana Jones*), with opportunities to win children's toys (Xbox), iPods, luxurious motorcycles, bicycles, boats or cars, tickets to Olympic events, as well as large sums of money. Located in many toy and department stores you can find handheld poker, bingo, blackjack, and Texas Hold'em electronic games. Other "games," often found in toy stores, include roulette wheels and poker chips. One can even find music CDs to listen to while gambling. Poker can be made more enjoyable listening to Kenny Rogers singing *The Gambler,* Lady Gaga singing *Poker Face,* or Elvis Presley crooning *Viva Las Vegas.* Chocolate candies shaped as casino chips and cards are readily available for your sweetheart (Walmart recently sold a Valentine's box shaped like a heart which read "Sweetheart, You're the Real Deal" with chocolates in the shape of cards and chips inside). If one searches on ebay.com and types in the word "poker," almost 80,000 items are listed daily. In Macau, they have structures on children's playgrounds that resemble a roulette wheel, and in many toy departments one can find "Professional Gambler and Dealer" kits. You can purchase gambling software games for Nintendo's Wii, Microsoft's Xbox, or Sony's PlayStation. The logos for PokerStars are as readily identifiable to today's teens as Mickey Mouse and Disneyland are recognizable to children.

To trace the origins of music, medicine, and prayer is difficult if not impossible because they predate our written historical accounts. Many historians would argue that this is similarly true for gambling. Today's historians who study the origins of gambling contend that gambling was available even before money and currency existed. Since recorded history, people were often willing to risk their personal possessions in order to win someone else's possessions. As such, the notion of "risk taking," as an integral component of gambling, can be traced back to our earliest ancestors. Initially, such early forms of gambling appeared to be related more to religion than recreation and entertainment.

During the past century, gambling has undergone a profound transformation in the types of games available, its widespread social acceptance, its accessibility, and its appeal. Once regarded as economically marginal, politically corrupt, and morally disdainful, it has now become widely adopted as a socially acceptable form of entertainment and a significant revenue generator for both the industry (now large corporations with holdings in many multinational properties) and governments. Within the past two decades, we have witnessed an unprecedented and enormous increase in the variety of gambling opportunities around the world. Casinos previously owned and operated by organized crime families in North America have been replaced by boards of directors of multinational corporations listed on the stock exchange. In short, gambling has become more popular than ever. Our games of chance have continued to evolve over centuries, changing, maturing, and adapting to technological advances and consumer demands.

While the growth of the gambling industry has helped the economy through the creation of employment and tourism opportunities and with governments being eager to generate new and increased revenues without direct taxation of its citizens, there is growing evidence that the expansion and proliferation of gambling has not come without ensuing social costs and problems. Gambling, once perceived to be an adult activity, has similarly been adopted by today's youth as an exciting, recreational, and entertaining pastime. While scholars and politicians continue to debate the wisdom of its proliferation and the concomitant economic benefits and social costs associated with gambling's expansion, there is little doubt that there are a growing number of individuals who have been negatively impacted as a result of their excessive gambling. Such human costs associated with problematic gambling permeate every aspect of an individual's life. For some, what begins as an enjoyable activity can quickly escalate into a myriad of problems: financial, social, psychological, interpersonal, familial, physical, and legal. In extreme cases, individuals have committed suicide as the result of massive gambling debts and associated mental health disorders.

The past decade has witnessed not only unprecedented growth in the gambling industry but has also generated a significant increase in research designed to better help our understanding of typical gambling patterns, problem gambling behaviors, ways to help minimize gambling-related problems, and strategies and techniques to help individuals afflicted with this disorder. Such research has enabled us to provide more scientific, empirically driven prevention and treatment programs while at the same time helping to better inform social policy.

A BRIEF HISTORY OF THE EVOLUTION OF GAMBLING

While most parts of the ancient world and historical artifacts point to some form of gambling, many of today's games (excluding the technology to deliver them) have their roots and underpinnings among the ancient Mediterranean people, in particular the Greeks and Romans. The earliest records of gambling seem to suggest a popular game focused on predicting "odds and evens." David Schwartz, in his comprehensive historical account of gambling, suggests that there is early evidence for many of our current forms of gambling in ancient texts and among early African tribes. Gambling in its infancy was often associated with religious beliefs and practices. While the specific religious details and customs varied across cultural groups, religious leaders often poured water over a number of elements to help their followers answer important questions. If the number of objects getting wet was even, the best answer to the person's question was yes. If the number was odd, then the appropriate answer to the question was no. This very primitive and crude form of gambling ultimately led to the development of modern day dice games, which could then be used to help individuals try to answer or predict outcomes. The Romans preferred calling the tossing of a coin "head or ship" rather than "heads or tails" as their coins had the head of the god Janus on one side, while the other side had a picture of a Roman galley. The Greeks preferred the terms "day and night" because their coins had both white (representing day) and black (suggesting night) sides.

DICE GAMES AND "CRAPS"

A number of early archeological sites throughout Europe, the Mediterranean, and the Near East have uncovered replicas of modern dice shaped from sheep knucklebones (often referred to as "bones"), with many historians suggesting that this could in fact represent an early form of dice or craps playing. Later versions had the "dice" made from stone, wood, amber, and even animal and human teeth. The Romans appeared to have experimented with five- or eight-sided dice rather than the typical six-sided cubical dice used today. They even unsuccessfully experimented with other shapes, including pyramids, which proved to be unpopular.

Many early works of art found in the excavations of the ancient ruins of Pompeii depicted Roman soldiers playing games of dice. History suggests that dice playing was a significant problem for soldiers who became so preoccupied with gambling that they reportedly neglected their responsibilities and duties. King Richard the Lion Hearted in 1190 became so upset with his soldiers' dice playing that he issued an order restricting games of dice among his troops. And, when the Europeans arrived in America, the early settlers found the Iroquois playing a game called "hubbub" consisting of dice.

Today's dice games, sometimes referred to as "craps," remain extremely popular in North America and can be found in almost every casino. It is interesting to note that dice games were prohibited in Canadian casinos under regulations of the Criminal Code of Canada until fairly recently. The Canadian Criminal Code was ultimately modified to accommodate patrons of casinos bordering the United States in an effort to compete with American casinos.

Today's game of craps includes a relatively complex sets of rules based on laws of mathematical probabilities. Unless someone is cheating, players using a pair of today's dice (a six-sided cube with numbers [dots] of one through six) may roll thirty-six different combinations of numbers. This game is known to result in considerable excitement, with players yelling and praying for certain numbers to come up on the dice. In most casinos, the game of craps is the only game in which dice are used. While gambling can occur on other games that use dice, for example Monopoly or backgammon, these games are rarely found in modern casinos. It is interesting to note that dice games, while very popular in North America, have not proved to be as popular in Australasia among certain cultural groups.

POKER AND CARD PLAYING

While dice playing has some very early historical roots, other forms of gambling similarly grew in popularity. In particular, card playing, which traces its roots back to the sixth century, represented a different type of gambling activity. Still today, gambling on a variety of card games remains very popular.

Early historical records point to the use of playing cards having evolved from games found in Korea and China. Other reports suggest Venice or Spain may have been the birthplace of card playing, given that the Spaniards and Venetians were insatiable card players. Unlike today's glossy paper cards, these early cards were made from oiled silk, were considerably larger and wider, were more cumbersome, and contained eight suits, with ten cards per suit, for a total of eighty cards. These cards included suits that consisted of a man, fish, crow, pheasant, antelope, star, rabbit, and horse. Tarot cards, used for telling one's fortune, appeared during the sixth century and were also used for gambling by both men and women. Other parts of Europe and Asia began to use their own variations of cards. Historians have even suggested that Marco Polo may have brought playing cards back with him from his voyages to China. Nevertheless, during the fifteenth century, France became Europe's leading manufacturer of playing cards.

Today's modern cards most likely came from Italy, where fifty-two cards form the deck, using the current four suits. The cards were numbered from one through ten, plus three "court" cards—a king, a knight (*cavallo*), and a foot soldier (*fante*). Card games quickly became popular among the social elite in Italy. In France, the cards were printed in two colors, red and black, with the designations on the cards representative of the four classes of French society: hearts represented the church (indicative of the heart of the community); spades (originally called spears) were the symbol of the army; diamonds represented the wealth of the merchant class; and clubs were representative of the farmers and peasants (a number of theories suggested that farmers may have shaped their fields in the depiction of a club while some have argued that peasants were so poor they could not afford to have swords and thus used clubs as weapons when they were needed). French card makers preferred to produce cards that had uniform designs while the English wanted to ensure that the cards could be read from either end. Even in the 1300s, employers and the clergy began to see evidence that people had become so preoccupied with card playing that it interfered with their lives and work. The two vices that accompanied such playing were primarily focused on the wasting of both time and money. With the advent and popularity of card playing came a number of very early prohibitions during the late 1300s and early 1400s. In 1397, card playing became prohibited in France on working days, in 1423 St. Bernard of Siena, an Italian monk, denounced card playing as "an invention of the devil," and a royal decree in 1495 in England prohibited servants and apprentices from card playing except during the Christmas holiday period. This early notion of the prohibition of gambling would again resurface numerous times throughout history even to the present day.

Both commoners and nobility enjoyed card playing. King Henry IV reportedly became "cured of his gambling problem" only after losing a vast sum of money in a card game. Politically, cards were thought to have had a role in the American Revolution. In the early days of the American colonies, thousands of sets of playing cards were imported from England with a special tax levied on each deck of cards. This acquired tax money was reported to have been used to help fund the American Revolution. Among the American patriots, it was rumored that George Washington, Thomas Jefferson, and Benjamin Franklin were all avid gamblers and loved playing cards.

During the sixteenth century, the more formal study of mathematics evolved and mathematicians began to examine the concept of chance events using probability theory and models. While the Greeks continued to appeal to their gods, such as Tyche, goddess of fortune, and the Romans relied on Fortuna, some individuals proficient in what can be best termed probability theory began to use their understanding of the laws of probability to become "professional gamblers" ultimately trying to make their living from gambling. Playing cards also seemed to have a multi-dimensional use in the early colonial days of America, with the Colonists using the backs of playing cards as invitations to afternoon teas and society balls. In 1765, playing cards were also reportedly used as admission to classes at the University of Pennsylvania.

Poker playing is thought to have emanated from a French card game *poque* during the fourteenth century and has been popular ever since its inception. Today's version of poker appeared in the United States during the latter part of the eighteenth century and early part of the nineteenth century. It quickly became the pre-eminent game during the United States' early history and has been popular with adults and children alike. Today, due to televised tournaments, its popularity and growth has been unparalleled,

In the eighteenth century, gambling houses proliferated throughout the original thirteen states. Professional card players began to emerge, with some being less than honest. As more and more games grew in popularity, more cheats and professional gamblers seemed to have emerged. Gamblers began to take on colorful roles as the

United States expanded westward. James Butler Hickok, better known as "Wild Bill" Hickok, typifies the history of the "Old West." Ever present at the card table, there he was with a deck of cards in his hand, a bottle of whiskey on the table, and a gun in his holster. Unfortunately, Wild Bill's luck ran out one day when he was shot dead during a poker game. Killings during gambling disputes permeated the Wild West. If someone lost while playing cards, he could always call his opponent a cheat and shoot him. Legends quickly grew and individuals became equally known for their card playing prowess as well as their shooting ability. Card cheaters were dealt with swiftly and harshly, often ending up on the floor underneath the poker table.

Even in its early days, poker was played at all levels of society. Some of the American founding fathers, George Washington, Thomas Jefferson, and Benjamin Franklin, all enjoyed the game. In fact, the 44th President of the United States, Barack Obama, is said to very much enjoy playing poker. Famous Hollywood celebrities (e.g., Ben Affleck, Matt Damon, Jason Alexander), and sports stars (e.g., Michael Jordan, Charles Barkley) have been known to enthusiastically endorse and engage in poker playing for large sums of money. The Poker Players Alliance, an American nonprofit interest group, was formed in 2005 to provide a united front to promote poker and protect players' rights. This group, headed by Alfonse D'Amato, former senator from New York State, claims to have over a million members and represents the more than 20 million Americans who enjoy playing poker. While there has been much debate over whether or not poker is truly gambling or a game of skill (some even claim it is a sport because it is televised on sports networks and specialty channels), there is little doubt that its popularity has been dramatically enhanced by the increase and popularity of a number of Internet gambling sites (PokerStars, Party Poker, Absolute Poker, Full Tilt Poker, etc.), high stakes poker tournaments, and the expanded coverage of poker on sports television networks throughout the world. An entire new generation of youth can view their favorite players competing on television. What is remarkably different is that the current generation of players is considerably younger than in the past. These youth wear wrap-around sunglasses, baseball caps turned backwards, hoodies, jeans, and earrings. Not your typical old-time poker player.

The World Series of Poker (WSOP) is a world-renowned series of poker tournaments, ultimately ending in the final championship being played in Las Vegas (a similar championship is held in Europe by the World Series of Poker Europe, which began in 2007). The winner of the tournament receives a coveted gold and diamond bracelet and a monetary prize based on the number of entrants. This "Super Bowl" of poker has seen the number of participants continue to grow to record levels. The idea for the World Series event began in 1969 with an event called the Texas Gambling Reunion, an invitational event held among the best poker players in the world. The WSOP buy-in (the registration required for participation in the event) is $10,000, with the last two event winners in 2009 (Joe Cada) and 2010 (Jonathan Duhamel) both being under 21 years of age, college dropouts, and winning in excess of $8.5 million. In 2010, 7,319 entrants tried their luck and skill to walk away with the top prize. The widespread television coverage, and poker's enormous popularity along with the large number of Internet gambling sites offering tournaments has actually prompted casinos to vastly expand their poker rooms. Casinos tend not to prefer poker as they do not make a significant amount of money directly from the game but rather anticipate that poker players are gamblers and will gamble on other games while in their casino.

To help better "train" players, a videogame based on the tournament, titled the *World Series of Poker,* was released for several game and computer platforms. A sequel, *World Series of Poker: Tournament of Champions* was released in 2006 and the *World Series of Poker 2008: Battle for the Bracelets* has been subsequently released. The popularity of this event prompted the organizers to hold a World Series of Poker Academy (a poker school aimed at providing poker players with the skills required to "win a WSOP bracelet") and the Arizona Lottery has a scratch lottery ticket associated with the World Series of Poker. Go online at ebay.com and enter poker and you will find a plethora of poker-related items. From poker tables to chips with your picture on it, professional dealer kits, cards, clothing to wear when playing poker to help psych out your opponents, poker-related jewelry and charms, DVDs, educational books, poker skeleton figurines, cuff links, pitchers, glasses, and vases, just to name a few. In local toy stores you can purchase handheld poker and Texas Hold'em machines and, as previously noted, you can buy chocolates shaped as cards and poker chips and have special "poker" music. The widely popular series of books "for Dummies" has a number of gambling-related books including *Poker for Dummies* and *Texas Hold'em for Dummies*.

Poker's extreme appeal and popularity among youth prompted a group of entrepreneurs from the United States to attempt to hold a summer camp in 2006 for children ages 10-14 and 15-18 in Toronto, New York, Chicago, Miami, Las Vegas, Los Angeles, and Vancouver to "Teach Kids the Correct Way to Play Texas Hold'em." The program was billed as a two-day camp (one and a half days of training and a half day tournament) that was reported to be led by "top industry professionals in a safe and controlled environment." They purported that children would learn the intricacies of the game and important life skills including communication and social interaction, good sportsmanship, math and number-related skills, and how to perform after adversity. It was suggested that through well-rehearsed poker strategies these children would develop and enhance their analytical thinking, gain insight into personal limits and self-control, understand the risks and reward scenarios associated with poker playing, and acquire knowledge about the potential pitfalls of gambling and important preventive measures.

The normalization of poker has continued to expand. Adolescents admit playing poker for money with their parents and relatives, while some even report that their parents encourage them to hold poker tournaments and poker parties in their homes. Poker rooms have been widely advertising the availability of their venues in college newspapers and purchasing advertising space in school agendas and calendars. On many college campuses, fraternities and sororities regularly hold Texas Hold'em tournaments and it is not uncommon to see "charitable tournaments" to raise funds for worthy causes being widely advertised and very well attended.

With the introduction of televised poker, especially the World Series of Poker, its popularity has skyrocketed and poker currently exceeds all forms of gambling via the Internet. Land-based casinos have witnessed this explosion and have dramatically increased the number of tournaments and poker tables. Today, poker ranks among the most favorite forms of gambling. It has a strong cross-cultural following and is growing in popularity among both women and men internationally. Newer forms of poker can also be seen in casinos, such as *pai-gow poker*.

Other forms of games using cards are also popular. Today's version of Blackjack, typically referred to as "twenty-one," was thought to have begun in France where it was called *vingt-et-un*, and originated in the mid-fifteenth century from an earlier game called thirty-one. Its popularity actually rose when "card counting" became popular in the 1960s. Today, while not as popular in Asia as America, Blackjack still remains a favorite game in most land-based casino operations as well as many Internet gambling sites. Baccarat, a favorite of the French nobility and Asians, has its origins dating back to the seventeenth century. Its popularity grew in Monte Carlo and the French Riviera casinos during the early twentieth century and was made infamous by the immortal James Bond. Other card games remain in development. Such games must be attractive, interesting, and exciting, but most of all the odds must be in the casino's favor before they are ever implemented.

ROULETTE

In Europe, gambling spas, gaming towns, and new games began to emerge and grew in popularity during the later part of the seventeenth century and early part of the eighteenth century. Roulette, often referred to as "black and red," became extremely popular, with reports suggesting that it created as much of a craze as playing cards had a few centuries earlier. Empress Catherine the Great reportedly had multiple roulette wheels constructed for her palace, as did Sultan Selim III of Turkey. Today's roulette (there are slight differences between American and European roulette) has its origins in a game called *hoca* played during the seventeenth century. Roulette continues to be one of the leading types of gambling activities throughout Europe. It is often viewed as the rich man's pastime. Today's roulette has not changed that much except for the speed at which the game can be played and the electronic board attached to the gaming table that indicates the last twenty or so spins. By providing the player with past winning numbers, individuals believe it will help them predict the next winning number. This is what is referred to as the "gambler's fallacy." The American roulette table typically has 36 numbers plus a 0 and a 00, while the European roulette table has 36 numbers and only one 0. Today's modern casinos also provide the opportunity to gamble on roulette electronically on a variety of electronic gambling machines as well as on a traditional table with a croupier.

LOTTERIES

Lotteries, widely popular today, seem to have their origin in the fifteenth or sixteenth centuries (there is some controversy as to their actual date of origin), offering citizens an opportunity to become instantaneously rich while simultaneously helping and supporting educational and other worthy causes. The advent and widespread use of bank notes in Europe during the eighteenth century provided an easy way to exchange money won or lost. In spite of the controversy concerning gambling during this period, many aristocrats who condoned the "frivolous nature" of gambling still engaged in playing the lottery, and it quickly grew in popularity among individuals of all economic means and levels of society.

Lotteries became so popular in the British Colonies, and subsequently in the newly formed United States, that the Continental Congress developed a lottery to help finance and support the Independence effort. In the United States, lotteries have had a long, colorful, and less than glorious history. Its early origins came from a decree by King James I who gave permission for the colony of

Virginia in 1612 to use a lottery to raise much needed funds. The other colonies quickly began to see how lucrative this venture could be so lotteries quickly became organized and developed to pay for the construction of roads, bridges, schools, churches, and hospitals in all the colonies. Some of America's most famous universities (Harvard, Columbia, Yale, Dartmouth, William and Mary, and Rhode Island College [currently Brown University]) were initially aided and partially financed by the proceeds from lotteries.

Lotteries became popularized by churches and governments as an efficient way to help finance infrastructure projects, support religious institutions, and fund military operations. Legislators quickly realized the lotteries' potential for raising funds. While there is little doubt that purchasing a lottery ticket is a form of gambling (risking/wagering money to make money), many individuals vehemently opposed to gambling still purchase lottery tickets, probably because the tickets are relatively inexpensive, provide an opportunity to win significant sums of money, and the proceeds are typically used for worthwhile charitable or educational causes. In fact, most people do not equate lottery playing with gambling.

Throughout the 1800s, lotteries continued to grow in popularity both in the United States and Europe. However, by the mid-1800s strong opposition began to overshadow the positive benefits derived from the lotteries and in spite of their widespread popularity they began to be banned in certain countries. The earliest lotteries were also scandal-ridden, with corruption being commonplace. Retailers were chastised for cashing winning tickets and keeping the proceeds. This is not to suggest that today's lottery draws are corruption-free even though there are much stricter and more stringent controls. A major scandal in New York State occurred in 1975 when it was found that the numbers being drawn had not been sold, thereby increasing the state's revenues. More recently, in several Canadian provinces, a number of retailers were found to be cheating their customers by not disclosing winning tickets or falsely informing the individual that a ticket had not won or had won a smaller amount of money. This prompted provincial lottery corporations to install new electronic machines that provide lottery customers with auditory cues identifying winning tickets.

In spite of difficulties and corruption, we have recently witnessed an increase and explosion of state, provincial, and national lotteries being offered to the consumer. Internationally, the lottery remains one of the most popular forms of gambling as individuals continue to pursue the dream of winning the "big one" (a recent U.S. lottery in 2011 paid the winner $330 million, which was divided amongst two ticket holders). The Powerball in the United States, Maxi-Millions in Canada, and Euro-Millions in Europe, as well as other lotteries offering enormous jackpots, continue to thrive and attract incredible numbers of individuals trying to exercise their luck and capture the dream. Revenues from these games, in spite of the potential distribution of such large prizes, continue to increase. The World Lottery Association, representing 140 government-regulated lotteries in more than 70 countries, reported combined annual revenues in 2010 in excess of $120 billion. World lottery sales increased 6.3% between 2009 and 2010 and it is predicted that lottery sales will see an increase of over 12.5% for 2011 and beyond.

Lotteries continue to be a major source of revenue for worthwhile charitable causes in the United Kingdom, United States, Sweden, Spain, Brazil, Israel, France, Canada, China, and a score of other countries. One of the earliest and best-known lotteries is the Irish Hospital Sweepstakes which began in 1930. Held three times a year to support hospitals in Ireland, its popularity grew well beyond its borders. Within the United States, many state lotteries report that the revenues will be spent on education and providing scholarships for college students.

Lottery draws continue to capture the imagination and dreams of the public. This has led today's lottery corporations, typically owned and operated by governments (sometimes licensed by governments), to devise new ways to increase sales and revenues. Lottery draws are held more frequently with the opportunity to win huge prizes. A number of lottery corporations have begun selling tickets via the Internet and most now have instant low-cost scratch card tickets, where in addition to winning money a diversity of products can be won (e.g., motorcycles, Wii games, iPods, leather "Betty Boop" jackets, boats, and guitars). These scratch tickets are typically inexpensive although they can range from $0.50 to $20, and are particularly attractive to youth as they frequently incorporate familiar licensed games, movies, or cartoon characters (e.g., Monopoly, Battleship, Flintstones, and Raiders of the Lost Ark). Given the perceived relatively high rate of return (the largest number of prizes are for another free ticket), adolescents view their probability of winning as significantly greater than in other forms of gambling. More important, the tickets provide instant feedback to adolescents, and many people derive pleasure from merely scratching the ticket with the hopes of winning. In spite of age-regulated prohibitions in most jurisdictions, there is ample evidence to suggest that underage adolescents have little difficulty purchasing lottery tickets from licensed retailers. This has prompted lottery corporations to provide greater training for their vendors and increased vigilance concerning proper age identification for individuals who appear to be under the legal age to purchase tickets. It should be noted that the legal age to purchase tickets is independently regulated by the various states, provinces, and countries. Thus, the age varies widely, with each jurisdiction establishing its own minimum age to purchase a ticket.

SLOT MACHINES AND OTHER FORMS OF ELECTRONIC GAMBLING MACHINES

The early gambling machines have their roots in America during the 1870s and their development coincided with America's industrial revolution. Many of the early gambling machines interspersed elements of chance and skill. It was the national poker craze in the 1880s that prompted several ingenious American inventors to develop a machine in which poker could be automatically played. Because of poker's great popularity, machines were developed that automatically paid the winner a set number of coins while retaining all the losses. An early slot machine, originally called the Card Bell was later renamed the Liberty Bell. During the 1900s, slot machines became omnipresent throughout America. It was reported that in the early 1930s the infamous gangster, Frank Costello, controlled over twenty-five thousand slot machines in New York alone that generated over $25 million in profits a year. Today's machines are no longer "mechanical machines" but rather employ sophisticated electronic chips and processors. They have evolved from single games to multi-games, from three reels to multi-reels, from coin acceptors to bill acceptors, and from dispensing winnings through coins to providing a slip which is then redeemed at the cashier's window.

Slot machines can range from a penny to hundreds of dollars and consume most of the casino gaming floors in North America because they are the greatest source of revenues and require the least number of staff to monitor and operate them. Based on what the noted behavioral psychologist B. F. Skinner called "intermittent reinforcement" (variable ratio schedules), people keep playing because they never know when the machine will pay out. Most often, these machines pay small amounts rather than the larger progressive jackpots, thus providing the individual with small intermittent rewards and giving hopes of winning the jackpot. The more often individuals receive some payout (reinforcement), the more likely they are to continue to play. Behavioral psychologists have concluded that most individuals view the entertainment value of these machines as paramount. As such, operators do not want individuals to lose all their money quickly. Therefore, by providing them with periodic intermittent reinforcement, individuals continue to play for longer periods of time and retain pleasurable memories in spite of losing money.

Once called the "one-armed bandit" because the individual pulled a handle giving the person a perceived illusion of control, today's slot machines typically have a button which is depressed to begin the game. These electronic gambling machines (EGMs) are also called Video Lottery Terminals (VLTs) in Canada or Pokies in Australia and New Zealand, and still remain extremely popular among individuals of all ages, particularly women. They often incorporate licensed themes such as games (e.g., Monopoly), movies (e.g., *Top Gun, Ghostbusters, The Hangover*), and successful television game shows (*Wheel of Fortune, Sex and the City*) and frequently have progressive jackpots. It is not unusual in North American casinos to see luxurious cars placed in the middle of a bank of slot machines providing an incentive to the consumer to tempt their fate to win the "big prize." International Gaming Technology, a manufacturer of gaming machines, software, and network systems worldwide, has been in existence since 1981. It marked a significant milestone in the company's history in the autumn of 2010 in its production of its 2,000,000th slot machine, attesting to its popularity. While not as popular among Asian communities, electronic gambling machines can be found in virtually all casinos worldwide.

What can we expect to see in future slot machines? Key slot machine trends will incorporate more entertainment values, more depth of bonuses, and more interactive features between the player and the machine. Slots still represent the "cash cow" of the land-based gambling industry. We will likely see more skill-based joystick bonuses and innovative mechanical gun hardware. Additionally, a probable development will be the continued merging of videogame technology on these machines with more interactive videos and enhanced graphics. Player loyalty cards, prominent on these machines, will provide the individual with more bonuses, perks, and prizes.

SPORTS GAMBLING

While different sports are popular in different countries, sports betting has always been popular, especially among males. The early Romans reportedly wagered on chariot races and gladiator duels, while the Greeks wagered on the outcome of Olympic contests. Today's popularity of sports wagering is especially evident in the vast numbers of Internet gambling sites and casinos which accept sports wagers. In 2008, as an example, approximately $2.57 billion was gambled in Nevada's legal sports books (wagering in Las Vegas alone on the Super Bowl in 2010 topped $92 million), with an estimated

$380 billion being wagered through offshore gambling sites or with local bookmakers. According to an ESPN survey, approximately 118 million Americans gambled on sports during 2008, with current numbers continuing to rise (Nevada recently introduced mobile sports wagering via one's cell phone within the state and one can now wager from the comfort of a hotel room).

Sports wagering, on both college and professional sports, remains extremely popular among college-age students. Odds are published in newspapers and posted on Internet websites. Data from a number of studies suggest that approximately 65% to 70% of college students wagered on some sporting event, with sports wagering being only second in popularity to poker among college students. The following are some interesting, recent sports gambling-related statistics:

- Approximately 33% of all American men report having gambled on sports.
- A recent survey revealed that 44% of grade 12 high school males reported having gambled (for money) on a sporting event.
- It is estimated that 42% of Americans would support legalized sports wagering in all states, with 55% of those wagering on sports supporting its legalization.
- If legalized and regulated throughout the United States, sports betting would generate an estimated $10 billion per year and $100 million in tax revenues per state.

Unlike in the past where individuals wagered merely on the final outcome, today there are "proposition bets" where an individual can place wagers on multiple plays, players, and outcomes during the game. For example, in a recent Super Bowl football contest in the United States, individuals were able to wager on the following on a variety of Internet gambling sites:

- Which team won or lost and did they cover the point spread.
- Which team was leading by the end of the first quarter, first half, third quarter.

- Which player had the first reception.
- Which team experienced the first fumble.
- How many field goals were kicked in the first quarter, first half, third quarter, and in total.
- Which player was named the game's MVP (most valuable player).

Even during popular contests like the Super Bowl, Internet gambling sites took wagers not directly related to the sporting event but on a wide diversity of activities associated with the event. Some examples include:

- How long was the national anthem?
- How many times was the quarterback's girlfriend/wife shown on camera?
- Which team will win the coin toss?
- What color of Gatorade (a popular drink) will be poured on the winning coach after the game ended?
- The Who, a famous rock band, performed during the half-time Super Bowl show and several websites were accepting wagers on (a) whether a member of the band would smash his guitar, and (b) if someone smashed his guitar, which band member did so.

These proposition bets are not only associated with football but can be placed on most professional and college sports. During the most recent World Cup soccer tournament in South Africa, billions of dollars were wagered from around the globe. Also, other popular contests involve wagering on the annual National Collegiate Athletic Association (NCAA) basketball championship or football bowls. Each year, estimates are that wagering increases, with betting on the 2010 NCAA basketball tournament exceeding $300 million.

HORSE WAGERING/HARNESS RACING

Horse racing has been popular since 1500 BC. The beginning of organized racing events has been historically traced to China, Persia, and Arabia. The Romans were notorious for their chariot races and the even more hazardous races where the rider used two horses and had one foot placed on each of the horses as he rounded the circuit.

Horse racing became a popular sport and opportunity for gambling in colonial America. Several states, in particular Kentucky, Tennessee, Maryland, and Virginia, are noted for their major races. After the Civil War in the United States, horse racing truly began in earnest. Churchill Downs, home to the Kentucky Derby, opened its doors in 1875. The internationally known Kentucky Derby is also the first race of what is referred to as the "Triple Crown" (the other two races being the Preakness and Belmont). While harness racing is still popular in a number of countries, in particular Australasia, its popularity has waned throughout North America. In order to keep many race tracks open and to help support breeders, trainers, and racing staff, many jurisdictions have opened off-track betting parlors where individuals can wager and view, in real time, horse races from most parts of the world. In Canada, a new concept, racino, was developed, which combines horse racing and gambling games typically found in land-based casinos. These racinos, located at horse tracks, generate more money from slots and electronic gambling machines than the wagers on the harness racing. During the past several hundred years, horse racing has been plagued by scandal (fixing the outcome), with church groups who claimed it is immoral, and more recently pro-animal activists who have argued that it is inhumane to race these animals.

GAMBLING: A NEW DAY HAS COME—
INTERNET WAGERING

With technological advances and the advent and growth of the Internet along with significant reductions in the cost of personal computers and high-speed Internet connections and cell phones, gambling opportunities have become revolutionized. Unlike traditional forms of gambling, multiple games (poker, slots, blackjack, roulette, keno, sports wagering, bingo, and more) are now easily accessible from within the comforts and confines of one's home.

The commercialization of Internet gambling sites began in the mid-1990s, with the earliest confirmed date for an authentic Internet gambling site being September 1993 when the Swiss lottery (*Loterie Romande*) began selling its lottery tickets to individuals having a special (Videotex) terminal and software. In 1994, the government of Antigua passed legislation permitting online casinos to be established, regulated, licensed, and housed within their jurisdiction. Intercasino was the first online casino to accept actual money wagers and the World Sports Exchange launched a full-service Internet sports book in 1997. The Kahnawake Gaming Commission, located in Montreal, Canada, began to license Internet gambling sites, providing the necessary software and technical assistance to individuals, groups, or companies who wanted to establish their own gambling websites.

As online commerce in general became safer, more sophisticated, and reliable, individuals became more comfortable with this new technology. This resulted in the rapid expansion of Internet gambling. Since its early beginnings, the number of online gambling sites has increased at an astounding rate each year. In 1994 there were reportedly 30 gambling websites. Four years later there were approximately 90 online casinos, 39 lotteries, 8 online sites offering bingo, and 53 sports books. Five years later, the number of sites dramatically increased to 250 online casinos, 64 lotteries, 20 bingo, and 139 sports books. While still prohibited in certain jurisdictions, Internet wagering is both popular and plentiful around the globe and by 2006 it was estimated that there were 2,132 Internet gambling websites. As of June 2010, one survey found 2,679 Internet gambling sites owned by 665 different companies. These included 865 online casinos, 616 online poker rooms, 516 sports betting sites, 426 online bingo sites, and 187 lottery and other sites. Some software manufacturers even offer the public the opportunity to develop their own personal gambling site at a minimal cost.

Since the initial explosive market expansion, it appears that the increase in number of sites has somewhat tapered off as smaller companies amalgamate with larger ones. Sports and harness race wagering, online casinos, and poker rooms are estimated to account for 95% of the total market share, with individuals from the United States (in spite of legal prohibitions and the closing of some sites) and the Asia Pacific region comprising the largest markets, followed by Europe.

Global Internet gambling revenues have reportedly increased from approximately $2.2 billion in 2000 to nearly $30 billion in 2010. All indications are that it remains one of the fastest growing segments of the industry, with a growing number of land-based gambling operations anxiously entering the market and an increasing number of governments now licensing, regulating, or owning/operating gambling sites under their respective jurisdictions.

The market and legislative statutes are changing so rapidly that one needs to be updated almost daily. Several European countries, Canada, and Australia have strong regulatory bodies overseeing this form of gambling, and the United States will likely follow suit in spite of the Department of Justice's closing down access to several sites. Internet gambling can take many forms: online casinos similar to land-based casinos (having a diversity of table and slot games), poker sites, sports betting, wagering pools, Fantasy sports, lottery tickets, betting exchanges, and games of skill. You can wager on almost anything via the Internet, be it political races, celebrity marriages/divorces or child adoptions, the number of letters in the winning word of national spelling bee contests, the outcome of reality television shows and competitions, or who will become the next pope.

In spite of its many detractors and prohibitions in certain jurisdictions, Internet wagering continues to become the fastest growth area in the gambling industry. As the general public has become more accepting of security features associated with Internet commerce in general and as stricter regulations have been imposed on licensed gambling sites, individuals have become much more comfortable with wagering online.

It should be noted that Full Tilt Poker, a very popular gambling website, was closed and has refused to pay its account holders. Several independent accrediting bodies such as the e-Commerce and Online Gaming Regulation and Assurance group (eCOGRA) and the

Global Gambling Guidance Group (G4) now provide external audits and certification procedures to ensure the fairness and integrity of Internet gambling companies. As confirmation of their audits, their logos appear on the websites of many gambling providers. Equally important on many sites is the inclusion of responsible gambling strategies to help minimize the potential negative harm associated with excessive gambling.

While still relatively underdeveloped, the mobile gambling industry is poised for rapid growth. Several recent reports suggest that it may account for as much as 15% of wireless gambling revenues, especially with the growing number of iPhone, iPad, Tablet, BlackBerry, and Android applications. Gaming machine developers and manufacturers, in particular, International Game Technology and Aristocrat, have both created an online and mobile division. Recently, a number of Nevada casinos have begun accepting mobile sports wagers from individuals located in that state. While currently only available for BlackBerry devices within the state, this new technology is primed to take off. There remains little doubt that the interactive gaming arena will continue to experience steady growth over time as operators currently have the technology to offer multiple types of wagering via mobile platforms. In spite of current legislative statutes prohibiting the use of smart phones to gamble in many jurisdictions, policy experts have suggested that this is likely to change in the very near future.

GAMBLING: ITS PUBLIC ACCEPTANCE

Equally important to the growth of the industry has been the public's general acceptance of gambling. While not many people want a casino in their neighborhood or backyard, they do want one in close proximity. This general acceptance of gambling has been fostered and promoted by the industry, which prefers to use the term "gaming" rather than gambling. While the distinction may seem subtle, it represents a fundamental shift in our perception and thinking about gambling. The term gaming evokes an enjoyable, pleasurable, socially acceptable form of fun and entertainment while gambling still retains some of the negative associations with crime, smoke-filled card rooms, excessive alcohol consumption, and illicit behaviors. This shift in thinking has led gambling to become much more socially acceptable today than in the past. While still problematic to some, its widespread acceptance and popularity has influenced legislators and has spurred the industry's growth. Most governments have closely regulated gambling to ensure its honesty and integrity while using the revenues derived from gambling for the public good. This is consistent with this new general acceptance. According to a recent 2010 public opinion research poll in the United States, more than one quarter (28%) of American adults visited a casino during 2009. With the ever growing number of casinos in different jurisdictions, these numbers are likely to continue to increase.

In spite of its widespread appeal, there remains significant diversity in public opinion about government's role in gambling. Within some jurisdictions, such as the United States, all forms of gambling with the exception of the lottery are operated by private corporations with government oversight through stringent regulatory controls and commissions. In other jurisdictions, like Canada, the government can be the owner, operator, and regulator of all forms of gambling (including Internet wagering). The regulatory aspects associated with gambling differ widely across jurisdictions and countries and continue to evolve.

Another distinct shift in philosophy and practices of operators, legislators, and regulators has occurred during the past ten years. No longer is profit the single motivation of corporate policy; rather the inclusion of "responsible gambling practices" has become an integral part of daily operations. While there exists a wide diversity in corporate policies and practices around the globe, such policies are often predicated on the regulatory guidelines established in each state, province, or country and can differ between jurisdictions for the same gambling operator. Our understanding and knowledge of what are the "Best Practices" for responsible gambling is far from complete and there are many different international studies currently under way to determine what these practices should entail. Such practices are typically designed to help protect underage individuals from gambling, identify the needs of vulnerable populations, address how best to protect individuals with gambling problems, and identify ways to minimize the potential harms to the gambling public.

Such responsible gambling practices have been integrated into the daily operations of most licensed operators, lottery corporations, card rooms, casinos, tracks, electronic gaming rooms, as well as Internet and mobile gambling operators. Currently, these practices can include one or more of the following: providing informational brochures describing responsible gambling programs, removal of ATM/cash machines from the gambling floor, information explaining the probabilities of winning or losing on casino games and winning prizes via the lottery, help-line telephone numbers for individuals requiring assistance for a gambling or gambling-related problem, responsible advertising codes of ethics and standards, opportunities for patrons to request being removed from mailing lists for promotional materials being sent directly to their home, self-exclusion policies whereby the individual elects to exclude himself/herself from a gambling venue (a small number of jurisdictions have what is referred to as third-party exclusion where a family member may petition a gambling establishment or regulatory body to exclude a family member because of a gambling problem), smart cards and USB identifier keys for use on gambling machines whereby the individual can establish preset time and money limits and when these are exceeded the player's privileges are terminated immediately by closing the machine, and restricting alcohol on the gambling floor while individuals are gambling (this is not universal). In some jurisdictions, new innovations include the requirement for inserting a driver's license or government-issued identification card into lottery vending machines to preclude underage individuals from playing and the inclusion of Apps on smart phones which can receive responsible gambling awareness messages. Such devices can also be integrated into limit-setting for mobile gambling. Staff training in responsible gambling has become an integral part of most responsible gambling programs.

The expansion of land-based gambling in the United States and worldwide continues to grow. In 2009, thirteen states had commercial casinos, with 29 states having at least one tribal casino. In the United States, during 2009, commercial casinos had revenues of $30.74 billion and employed more than 328,000 people. When one adds in racetrack employees, lottery employees, and gaming equipment manufacturers, more than half a million people are employed in the gambling industry in the United States alone. It should be noted that not everyone is enamored with gambling and there has been strong opposition in many states and countries. This opposition, while moderately successful in some places, is often predicated on moral and religious grounds and has been losing momentum. The pendulum of acceptance of gambling has strongly swung in the pro-gambling movement's favor.

Around the world, land-based casinos and Internet gambling sites dot the globe. Gambling's popularity seems to have no geographical boundaries. In the next decade, we will continue to see increased expansion of land-based forms of gambling, innovative games of chance, and technological advances that will no longer necessitate travelling to gamble. The destination casinos will continue to evolve into a new era of multifunctional entertainment complexes.

While most individuals gamble in a responsible manner, setting and generally maintaining their limits, this gambling expansion will also bring a host of new social problems. These problems will impact not only adults but adolescents as well.

The early colorful characters of the Wild West and gangsters like Benny Siegel and Meyer Lansky have been replaced by legitimate executives and entrepreneurs including Howard Hughes, Bill Harrah, Steve Wynn, Sheldon Adelson, and Gary Loveman. The boards of directors of multinational gaming corporations have successfully changed gambling into gaming, with casinos housing huge entertainment complexes, shopping centers, and exclusive restaurants. A new day has come.

REFERENCES

American Gaming Association. (2010). State of the States: The AGA Survey of Casino Entertainment. Washington, DC: American Gaming Association.

American Gaming Association. (2011). State of the States: The AGA Survey of Casino Entertainment. Washington, DC: American Gaming Association.

Durham, S., and Hashimoto, K. (2010). *The history of gambling in America.* Prentice Hall.

Fleming, A. (1978). *Something for nothing: A history of gambling.* Delacorte Press.

H2 Gambling Capital. (April 2010). United States: Regulated Internet Gambling Economic Impact Reports.

H2 Gambling Capital. (April 2011). National Summary Sheet Report.

H2 Gambling Capital. (August 2011). Mobile Gambling Report.

Monaghan, S., and Derevensky, J. (2008a). An appraisal of the impact of the depiction of gambling in society on youth. *International Journal of Mental Health and Addiction, 6,* 1557–74.

Monaghan, S., and Derevensky, J. (2008b). A Critical Review of the Internet Gambling Literature: Some Policy Recommendations. Report prepared for the Nova Scotia Gaming Corporation, 88 pp.

Partucci, C. (August 2009). The True Statistics of Sports Gambling. http://www.articlesbase.com/online-gambling-articles/the-true-statistics-of-sports-gambling-1097238.html.

Pew Research Center. (May 2006). Gambling: As the Take Rises, So Does Public Concern. Pew Research Social Trends Reports.

Reith, G. (1999). *The age of chance in western culture.* London: Routledge.

Schwartz, D. G. (2006). *Roll the bones: The history of gambling.* New York: Gotham Books.

Stewart, D. O. (May 2011). Online Gambling Five Years After UIGEA. American Gaming Association White Paper.

Thompson, W. (2001). *Gambling in America: An encyclopedia of history, issues and society.* California: ABC-CLIO.

GAMBLING BEHAVIORS AMONG ADOLESCENTS

GAMBLING

There are multiple definitions of the term "gambling." While some individuals include the wagering or gambling of personal possessions in order to win something of value as a form of gambling, within the context of this book gambling or gaming (not to be confused with videogaming) is defined as wagering money on an outcome of an uncertain event in order to win money. Clearly, all forms of gambling include some element of unpredictability and risk, otherwise it would not be considered gambling. Even those games typically thought to be more skill-based, such as poker or blackjack, have elements of risk, given the cards are randomly dealt. It is also not unusual for individuals to wager on games of skill including sporting events, with some youth occasionally wagering on the outcome of their performance on videogames. Some online gambling companies have recently even taken wagers on college students' academic performance where students can bet on their own final grades.

While it is not the intention to get into the semantics of the term "gambling," it is well accepted that gambling can occur on a continuum with most people either not gambling at all, gambling occasionally, or gambling frequently and experiencing minimal negative financial or social consequences. Others, who gamble even more often and who gamble with increasing amounts of money and are unable to set and adhere to their own preset limits, both in terms of time and money, may experience a number of gambling-related problems. It is important to note that for some individuals losing control may be episodic and short-lived (there has been some recent attention given to the concept of "binge gambling" where individuals get overly involved for short periods of time and then return to their natural levels of gambling) whereas for others it is more representative of a progressive disorder. This gambling disorder, often referred to as pathological gambling, problem gambling, compulsive gambling, or disordered gambling, has many accompanying problems.

There is little doubt that the amount of expendable and available money individuals have can differ widely. For a very wealthy person to lose what some may perceive as a large sum of money may not be as problematic as for the individual who is wagering his or her grocery or rent money. Throughout this book, the risk factors associated with gambling, and in particular adolescent problem gambling, will be identified as well as some treatment issues and prevention programs aimed at minimizing such harms. For now, the following illustration provides an example of what is often referred to as the continuum of gambling.

As can be seen from the diagram in figure 2.1, gambling can range from non-gambling to social or recreational gambling to at-risk gambling (this denotes individuals who are starting to develop a number of gambling-related problems but fail to reach the established crite-

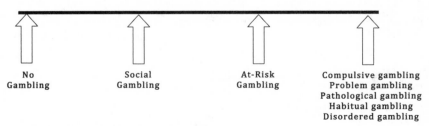

No
Gambling

Social
Gambling

At-Risk
Gambling

Compulsive gambling
Problem gambling
Pathological gambling
Habitual gambling
Disordered gambling

Figure 2.1.   Continuum of gambling behavior.

ria determined by clinicians for a gambling disorder) and finally to compulsive, habitual, problem, pathological, or disordered gambling.

Within the field of gambling studies, a nomenclature issue currently exists with respect to what constitutes "problem gambling." While we can all agree that some individuals have gambling and gambling-related problems, clinicians, treatment providers, and researchers have yet to agree on the appropriate term to best describe these individuals. In the most recent American Psychiatric Association's *Diagnostic and Statistical Manual*, Fourth Edition (DSM-IV), individuals with an excessive number of gambling and gambling-related problems are referred to as "pathological gamblers." As the DSM-IV gets revised, there still remains controversy over the actual terminology that will be selected to describe individuals experiencing significant gambling and gambling-related problems. A number of clinicians and members of the subcommittee examining this issue have suggested that a new term, "disordered gambling," may be more appropriate to describe individuals experiencing significant gambling and gambling-related problems. While no distinctions have been made between adult and adolescent gamblers, these distinctions will likely have to be articulated in the gambling screens used to identify individuals with gambling problems.

ADULT GAMBLING PREVALENCE

There are numerous reports from internationally based research studies revealing that approximately 80% to 90% of adults have gambled during their lifetime. Among those adults who report gambling, almost one third indicated having visited a casino and even larger numbers report playing the lottery. The percentage of individuals gambling, often referred to as the prevalence rate, has been shown to vary significantly depending on the accessibility, availability, and minimum age requirement for gambling. Different geographical jurisdictions allow different forms of regulated gambling. Some states have casinos while others have prohibited them, at least temporarily. In the United States, only Utah and Hawaii currently have no form of regulated gambling. As well, it is important to note that the age permitted for gambling may not only differ between jurisdictions but also within jurisdictions themselves based on the types of games offered (e.g., typically the age for purchasing lottery tickets is often lower in many jurisdictions than for casino gambling). As previously indicated in chapter 1, there are a growing number of studies suggesting that more and more adults are not only gambling but gambling frequently. Yet, the incidence and prevalence rate of adult pathological gambling is approximately 1% to 3% depending on where the research is conducted.

ADOLESCENT GAMBLING PREVALENCE RESEARCH

Adolescent gambling prevalence research in North America has spanned three rather distinct periods. The earliest research began during the 1980s just when the introduction of lotteries began to proliferate throughout the United States and Canada. These early prevalence studies tracked adolescent gambling and were typically conducted using self-administered surveys and questionnaires with information collected in high school classrooms. It has been suggested that in all likelihood these early studies were not truly representative of the general population of adolescents, but merely provided an early glimpse into adolescent and teen gambling. These studies revealed significant variability in gambling prevalence rates depending on the age of the adolescents assessed, the types of accessibility and availability, and the geographical region in which the study was collected. Nevertheless, there was little doubt that these studies pointed to the fact that adolescents were indeed gambling for money on multiple forms of regulated and nonregulated activities and that there was a developmental trend such that as children aged they engaged in gambling more frequently and on more varied types of activities. These studies, while not truly representative of the general population, clearly pointed to the necessity for further investigations. They also became an early benchmark for tracking prevalence rates of teen gambling.

The early adolescent gambling studies in the 1980s were followed by an increased number of studies in the 1990s in North America and the United Kingdom using similar methodologies but sometimes different instruments and measurement tools, which had been developed to assess both the prevalence of adolescent gambling behavior and that of problem gambling. The median level of adolescent gambling appeared to rise during this period from 45% in the 1980s to an average of 66% in the 1990s. Durand Jacobs, in his analyses of multiple prevalence studies, concluded that during the 1990s juvenile gambling had increased dramatically in the United States, with comparable increases in Canada resulting from expanded availability and ease of accessibility. These studies began to raise serious concerns as to the frequency and types of gambling engaged in by adolescents. As well, the research scope expanded to address issues related to adolescents' underlying motivations for gambling, why there seemed to be an apparent lack of parental monitoring of their children's gambling behavior, and to identify concerns related to the comorbidities and co-occurring disorders and problems associated with gambling. Finally, and most important, it became evident that a small but identifiable number of youth seemed to be experiencing serious gambling-related problems similar to their adult counterparts. Studies of adolescent gambling were also beginning in Europe, Australia, and New Zealand around this time.

Since the turn of this century, many more jurisdictions, on an international level, examining adolescent risky behaviors have begun to include gambling modules as a way to ascertain the prevalence and incidence of adolescent gambling behaviors. In a number of countries, including the United States, Canada, United Kingdom, Estonia, Lithuania, Romania, Germany, Belgium, Denmark, Finland, Iceland, Norway, Sweden, Australia, and New Zealand, rather large gambling prevalence studies among adolescents and young adults have been completed. All studies tended to report similar findings: (a) while there is significant variability depending on the jurisdiction in which the study has been conducted, the available research seems to report an increasing number of adolescents gambling, (b) there is clear evidence that males are more likely to gamble and be susceptible to gambling problems than females, (c) the types of gambling activities in which adolescents participate are a factor of ease of accessibility, availability, gender, and age, (d) certain cultural groups may be more vulnerable to both gambling and problem gambling issues, and (e) parental attitudes and behaviors appear to influence both adolescent gambling and problem gambling.

ADOLESCENT GAMBLING PREVALENCE RATES

Gambling, once thought to only be an adult activity, has been shown to be popular among children and adolescents. Whether betting among themselves (it is not unusual to hear children betting on a school playground), purchasing lottery tickets, playing poker with friends, or sneaking into casinos or gaming parlors, gambling's popularity with teens is clearly on the rise. Recent data from Rachel Volberg and her colleagues, concerning youth gambling on an international level, suggest that upwards of 80% of youth report having gambled for money during their lifetime, with the median percentage being 66% during the past year in the United States, 63% in Canada, 66% in Europe (excluding Scandinavia), 72% in the Nordic countries, and 62% in Australia and New Zealand. Similar findings have been found for adults. These numbers certainly attest to gambling's popularity for both adults and adolescents alike. As the growth and diversity of both regulated and unregulated (games played among peers) types of gambling activities continue to grow and gambling becomes normalized in our society, we are very likely to see the number of youth engaged in this behavior increase. Gambling opportunities have never been more varied, easier to find, and accessible in spite of legal prohibitions.

GAMBLING BEHAVIOR

While the vast majority of adults and teens gamble in a fairly responsible manner, some do it in excess, which can result in a wide range of problems—emotional, familial, psychological, interpersonal, financial, and legal. Most adults and teens, when gambling, typically set and generally adhere to time and money limits. Occasionally, time and/or money limits may be exceeded but the vast majority of individuals will quickly readjust their gambling and spending and not suffer many long-term gambling-related problems. While the issue of problem and pathological gambling will be explored in greater depth in chapter 3, for some individuals, moderate and/or social gambling ultimately leads to excessive gambling and a host of associated problems. The best analogy may be to that of drinking alcohol. If done in moderation, within certain well-accepted limits (drinking and driving being an exception), few health-related, social, or interpersonal problems arise (some scientists have argued there actually may be health benefits to drinking red wine in moderation). Yet, if done excessively, often referred to as alcohol abuse or dependency, then a wide variety of alcohol-related problems generally occur. Similarly, gambling can be viewed within a potentially high-risk framework, with problems often occurring if done excessively.

The Center for Substance Abuse Prevention and the Substance Abuse and Mental Health Services Administration in Washington, D.C., has articulated a strategy to address adolescent risky behaviors by attempting to identify the risk and protective factors associated with alcohol abuse, substance use, teenage suicide, and delinquency. Following this model, researchers at the International Centre for Youth Gambling Problems and High-Risk Behaviors have incorporated pathological gambling within this framework to make it more comprehensive. During the past twenty years, the researchers and clinicians at the International Centre for Youth Gambling Problems and High-Risk Behaviors at McGill University in Montreal have been trying to identify the correlates as well as the risk and protective factors associated with youth pathological gambling to have a better understanding of adolescent gambling and problem gambling. Such acquired knowledge can then be put into efforts to develop more effective science-based prevention programs. It is important to view gambling behavior among adolescents as just one more potentially risky behavior which may begin innocently

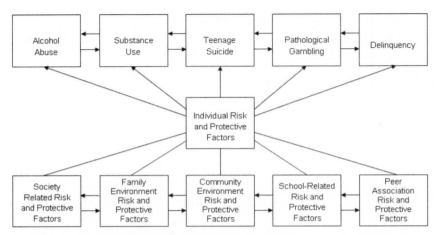

Figure 2.2. An adolescent high-risk model. Adapted from P. Brounstein and J. Zweig, *Understanding Substance Abuse Prevention: Toward 21st Century Primer on Effective Programs,* **1999, Center for Substance Abuse Prevention (CSAP) & Substance Abuse and Mental Health Services Administration (SAMHSA); Dickson, Derevensky, and Gupta 2002.**

enough and spin out of control. This is evident in figure 2.2 where adolescent pathological gambling is placed within a general high-risk framework.

Given that many individuals begin gambling at a relatively young age, it is not unusual that a certain segment of the population experiences problems. While the typical stereotype of an individual with a gambling problem is a middle-age male; likely a horse race, slot machine, or casino player; someone who has experienced marital and familial problems; and possibly may have committed criminal and/or illegal acts to finance his gambling, nowhere in this description are adolescents or teenagers mentioned. Yet, as previously noted, there is ample evidence that large numbers of adolescents are engaged in multiple forms of both regulated and unregulated gambling. As gambling becomes more accessible, the number of gambling venues increases, and the normalization of gambling becomes widely adopted, there remains a growing concern that not only will adolescents engage in this behavior more frequently but that an increasing number of these youth will ultimately experience multiple gambling-related problems.

Much of this concern has emanated from research which has focused on adult gambling and adult problem gambling. In research studies with adult problem and pathological gamblers, most universally report that gambling for money began at a relatively early age—approximately ages 10 to 12. There is also a growing body of evidence that adolescents tend to begin gambling well before they begin experimenting with smoking, alcohol, drugs, or sexual behavior.

As can be observed in table 2.1, recent results show a growing percentage of adolescents engaging in potentially risky behaviors as they get older. Both total use during one's lifetime as well as weekly use can be observed in this table. As depicted in the table and as expected, the percentage of adolescents engaging in any of these behaviors weekly is less than their total lifetime use. However, when examining the patterns of gambling behavior, gambling is relatively stable at an earlier age and is more likely to be endorsed than alcohol or illicit drug or cigarette use. When interpreting these results it becomes evident that there are considerably more teenagers engaged in gambling than in any of the other potentially risky behaviors presented. Furthermore, by the time children are 12 years old, almost 80% of teenagers report having engaged in some form of gambling for money, whether among their peers or family members or in other common forms of gambling activities. If one examines this behavior on a weekly basis, as expected, fewer youth appear to be engaged in gambling. However, the percentage of youth gambling weekly similarly increases as they get older. Examining the prevalence information presented in this table, it is evident that more youth seem to be engaged in gambling

Table 2.1. Involvement in Addictive Behaviors

	Total Use			Weekly Use		
	Grade 7	Grade 9	Grade 11	Grade 7	Grade 9	Grade 11
Alcohol	36.8 %	62.2 %	79.8 %	7.4 %	14.0 %	20.2 %
Drugs	3.5 %	13.4 %	26.5 %	2.7 %	2.1 %	9.0 %
Cigarettes	18.2 %	34.5 %	48.4 %	7.0 %	16.1 %	31.4 %
Gambling	79.1 %	78.9 %	83.4 %	30.4 %	37.4 %	37.1 %

on a weekly basis than consuming alcohol, drugs, or cigarettes. While these data come from studies in Canada, similar findings have been reported in numerous jurisdictions.

Other research and clinical findings further suggest that adolescent gambling tends to co-occur with other risky behaviors. Additional research has concluded that adolescents and young adults have the highest rates of problem gambling, even more so than adults. While most regulated forms of gambling (those activities that are available and regulated by governmental agencies) have some age restrictions, typically varying between jurisdictions and the type and form of gambling activities, there is ample evidence that underage youth have managed to engage in most forms of gambling in spite of existing laws and restrictions.

ADOLESCENT GAMBLING ACTIVITIES

The most popular forms of gambling among adolescents include card playing (poker has become a huge pastime on an international level), lottery ticket purchases (scratch cards are far more popular than lottery draws), bingo, sports pools and sports wagering, electronic gambling machines, sports lottery tickets (where applicable), and interpersonal games of skill. Sports wagering activities remain far more popular among males, whereas females are more likely to purchase lottery tickets and play bingo for money, with a recent increase in card playing being reported. It is also important to note that those gambling activities perceived as "less harmful" typically have lower age restrictions. Lotteries, raffles, and bingo are often considered as less harmful but nevertheless still represent an enjoyable and exciting form of gambling for adolescents, while casinos often are the most restrictive. Most forms of regulated gambling have some age restrictions.

The percentage of children and adolescents engaging in various gambling activities can be observed in figure 2.3. As children get older, they gain greater access to gambling venues and are more prone to gamble on a diverse number of different restricted activities.

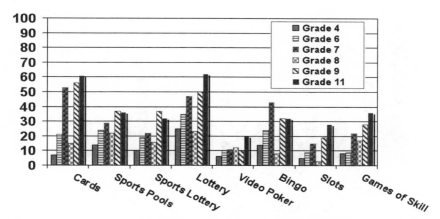

Figure 2.3. Percentage of children and adolescents engaging in various gambling activities.

It is evident that gambling on some of these activities is highly dependent on both their accessibility and availability. For example, sports lottery ticket purchases (wagering on the outcome of two sporting events, e.g., two hockey games, which is available through the Canadian provincial lotteries), while legal in Canada, is currently not permitted in the United States. Similarly, not all jurisdictions have video poker machines or electronic gambling machines outside a casino. However, it is quite evident that lottery purchases, card playing, and sports wagering remain among the most popular forms of gambling among youth. A similar trend is found when examining occasional and regular (once per week or more) adolescent gambling behavior.

Examining the recent research data presented in figure 2.4, one can readily observe how Internet gambling, for fun (using actual gambling activities for fun/points and not real money), has become a growing favorite pastime. This will be more thoroughly discussed later.

AGE AT ONSET OF GAMBLING AMONG CHILDREN AND ADOLESCENTS

Evidence from Europe, North America, Australia, and New Zealand all point to the early age at which children report beginning

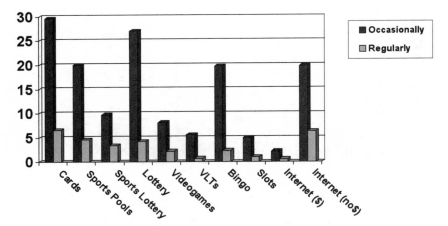

Figure 2.4. Frequency of adolescent gambling. VLTs are multi-game electronic machines similar in many ways to slot machines. Regularly is defined as at least once per week.

to gamble for money. Multiple research studies conducted in these countries have revealed that children as young as age 9 and 10 have gambled for money, primarily with family members. In several early studies of high school students, it was reported that 73% of adolescents gambled during the past year with friends, 65% gambled with family members (including parents, siblings, and extended relatives such as grandparents, aunts, uncles, and cousins), 24% gambled alone, and 5% gambled with strangers, with many teenagers reporting gambling for money in their own homes. It is important to note that these categories are not mutually exclusive such that a large percentage of adolescents reported gambling with multiple family members and their friends. An example of these findings is presented in figure 2.5.

Females were found to be more likely to indicate gambling with family members, whereas males were more likely to try to hide their gambling from family members. As these youth become older, gambling with family members seems to decrease with more peer and independent gambling emerging. Such findings were more recently confirmed in a Canadian national study which asked parents about their children's gambling behaviors.

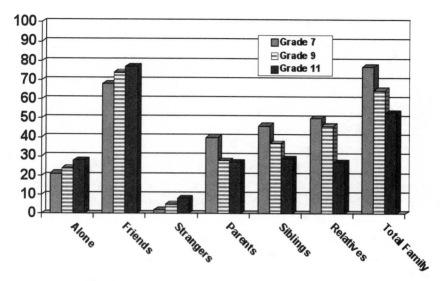

Figure 2.5. With whom adolescents are gambling.

REASONS FOR GAMBLING

Gambling by its very nature involves risking money in order to make money. Is the opportunity to win money the predominant reason individuals gamble? If that were the case, individuals who won a specified preset amount of money would likely quit and walk away a winner. Conversely, for adolescents who lost their money, one would think they would stop and not continue as the result of their losses. Yet, for many adults and adolescents they persevere and continue gambling, often gambling away their winnings and incurring repeated losses and growing debt. So why do individuals persist at this activity in spite of the fact that most people understand the odds of winning are not in their favor? In a number of research investigations with adolescents, the findings reveal that the primary reasons cited for gambling among adolescents include enjoyment (80%), followed by the desire to make money (62%), excitement (59%), social involvement (12%), relaxation (8%), to escape daily problems (4%), to feel older (3%), to alleviate depression (2%), and to help deal with loneliness (1%). It is important that these findings not be interpreted to mean that individuals only have one motive for gambling. At any given time, individuals may have multiple reasons for gambling, all of which can change over time. Yet the three primary reasons reported by adolescents for gambling, entertainment/enjoyment, to win money, and for excitement, are in fact the same reasons cited by adults when asked why they gamble.

Some of the more popular reasons given for gambling by children in grade 4 (ages 9 to 10) through grade 11 (ages 16 to 17) can be observed in figure 2.6. While some differences are noted, the primary reason for gambling endorsed by these children and adolescents relates to the enjoyment and entertainment value received from participating. Money, while important, does not appear to be the primary motivation for gambling. This is important in helping understand why certain individuals will continue to gamble in spite of their repeated losses. Trying to achieve the same level of excitement and enjoyment propels individuals to keep gambling. Yet, we also know that individuals continually need to increase their bet size and frequency to maintain a level of excitement.

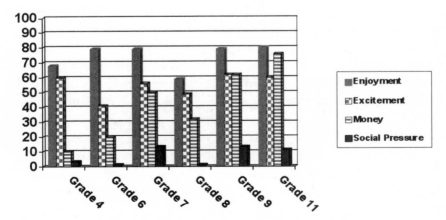

Figure 2.6. Reasons children and adolescents report gambling.

FAMILIAL FACTORS RELATED TO YOUTH GAMBLING

The results from a number of research investigations suggest that the majority of youth report gambling with family members (40% to 68%) as well as with friends (55% to 82%). Teenagers tend to report that their parents do not appear to be overly concerned with their gambling. In general, adolescent reports suggest that approximately 80% to 90% of parents are aware their adolescent children are gambling for money and do not object. In a study examining lottery ticket purchases in Canada, the researchers found that 77% of adolescents indicated that their parents actually purchased scratch lottery tickets for them, with another 50% purchasing lottery draw tickets (e.g., Lotto 6/49) for their children. Surprisingly, 70% of adolescents also reported having received a lottery ticket as a present (most notably for birthdays, Christmas, holidays, or special occasions). Among children aged 9-14, 40% had indicated that they had gambled for money with their parents and only 20% seemed fearful that their parents or another authority figure would discover their gambling. By the time children were age 13 or 14, less than 10% were concerned that their parents would find out about their gambling behavior.

In order to corroborate some of these findings, a recent national survey among parents having a teenage child was conducted in Canada. These findings confirmed earlier youth reports that parents do not seem overly concerned about their children's gambling. Less than half (40%) of the parents expressed any meaningful concern about their child's gambling. Furthermore, 60% of parents of teenagers readily admitted engaging in some form of gambling with their child. The most common forms of gambling engaged in by parents with their children included purchasing lottery tickets, raffles for fundraisers, and joint lottery draw tickets. Parents revealed that they tended to wager more with their adolescent sons than with their daughters, and a small number admitted gambling on electronic gambling machines, the Internet, and casino games with their underage children. Fathers, overall, were found to be considerably less concerned than mothers about their children's gambling. Interestingly, only 12.5% of parents reported they were aware their child was gambling for money, while the actual known gambling prevalence rate among adolescents is considerably higher.

Parental gambling behaviors have also been shown to have an important impact on their children's overall attitudes toward gambling as well as their own gambling behavior. Adolescents whose parents are accepting of their children's gambling have been found to be more likely to gamble as well. The normalization and social acceptability of gambling has certainly impacted child and adolescent gambling.

Paternal gambling problems have been consistently shown to be highly correlated to the frequency of their children's gambling, thus constituting one risk factor for the development of a gambling problem. Retrospective studies further suggest that between 25% and 40% of adult pathological gamblers report their own parents had similar gambling problems.

The impact of parental gambling can have far-reaching consequences for the gambler and the entire family. Along with the effects of having increased family debt, children from homes where parental gambling is a problem continue to report feelings of insecurity, poor self-esteem, low self-image, and in general have a greater need for acceptance. Unfortunately, a growing number of very young children have been reportedly left alone in cars in casino parking lots while their parents were gambling for hours. The casino in Capetown, South Africa, which operates a child daycare on its site, had to initiate a pager system because parents left their children in the daycare for excessively long periods without checking or inquiring about their well being.

PEER INFLUENCES

Friends and peers play an equally important role in shaping a wide range of behaviors. As with peers being influential in drug/alcohol use, cigarette smoking, and other potentially risky behaviors, gambling behavior is no exception. Early studies have revealed that in addition to parents and family members, individuals seek to gamble with their peers and friends. A number of research investigations have reported that upwards of 75% of 9 to 14 year olds who regularly gambled did so with their peers, typically on unregulated activities. These studies also indicated that there was a distinct tendency to gamble at a friend's home and at school with peers as they became older.

The recent proliferation of young people's poker playing among friends further supports these findings. Youth frequently report that their parents encourage them to play poker on weekends in their homes as a way of minimizing their going out with friends and getting involved in "more serious risky behaviors" (e.g., use of alcohol and drugs). Unfortunately, typically parents never warn their children about the potential risks associated with excessive gambling. What begins as a social, enjoyable, and exciting activity actually can get out of control and become problematic. One teenager in treatment remarked how angry he was with both his parents and school because, while they had continuously reinforced the risks associated with excessive alcohol consumption, drug use, and unprotected sex, they never discussed potential problems associated with gambling. So while gambling appears to be a fun and exciting activity, unless closely monitored, it can escalate and result in serious problems. There is little doubt that adolescents are gambling on a diverse range of activities, are influenced by parents and peers, are highly attracted to gambling advertisements, and may be gambling excessively in spite of restrictions and prohibitions. The number of young people gambling continues to grow at alarming rates.

REFERENCES

Abbott, M., Volberg, R., Bellringer, M., and Reith, G. (2004). A Review of Research on Aspects of Problem Gambling. Report prepared for the Responsibility in Gambling Trust, U.K.

Australian Government Productivity Commission. (2010). *Gambling Inquiry.* Australian Government.

Australian Government Productivity Commission. (1999). *Australia's Gambling Industries*: Australian Government.

Campbell, C., Derevensky, J., Meerkamper, E., and Cutajar, J. (2011). Parents' perceptions of adolescent gambling: A Canadian national study. *Journal of Gambling Issues, 25*, 36–53.

Delfabbro, P. (2007). *Australasian Gambling Review Third Edition (1992–2007)*. A report prepared for the Independent Gambling Authority of South Australia. Adelaide: Independent Gambling Authority.

Derevensky, J. (2008). Gambling behaviors and adolescent substance use disorders. In Y. Kaminer and O. G.Buckstein (Eds.). *Adolescent substance abuse: Psychiatric comorbidity and high risk behaviors*. New York: Haworth Press, 403–33.

Derevensky, J., and Gupta, R. (Eds.). (2004). *Gambling problems in youth: Theoretical and applied perspectives*. New York: Kluwer Academic/Plenum Publishers.

Dickson, L., and Derevensky, J. (2006). Preventing adolescent problem gambling: Implications for school psychology. *Canadian Journal of School Psychology, 21*(1/2), 59–72.

Ellenbogen, S., Derevensky, J., and Gupta, R. (2007). Gender differences among adolescents with gambling related problems. *Journal of Gambling Studies, 23*, 133–43.

Felsher, J., Derevensky, J. and Gupta, R. (2003). Parental influences and social modeling of youth lottery participation. *Journal of Community and Applied Social Psychology, 13*, 361–77.

Griffiths, M. (1989). Gambling in children and adolescents. *Journal of Gambling Behavior, 5*, 66–83.

Griffiths, M. (1990). Addiction to fruit machines: A preliminary study among young males. *Journal of Gambling Studies, 6*, 113–26.

Griffiths, M. (1994). An exploratory study of gambling cross addictions. *Journal of Gambling Studies, 10*, 371–84.

Griffiths, M. (1995). *Adolescent gambling*. London, UK: Routledge.

Griffiths, M., and Sutherland, I. (1998). Adolescent gambling and drug use. *Journal of Community and Applied Social Psychology, 8*, 423–27.

Gupta, R., and Derevensky, J. (1997). Familial and social influences on juvenile gambling. *Journal of Gambling Studies, 13*, 179–92.

Gupta, R., and Derevensky, J. (1998). Adolescent gambling behavior: A prevalence study and examination of the correlates associated with problem gambling. *Journal of Gambling Studies, 14*, 319–45.

Hardoon, K., Derevensky, J., and Gupta, R. (2001). Social influences involved in children's gambling behavior. *Journal of Gambling Studies, 17*(3), 191–215.

Hardoon, K., Gupta, R., and Derevensky, J. (2004). Psychosocial variables associated with adolescent gambling: A model for problem gambling. *Psychology of Addictive Behaviors, 18*(2), 170–9.

Huang, J-H., Jacobs, D., Derevensky, J., Gupta, R., and Paskus, T. (2007). Gambling and health risk behaviors among U.S. college student athletes: Findings from a national study. *Journal of Adolescent Health, 40*(5), 390–7.

Jacobs, D. F. (2004). Youth gambling in North America: Long-term trends and future prospects. In J. Derevensky and R. Gupta (Eds.), *Gambling problems in youth: Theoretical and applied perspectives.* New York: Kluwer Academic/Plenum Publishers.

Ladouceur, R. and Mireault, C. (1988). Gambling behaviors amongst high school students in the Quebec area. *Journal of Gambling Studies, 4*, 3–12.

Lesieur, H. R., and Klein, R. (1987). Pathological gambling among high school students. *Addictive Behaviors, 12*, 129–35.

Meyer, G., Hayer, T. and Griffiths, M. (Eds.) (2009). *Problem gambling in Europe: Challenges, prevention and interventions.* New York: Springer.

Mooss, A. D. (2009). *Gambling behaviors among youth involved in juvenile and family courts.* Psychology dissertations, Paper 63. Georgia State University.

National Research Council. (1999). *Pathological gambling: A critical review.* Washington, DC: National Academy Press.

Poulin, C. (2000). Problem gambling among adolescents in the Atlantic provinces of Canada. *Journal of Gambling Studies, 16*, 53–78.

Shead, N. W., Derevensky, J., and Gupta, R. (2010). Risk and protective factors associated with youth problem gambling. *International Journal of Adolescent Medicine and Health, 22*(1), 39–58.

Shead, N. W., Derevensky, J., and Meerkamper, E. (2011). Your mother should know: A comparison of maternal and paternal attitudes and behaviors related to gambling among their adolescent children. *International Journal of Mental Health and Addiction, 9*, 264–75.

Volberg, R., Gupta, R., Griffiths, M., Olason, D., and Delfabbro, P. (2010). An international perspective on youth gambling prevalence studies. *International Journal of Adolescent Medicine and Health, 22*, 3–38.

3

ADOLESCENT PROBLEM GAMBLING

With the increased number of venues, ease of access, and social acceptance of gambling, it is not surprising that many youth are gambling. The thrill and excitement, glitz and glamour, and lure of riches and prizes propel most people to gamble. While most adults and adolescents can best be described as occasional, infrequent, or social gamblers, a number of these individuals go on to experience multiple gambling-related problems resulting from excessive gambling. It is not necessarily the gambling itself that is problematic but all the negative consequences closely associated with the time and money spent gambling. In some ways, it may be analogous to youth who spend countless hours playing videogames. While in this instance there is no money associated with videogame playing, youth who appear to be addicted to these games frequently suffer interpersonal, academic, and social problems. Interestingly, a growing group of researchers studying videogame playing and other behavioral addictions are using gambling as the model on which to base their investigations, given the similarity in their associated behaviors and consequences. There is a growing body of evidence suggesting that both excessive videogame playing and gambling behavior can best be viewed on a continuum, with some individuals not engaging in this behavior at all, to those who are excessively involved and experiencing a wide array of problems associated with their behavior, with these individuals experiencing a form of behavioral addiction. What differentiates youth gambling problems from a videogame addiction is typically related to the myriad of financial and associated consequences (loss of money, lying, stealing, etc.).

There is an old adage within the gambling industry: "the more you gamble, the more you lose." With repeated playing, most youth with gambling problems ultimately lose all their money no matter how smart or intelligent they think they are. And, in order to continue gambling, individuals are forced to acquire more funds. This frequently leads youth with gambling problems to sell personal possessions, use all their savings, borrow money from friends and family members under false pretences, and steal money from those close to them. For some individuals, when the money is depleted they stop gambling, but for others the need and urge to continue gambling is too great and they go to any lengths to get money to maintain their gambling. Many adolescents with gambling problems report initially stealing from their parents or siblings because it is easier and there is a general perception that if caught stealing by a family member, they will not call the police or the youth will not face legal repercussions. One youth reported stealing thousands of dollars from his parents and when asked if he had any remorse he replied "Sure I have remorse, it is nothing personal. I wasn't deliberately trying to hurt my parents, I just needed the money."

While there are considerable differences in the methodologies used to ascertain the prevalence rates of adolescent problem gambling (discussed in chapter 4), the rates of adolescent problem and pathological gambling are actually considerably higher than those of adults. Nevertheless, methodological concerns over instrumentation, designations of what constitutes "adolescence," accessibility, and availability of gambling activities have led to some rather wide discrepancies in reported prevalence rates. Based on a recent comprehensive review of international studies by Rachel Volberg and her colleagues, the median prevalence rate of adolescent problem and pathological gambling was found to be approximately 3.0% in the United States and Canada, with non-Scandinavian European studies reporting 4.8%, Nordic countries reporting 2.2%, and those from Australia and New Zealand indicating prevalence rates of 3.7%. It should be noted that the average prevalence rate for problem and pathological gambling among adults in most Western countries is approximately 1% to 2%. For both adolescents and adults, the prevalence rates for males are considerably higher (three to four times) than those for females. It should also be noted that among adults, those individuals between the ages of 18 and 25 have the highest prevalence rates of problem gambling. While there are disagreements about how best to measure problem gambling, there is nevertheless strong agreement that adolescents represent a highly vulnerable population for gambling problems.

There is a correlation between youths having a friend with a gambling problem and the severity of their own gambling problem. This is not surprising given the strong influence of the peer group at this age. In a recent study conducted at the International Centre for Youth Gambling Problems and High-Risk Behaviors, we found that over 40% of youth with serious and extensive gambling problems and over one-third of at-risk gamblers (those exhibiting some problems on gambling severity screens but not reaching the clinical criteria for pathological gambling) had a close friend with a gambling problem. This is in stark contrast to individuals who gamble occasionally or never gamble. Among occasional gamblers, only 10% of these individuals reported having a friend with a gambling problem and this was even lower for youth who never gamble (6%). Not only does having a friend who gambles increase the likelihood of gambling involvement, a large number of clinical reports suggest that adolescents with gambling problems tend to sever ties with their non-gambling friends because they frequently borrow money and fail to repay these loans, lie and steal from friends, and gradually begin to spend more time with fellow problem gamblers who have similar interests. Once these old, stable relationships have been destroyed, it is often very difficult to rebuild previous friendship patterns. Similar findings have been found for individuals who have friends who are either using or abusing a variety of substances. Problem gamblers have also reported having friends who frequently use/abuse alcohol or drugs on a regular basis.

As previously mentioned, problem gambling often begins at an early age and results in many problems. Arnie Wexler, now a gambling counselor who works with both adolescents and adults, is in some ways typical of an individual who developed significant gambling problems. Fortunately, he turned his life around and is now helping others in need. Arnie's testimonial typifies the progression of the disorder from adolescence throughout adulthood. It also reveals how problem/pathological gambling can be an all-encompassing and unrelenting disorder that seems to have no beginning and, for some, no end.

ARNIE'S STORY

I am a recovering compulsive gambler who placed my last bet on April 10, 1968.

I started gambling at about age 7 or 8 as a kid in Brooklyn, NY. It started with flipping baseball cards, pitching pennies, shooting marbles, and playing pinball machines. That kind of gambling continued until about age 14. At that point, I started to bet on sporting events with a bookmaker and I got into the stock market.

As a young kid growing up, I always felt that everyone was better than me. The only time I felt okay about myself was after I had a win, whether it was marbles or baseball cards or pennies. Then at 14, I went to the racetrack for the first time (that was Memorial Day, 1951, Roosevelt Raceway). At that time in my life, I was making 50 cents an hour after school, working about 15-20 hours a week. That night at Roosevelt Raceway, I had my first big win and walked out of the track with $54. Looking back today, I think it was that night that changed my life. Even though it was only $54, it was about five weeks' salary to me at that time. That night gave me the belief that I could be a winner from gambling and eventually become a millionaire. I can still recall that high feeling walking out of the racetrack that night.

By 17, I was already stealing to support my gambling. It started with stealing comic books to play cards with from the local candy store. Before long, I was stealing money from my family to pay for gambling. By then, I was taking the bus to the racetrack a few nights a week on a regular basis. In those days they closed the track in the winter months in New York, so on weekends I would take the bus or the train to Maryland to gamble. I was betting sporting events and horses with the bookmaker on a daily basis. In those days, each sport had its own season. I remember calling the bookmaker one day and the only thing that was available to gamble on was hockey. I had never seen a hockey game, but bet on it anyway. It wasn't until months later when I did see my first hockey game that I realized that hockey was played on ice.

Somewhere between age 17 and 20 I went to the racetrack one night and won $6,000. Wow! Another big win. It was the equivalent of two years' salary. This reinforced my belief that I could be a winner at gambling.

By my early 20s, I was betting big amounts on lots of games that I didn't really know much about and probably couldn't name more than a handful of players who played in these events. In some of the college games I bet on, I couldn't name one player or even tell you where the college was located, but I needed to be in the action. By then I was a regular at the old Madison Square Garden every week. I was watching and betting on college and professional basketball on a regular basis. At this point in my life, I was working full time in a shipping department in the garment center and every Tuesday when we got paid there was a regular crap game out in the hallway. Almost every week I would lose my pay in this game. I began stealing supplies and merchandise on a daily basis to pay for my gambling. By then, I had a bank loan and a loan with a finance company. I was also borrowing from coworkers.

At 21, I met my future wife. Our first date was to the movies and most of the rest of our dating was at the racetrack. We had a joint checking account, saving for our wedding. She would put money in and I wouldn't. I needed to use my money for gambling. I was still looking for another big win. I thought the perfect place for our honeymoon would be Las Vegas or Puerto Rico, since I knew both places had casinos. My wife-to-be didn't think that was a good idea. I guess she understood enough about my gambling already. At 23, we got married and I wanted to stop gambling at that point. I thought that I could. Within a short time I was already back to gambling. Even though I wanted to stop, I realize today that I couldn't. I needed to gamble like any drug addict needed to stick that needle in their arm, or an alcoholic needed to have that drink.

CHAPTER 3

Four weeks after we got married, I went away to the Army Re-
serves at Fort Dix, New Jersey, for six months. During those six
months, I gambled every day, fast and furious, from placing bets by
phone with the bookmaker to shooting craps and playing cards, every
waking minute. When I came home in December 1961, I owed $4,000
and didn't even have a job.

I got a job eventually, working in the garment center. In the show-
room that I worked in, there were a few compulsive gamblers whom
I quickly got friendly with. They became my buddies. We would
play cards during the day, and go to the racetrack at night and on
weekends. My wife thought I was at business meetings some of these
nights and all of us would lie for each other.

In 1963, my first daughter was born. My wife was in labor 37 hours.
During that period, I went to the racetrack twice. When the doctor
finally came out and told me that we had a baby, the only question
I really was concerned about was how much did she weigh. He told
me 7 lb, 1 oz. You would think that the concern should have been
how is my wife or how is the baby. The first call I made was to the
bookmaker. I bet 71 in the daily double. The next day when I picked
up the newspaper, the daily double hit. I was convinced that day that
God was sending me a message that I was now going to be a winner.

One year later, my boss gave me an option to buy 500 shares of
stock in the company for $7,500. Within a year that stock was worth
$38,000. In those days you could buy a car for $2,000 and a house for
about $10,000. Within three years this money was gone due to my
gambling. By now, I was a plant supervisor for a Fortune 500 company. My gambling was already so out of control that I was stealing
everything I could to stay in action. I set up a room in the factory that
we used for playing cards (all day long). I was starting to do illegal
acts (manipulating stocks) in the stock market.

Our home life was deteriorating. Gambling was more important
than anything else that was going on at home. I was lying about almost everything and I would come home and pick a fight so I could
go out to gamble. Nothing else at that point in my life was more
important than gambling: not my family or my job. Gambling came
first. At this point even though I was doing illegal acts, I was still borrowing money from only legal sources.

My gambling continued to get progressively worse. I was now a
plant manager, supervising 300 to 400 people. My boss worked in

New York, and I was in the factory in New Jersey. Most of the time he didn't know what I was doing. Besides stealing and borrowing money from coworkers, I now had three bank loans and three loans to finance companies. I owed a loan shark an amount of money equal to one year's salary. I was involved with three bookmakers, both working for them and betting with them. I directed a lot of people who gambled in my company to my bookmaker and got a piece of the action. I even got involved in a numbers operation. Between this and stealing, I was supporting my gambling. There were times I would bet 40 or 50 games on a weekend, and believe I could win them all. One weekend, just before I hit my bottom, I called a bookmaker and took a shot by betting a round robin which amounted to about two years' annual salary. At that moment, if I lost that bet, there was no way I could pay it. Things were getting so bad, I remember calling a bookmaker one day and being told that if I didn't bring him the money I owed him, he would not take my bet for that night. I went home and sold our car to a neighbor.

By now I wasn't going home to pick a fight with my wife, I was doing it over the phone so I wouldn't waste the trip home. Most of the time I was out gambling, but when I was home we were constantly fighting. We had sex very rarely. When I won, I was so high I didn't need it and if I lost I didn't want it. But there were times we had sex and my wife would say to me "do you hear a radio?" Of course I would tell her she was crazy, but I had a radio on under the pillow so I could listen to a game. We were trying to have another child, but couldn't. My wife came to me with the idea of adoption. I didn't like that idea especially when I was told it would cost money. I needed that money for gambling. After three months of her bothering me, I finally went along with the idea of adoption, because I thought she would be so busy with the two kids that she would leave me alone. I borrowed the money we needed from my boss and relatives. On the day we were bringing our son home on a plane, it was the seventh game of the 1967 World Series. My wife was busy looking at this beautiful new baby. I had no interest in him. I had a large bet on the game. The pilot was announcing the score every 15 minutes, or so. I was so upset that we were on this plane. I wished and prayed that the plane would land so that I could see or hear every minute of this game.

In the next few months, the bottom fell out of my world even though I still had my job and still looked okay. There were no track marks on my arm, I wasn't smelling from my gambling. No one could really tell what was going on. I would come home from gambling and see my wife crying all the time, depressed, sick. Our daughter was 4 years old and I don't remember her walking or talking. I either wasn't home or when I was, my head was consumed with the gambling. At that point in my life, I owed 32 people three years' annual salary. I had a life insurance policy and constantly thought about killing myself and leaving my wife and two kids the money. I would do anything to keep gambling. As long as I could get my hands on some more money to stay in action, I still thought that the big win was just around the corner. I was trying to find out where I could get drugs to sell and looking around at gas stations to rob. I was asking people about making counterfeit money. I was running out of options. My boss came to me one day and told me that a detective was following me and he had a report on my gambling. He knew I was betting more money than I earned and he was sure that I was stealing from the company and that if he found out he would have me arrested. Three hours later, I was stealing from the company again. I needed to go to the racetrack that night. On February 2, 1968, my wife was having a miscarriage and I was taking her to the hospital. I was wishing and praying all the way that she would die. I thought that would solve all my problems (I wouldn't have to tell her how bad things were). That morning I called my mother to watch my kids, I called my boss and told him I couldn't come to work because my wife was in the hospital. That afternoon I went to the racetrack. After the track I went to see how my wife was. When I got to the hospital the doctor told me that my wife was in shock and had almost died. I was so deep into my addiction that I really didn't care about her, the two kids, or myself. The only important thing was making a bet.

I thought that I was the only one living the way I was living and doing the things that I was doing. I found out that I was not alone and that I could stop gambling with the help of other people. I had hope for the first time. It's been over 40 years since I last gambled. Today I have everything I dreamed about getting from gambling and then some. I have a wonderful family that is still intact and even have been blessed with four grandchildren whom I love very much. In the last 30 years, I have been able to devote my working life to helping others who have this problem and educating people on the disease of Compulsive Gambling. This has been a dream come true.

Arnie Wexler's story typifies the progression of a gambling problem, the preoccupation to gamble and the inability to stop in spite of the adverse consequences. Fortunately, through the help he received from Gamblers Anonymous he was able to turn his life around. Today, he has been responsible for helping many hundreds of individuals with a similar problem.

BEHAVIORS ASSOCIATED WITH PROBLEM/EXCESSIVE GAMBLING: SOME IMPORTANT WARNING SIGNS

Similar to other mental health disorders, problem gambling has multiple risk factors and warning signs, but no single constellation of risk factors can alone predict with a great deal of certainty that a particular problem will exist. Some of the risk factors and warning signs associated with problem gambling are also common to a number of other disorders, including other addictive behaviors, whereas some are more relevant to those individuals with a gambling problem. While there are multiple constellations of risk factors that in conjunction with the right opportunity can place certain individuals at high risk for a gambling problem, there is a growing recognition that the causes underlying gambling problems are not universal, that the constellation of risk factors may be different for each individual, that biological and environmental factors play an important role, and that different pathways may exist that lead to problem and pathological gambling.

After years of research and reviews of existing studies, the International Centre for Youth Gambling Problems and High-Risk Behaviors has concluded that a number of behaviors are indicative of someone with a gambling problem. As such, the following behaviors constitute potential warning signs:

- Spends large amounts of time gambling
- Places larger and more frequent wagers
- Frequently returns to gambling in order to win back lost money (often referred to as "chasing behavior")

- Has growing debts
- Pins hope on the "big win"
- Promises to reduce gambling
- Refuses to explain behavior or lies about it
- Has frequent mood swings
- Boasts about gambling winnings
- Prefers gambling over other activities
- Repeatedly seeks to gamble with friends and/or parents
- Appears "spaced out" (psychologists often refer to this as dissociation) while gambling
- Is very anxious when gambling
- Continues to seek new opportunities and venues in which to gamble
- Shows an interest in the gambling of parents, siblings, or others
- Prefers to watch poker tournaments on television
- Plays gambling-simulated programs frequently on videogame machines or on the computer
- Engages in Internet gambling practice/fun sites without money
- Asks parents to place a wager for them when they are gambling
- Is interested in selecting lottery tickets and/or winning numbers
- Has been observed to have a considerable number of lottery tickets, bingo cards, and/or gambling literature
- Has abused other substances (e.g., drugs and alcohol)
- Repeatedly seeks activities which result in increasing levels of excitement
- Has borrowed or stolen money and "can't recall" how the money was spent
- Carries large amounts of cash
- Talks about gambling
- Frequently seeks out movies and/or television shows related to gambling
- Becomes excessively angry or shows signs of anxiety when watching sports on television
- Has sudden failing grades, poor academic performance, and absenteeism at school

- Is obsessed with playing poker
- Has friends or strangers calling the house asking about money owed
- Quickly minimizes the computer screen when parents walk into the room
- Refuses to install software that blocks gambling on either the home or personal computer

While the endorsement of one or more of these warning signs *may* be indicative of a gambling problem, only a clinical assessment can confirm whether a problem exists and the severity of the problem. It should also be noted that certain behaviors may be specific to different forms of gambling (e.g., poker playing or sports wagering) while others may be more related to other forms of gambling (e.g., casino or Internet gambling).

CORRELATES OF A GAMBLING DISORDER

Adolescent problem gamblers have been shown to be prone to engage in multiple, co-morbid addictive behaviors (smoking, drinking, and/or drug use/abuse). In general, they are also more likely to exhibit other behavioral and mental health problems including conduct, antisocial, and oppositional disorders which will be discussed in more detail later. Some of these behaviors are the result of excessive gambling, while for others gambling is used as a way of minimizing and distracting the individual from other personal problems. Ultimately, a considerable number of these youth experience academic and peer-related difficulties, with increased truancy, delinquency, and social problems ensuing. While adolescents with gambling problems frequently report having a good support group, a closer examination reveals that their old friends are often replaced by "gambling associates" (people who have similar interests and friends who enjoy gambling). Problem and pathological gambling has been shown to result in increased criminal behaviors and disruption of familial and personal relationships.

Youth with gambling problems have a tendency to be preoccupied with their gambling, planning their next gambling activity or gambling trip, lying to their family and friends, and become obsessed with obtaining increasing amounts of money with which to gamble. Trying to recoup one's losses becomes a reoccurring preoccupation and behavior in order to "catch up," get even, and repay debts. Such debts can escalate quickly and can be in the thousands or tens of thousands of dollars, even for an adolescent. Ultimately, problem gamblers continue to gamble in an attempt to recoup lost money, getting deeper and deeper in debt in what appears to be a bottomless pit. This behavior is often referred to as "chasing behavior" where the individual keeps gambling to try to recoup losses, and ultimately enters a downward cycle toward pathological gambling. Some clinicians have argued it is only when individuals hit the bottom of this cycle that they will seek help and realize their gambling is truly problematic.

Over the past fifteen years, researchers at the International Centre for Youth Gambling Problems and High-Risk Behaviors at McGill University, Nottingham Trent University, University of Minnesota, Laval University, and others have been trying to identify the risk factors associated with excessive gambling problems and possible protective mechanisms as a way of minimizing gambling problems. Their work has led to a growing body of research focusing on behavioral patterns, correlates, and risk factors associated with adolescent gambling and problem gambling. While there are always studies that result in conflicting findings, there remains considerable evidence pointing to the following:

- Gambling is more popular among males than females (although there are differences in the types of gambling preferred by both males and females) and more adolescent males than females exhibit pathological gambling behaviors.
- Pathological gambling among male adolescents has been found to be approximately two to four times as prevalent compared with adult males. There is also evidence suggesting that young adult males (ages 18-25) have a considerably higher

prevalence of gambling and gambling-related problems than their older adult counterparts.

- Males typically have been found to make higher gross wagers, begin and initiate gambling earlier, gamble on more diverse types of activities and games, gamble more frequently, and spend more time and money gambling. Parents of boys are also more likely to encourage their son's gambling, with more males than females reporting gambling with their parents.

- Among adolescents, there often is a rapid movement from social, occasional, and recreational gambling to problem or pathological gambling.

- Adolescent problem gamblers report beginning gambling at an early age (approximately 10-11 years of age) as compared with peers who report gambling but who have few gambling-related problems. There have recently been a number of studies examining "late-onset" gamblers (individuals who develop problems but who have begun gambling much later) that reveal similar behaviors as the "early-onset" gamblers.

- Many youth problem gamblers report having had an early "big win" (remembering a big win for a child or teenager is considerably different than for an adult).

- Adolescents experiencing gambling problems often report that they began gambling with family members in their own homes.

- Older siblings (both brothers and sisters) have an important impact on their younger siblings' gambling behavior. However, as children get older, their patterns of gambling change such that youth gamble considerably less with family members (parents, relatives, and siblings) and more with friends.

- Adolescents with gambling problems in general population surveys are also more likely to report having parents whom they perceive gamble excessively, may be involved in other addictive behaviors, and have been involved in illegal activities.

- Similar to adults, children and adolescents often have a positive attitude toward gambling. While they often fail to completely understand the risks or odds associated with gambling, many are cognizant of the problems associated with excessive gambling but view them as long-term negative consequences and not of immediate concern. They typically believe that by the time problems emerge, their gambling will have stopped.

- While there is a paucity of research examining cultural differences among adolescents, a number of large scale studies of Minnesota adolescents reported that 30% of Native American adolescents gambled weekly, and 22% of Mexican-American and African-American youth gambled weekly, while only 4% to 5% of Asian and Caucasian youth gambled on a weekly basis. One study of adolescents in Texas reported that Hispanics gambled more frequently than Caucasians, while some Canadian research has revealed significant cultural differences among Francophones (those whose native language is French), Anglophones (adolescents predominantly from English-speaking families), and Allophones (adolescents whose native language is neither French nor English [e.g., Italian, Vietnamese, Chinese, and Portuguese]) with Allophones gambling more often and having more gambling problems. There is significant concern among Asian communities, given the appeal of gambling in their culture. Several prevalence studies in Asia, Australia, and New Zealand attest to increased prevalence rates of problem gambling among certain cultural groups. A recent finding in Australia also points to the high risk of gambling problems among Aboriginal youth.
- Personality traits reveal adolescent pathological gamblers often have difficulty conforming to societal norms and experience difficulties with self-discipline in many aspects of their lives.
- A growing body of literature suggests genetic influences on brain functioning may lead to vulnerability of multiple addictive disorders including pathological gambling. This would suggest that some adolescents may be more susceptible to gambling problems than others.
- Adolescents with gambling problems are typically more likely to experience a multiplicity of school-related problems including increased truancy and poor academic performance, are

more likely to have repeated a grade in school, and report a greater frequency of attention-deficit hyperactive disorder and conduct-related problems. What is not known is whether there is a cause-effect relationship.

UNDERSTANDING ADOLESCENT PROBLEM GAMBLING BEHAVIOR

In recent years, there has been a movement toward understanding youth gambling problems using a biopsychosocial model. This model posits that biological, psychological, and social factors play a significant role in understanding a particular disorder or problem. This model is not unique to explaining gambling disorders. The model can be traced back 35 years to George Engel, an American psychiatrist, who articulated that a new medical model was needed for understanding and explaining medical diseases. Helping to explain problem gambling using this model suggests that understanding the underlying causes and interactions is indeed complex. There is little doubt that no one particular theoretical perspective can best explain why certain individuals gamble excessively in the face of repeated losses. As such, viewing gambling as a complex issue consisting of genetic, biological, psychological, social, and environmental factors may help explain pathological gambling in general and adolescent gambling in particular.

This biopsychosocial model has led to considerable research in the field of adolescent gambling in an attempt to explain and identify the alternate pathways symptomatic of individuals with gambling problems, as well as to the acceptance that there may be multiple subtypes of problem gamblers. Alex Blaszczynski and Lia Nower have aided articulating a "Pathways Model" to help explain differences among adolescents experiencing gambling problems. Incorporating the underlying factors associated with problem gambling in a large study of adolescents, Gupta, Blaszczynski, Nower, and I found strong evidence and empirical support for this approach. Understanding the complex interactions from a biological, psychological, social, and environmental perspective will ultimately lead to more effective prevention and treatment initiatives. As will be discussed later in this book, it remains essential to not only understand the comorbid behaviors and disorders accompanying pathological gambling but to simultaneously address mental health and substance abuse issues along with the gambling problems in order to best help the individual.

BIOLOGICAL AND GENETIC FACTORS ASSOCIATED WITH PROBLEM GAMBLING

A growing body of evidence has been assessing differences in neurological brain functioning between individuals with gambling problems versus those that do not seem to have a problem. Rather than going into great detail, it is important to understand that significant breakthroughs in our understanding of the underlying brain mechanisms associated with problem gambling are occurring. A growing amount of research has also looked at specific genetic factors and has tried to link receptor genes and neurotransmitter regulation to an individual's level of arousal, impulsivity, and pathological gambling. Preliminary evidence suggests that serotonin (which is responsible for mood regulation), norepinephrine (responsible for mediating and controlling arousal), and dopamine (responsible for reward regulation) seem to play an important role in mood disorders (e.g., depression), impulsivity, and impaired control—all of which have been shown to be intricately linked to the definition of problem gambling. Much of this ground breaking work is currently being done by Dr. Marc Potenza at Yale University. On a genetic level, considerably more research is under way and there is some evidence suggesting that possession of a specific receptor gene (D2A1 allele) is related to pleasure-generating activities (i.e., gambling).

The Role of Impulsivity

Our current conceptualization of gambling problems views pathological and problem gambling as an impulse control disorder. In essence, it is an inability or impaired ability to control one's gambling in spite of repeated losses. Some people refer to the urges to gamble as an impulsive trait. A large number of investigations, with both adults and adolescents, have concluded that individuals experiencing gambling problems exhibit considerably higher scores on a variety of self-report and observational measures of impulsivity. In one interesting study, teacher ratings of impulsivity when boys were age 13 were reasonably accurate predictors of problem gambling when these youth were age 17.

Impulsivity has often been related to attention deficit hyperactivity disorder (ADHD), a disorder common among male children and adolescents. There have been a number of research investigations conducted internationally which have pointed to the relationship between ADHD and problem gambling. Anecdotally, many of the clients who come to the McGill University treatment clinic for a gambling problem either currently have symptoms of ADHD or were previously given a diagnosis of ADHD as children. A number of these studies have shown rates as high as 30% of those seeking help for a gambling problem who reported some history of ADHD. There is also considerable behavioral and neurological support suggesting that individuals with persistent ADHD are clearly at risk for developing a gambling problem. Childhood behaviors related to over-activity, destructibility, and the inability to control one's behavior are important correlates associated with adolescent problem gambling. In a number of investigations, problem gambling was found to be highly related to inattention and hyperactive-impulsive traits.

Many of the impulse control problems and disorders among adolescents have also been found to be associated with sensation-seeking behaviors (the desire to seek varied, novel, complex, and intense sensations and experiences), which are common among adolescent problem gamblers. It is important to note that problem gamblers may not be high sensation seekers in a variety of contexts, but rather use only gambling as a way of satisfying the need for intense and novel stimulation.

PSYCHOLOGICAL AND MENTAL HEALTH ISSUES ASSOCIATED WITH PROBLEM GAMBLING

Of significant concern are the myriad of mental health issues associated with individuals having a pathological gambling disorder. We are only beginning to have an understanding of the mental health factors that contribute to problem gambling, but we currently realize there are a number of psychological factors associated with problem and pathological gamblers.

Depression and Mood Disorders

There is strong evidence and support indicating that pathological gamblers, whether they are adults or adolescents, have increased levels of depression and depressive symptoms. In fact, in a large national study in Australia, it was found that approximately 22% of problem gamblers reported having experienced some form of depression. Other studies report that as many as 75% of problem gamblers experience some form of clinical depression. These rates are considerably higher among individuals seeking help for a gambling problem and are consistent with reports by members attending Gamblers Anonymous meetings. Rates of major depression among problem gamblers have been shown to be almost twice that of the general population. What still remains unclear is whether depression causes some individuals to gamble as a way of coping with their depressed mood or whether pathological gamblers become depressed because of the many ensuing gambling-related problems. While there is evidence supporting both sides of the argument, it is likely that it may well be a combination of both perspectives. For some individuals, the depression may have resulted in excessive gambling to relieve depression, while for others there may have been few signs of depression before the individual's gambling became excessive. Independent of the sequence and order, from a pragmatic perspective, the individual remains depressed. Merely getting the individual to stop gambling frequently can serve to exacerbate the depression, rather than relieve the depression, as this may have been one of the few forms of enjoyment the person experienced.

In a large number of studies of adolescents and young adults, researchers at the International Centre for Youth Gambling Problems and High-Risk Behaviors report similar findings, such as that as gambling severity (both frequency and number of problems) increases so does the rate and severity of depression. Among their clinical population, depression is the leading co-occurring mental health issue.

Anxiety Disorders

A number of research investigations have sought to better understand the relationship between anxiety disorders and problem gambling. These studies have in general revealed that a large percentage (approximately 38%) of individuals seeking help for a gambling problem had an anxiety disorder. In one large national epidemiological study of adults in the United States, over 40% of problem gamblers were reported to have experienced an anxiety disorder (compared to 29% for non-problem gamblers) at some point in their life, while in yet another study it was reported that 71% of problem gamblers reported some form of anxiety disorder. Several adolescent studies examining the relationship between anxiety and problem gambling have found similar results. In one study which examined multiple types of anxiety, between 14% and 48% (the variability is reflected in the specific type of anxiety disorder) of severe problem gamblers reported a high incidence of anxiety. Almost twice as many adolescent problem gamblers reported significant social stress compared with non-gambling adolescents. As will be discussed in chapter 6 concerning helping youth with gambling problems, while the individual's cumulative debts increase and concerns about lying to friends and family members about their gambling likely precipitate and increase their anxiety, anxiety during the actual gambling is possibly diminished because gambling provides an escape from mounting problems.

Personality Characteristics and Problem Gambling

When examining personality disorders or personality characteristics, certain personality traits are thought to contribute to problem gambling. In a comprehensive study examining personality differences between adolescents with severe gambling problems and typical adolescents, the researchers reported that problem gamblers scored higher on measures of excitability, conformity, self-discipline, and cheerfulness. Adolescents experiencing gambling problems appeared to exhibit less ability to self-regulate their behavior, tended to be more impulsive, easily distractible, self-indulgent, and had considerable difficulty in conforming to rules while exuding the impression that they are carefree, sociable, and happy. Other investigations have revealed that adolescent problem gamblers have lower self-esteem and may want to use their gambling as a way of attracting friends or displaying their bravado. Often adolescents talk of themselves as being considered the "big shot." There is also an abundance of evidence linking problem gambling and risk taking, frustration, impatience, and irritability.

Questions continue to be asked as to whether there exists an addictive personality trait and if so, does problem gambling fall within this framework. While there is no doubt that there is commonality between gambling problems and other addictive behaviors and that problem gamblers are more likely to experience substance use disorders, there is little support at this time suggesting an overall addictive personality trait. It has also been well established that boys tend to engage in many of these behaviors more frequently than girls and tend to be greater risk takers in general. Whether this is a predetermined personality trait remains unclear.

Antisocial and Delinquent Behaviors

A variety of what might be described as antisocial, delinquent, or deviant behaviors have been associated with problem gambling. Such behaviors include borrowing and stealing money to support gambling, selling personal possessions, and using school lunch money to gamble, lying to family members and friends, truancy from school, and criminal behaviors. In order to maintain their gambling, individuals require money. Given adolescents have a limited number of ways to acquire money because they typically are not employed or have jobs paying minimum wage, adolescent problem gamblers are prone to engage in a variety of illegal acts to acquire money for gambling.

Youth with significant gambling problems often begin by stealing money from their parents and report how easy it is to acquire money from their home without their parents' knowledge. Their belief is that if they get caught, their parents will not call the police. In the McGill clinic, many youth report borrowing money from friends and relatives with the sincere intention of repaying them, but ultimately their gambling losses and debts mounted. Some resort to shoplifting products from stores and selling the merchandise to friends in order to get money to gamble. Others pawn or sell personal possessions. One teenager reported how he would steal bottles of cognac from a liquor store and then sell them in order to get money to gamble while another was caught embezzling $10,000 from his father's bank account.

A number of research investigations have found that there is a disproportionately higher percentage of youth experiencing gambling problems that also have criminal records. This has resulted in a number of jurisdictions establishing a "gambling court" where judges, sensitive to the criminal behaviors associated with gambling, try to get the individual the therapeutic help they need to reduce the rate of recidivism rather than merely incarcerate these youth.

In a recent large national survey in the United States, a strong positive relationship between current problem gambling and conduct/oppositional disorders was found. Interestingly, the relationship was strongest among individuals whose problem gambling began in their early to mid-teens rather than for those whose disordered gambling began later.

The Impact of Childhood Maltreatment and Major Life Stressors

A number of theories have been proposed suggesting that the underlying etiology of this disorder may originate from some form of childhood maltreatment (i.e., physical abuse, sexual abuse, emotional abuse, or physical and emotional neglect). The basic assumption of these theories is predicated upon the premise that negative early childhood experiences have been shown to have a major impact on later behavior and an individual's mental health and psychological well-being. While there is strong evidence revealing the long-term negative impact of early maltreatment on later substance abuse, a number of clinicians have argued that the strength of the impact of childhood or adolescent maltreatment is probably dependent on the frequency, degree of severity, type of maltreatment, the individual's resilience in light of the maltreatment (of great importance is the child's understanding that they are the victim and not responsible for the maltreatment), the specific perpetrator, and the developmental level of the child. In a large study conducted at the International Centre for Youth Gambling Problems and High-Risk Behaviors, it was reported that all forms of maltreatment (emotional/physical abuse, sexual abuse, emotional and physical neglect) were related to problem gambling. Problem gamblers were more likely to report some form of maltreatment and more severe (in frequency and intensity) levels of childhood abuse. More recent findings from an Australian study also support these conclusions.

There is other evidence pointing to the findings that adolescent problem gamblers have suffered multiple major life stressors (e.g., parental divorce, death of a close family member, incarceration) and more daily hassles (e.g., school, family or peer-related problems). It is likely that these stressors may prompt individuals to use gambling as a strategy to repress or forget these events. It has also been well established that gamblers, especially problem gamblers, dissociate or enter a "zone" when they are gambling, such that they lose track of time, become oblivious to their surroundings, and forget their problems for the moment. A large number of clinicians have argued that this becomes the primary reason for gambling. Adolescents typically report being inclined to gamble more frequently when they are stressed at school or home, have had disputes with friends, or have had abruptly terminated relationships.

Suicide Ideation and Attempts

Given the emotional vulnerability of problem gamblers, their huge debts, perceived insurmountable problems, and high rates of depression, there is concern whether individuals, adolescents in particular, may contemplate suicide as an alternative to addressing their gambling and gambling-related problems. Suicidal thoughts, sometimes referred to as suicidal ideation, are not uncommon among adolescents and have been clearly linked with depression. While the majority of studies examining suicidal ideation and suicidal attempts have looked at co-occurring mental health disorders amongst adults, the mental health community has always been concerned about the alarmingly high rates of suicidal behavior among adolescents.

The Australian Productivity Commission survey of counseling centers in the late 1990s revealed that approximately 58% of adult problem gamblers reported having seriously contemplated suicide due to their gambling-related problems, with another 15% having made a serious attempt. Other studies of adults have suggested even higher rates of suicide ideation and attempts by problem gamblers. Several forensic autopsies have also reported a disturbing number of gambling-related suicides and there is evidence linking an increased number of suicides for both residents and tourists in gambling resort cities such as Las Vegas, Reno, and Atlantic City.

In a number of national and international studies examining adolescent problem gambling and suicidal ideation, the researchers concluded that there was a clear relationship between reported suicide ideation and the severity of gambling problems. As gambling severity increased so too did thoughts of suicide, independent of levels of depression. Still further, the incidence of reported suicide attempts was found to be highest among adolescent problem gamblers. What is somewhat limiting in the studies examining suicide ideation was that no questions asked whether individuals had made a serious plan to commit suicide, thought to be an important predictor of suicidal attempts.

While many youth with gambling problems often report that they have contemplated suicide, the same is similarly true for youth who have disagreements with peers or partners or who experience severe mental health issues. Nevertheless, this remains a growing problem and treatment providers and individuals helping adolescents with gambling problems are well advised to take suicide threats seriously.

SUBSTANCE USE/ABUSE AND PROBLEM GAMBLING

Multiple investigations, involving both adolescents and adults, have addressed the issue of the association between addictive behaviors, most notably drug abuse, alcohol abuse, and smoking, and pathological gambling. Studies of adult pathological gamblers have revealed increased prevalence rates of all forms of substance use (e.g., alcohol, tobacco, and drug use) as well as higher rates of substance abuse and dependency. Similar to the discussion on the relationship between depression and pathological gambling, it still remains unclear whether pathological gambling and/or other mental health disorders result in elevated rates of substance use and abuse or the reverse is true. Nevertheless, there is evidence that between 25% and 75% of adult pathological gamblers have reported a past history of substance use problems. Similarly, when asking individuals with substance abuse problems about their gambling behaviors, between 10% and 25% also report a serious gambling problem.

Most often, adult problem gambling has been associated with cigarette smoking and alcohol consumption. Cigarette smoking among problems gamblers has been reported to be as much as three times that of the general population of cigarette smokers. In an effort to help minimize these problems, some countries have instituted bans on cigarette smoking in casinos. Some have even established sealed dedicated smoking areas for gaming in their casinos with extra ventilation.

There is ample evidence also suggesting a significant relationship between problem gambling and alcohol consumption. Approximately 30% to 50% of adults who seek treatment for a gambling problem have been reported to also have a comorbid alcohol disorder. Clinicians and researchers have long suggested that the combination of gambling and alcohol may exacerbate a gambling problem and some regulators have restricted alcohol on the gaming floor.

Among adolescents, substance use and abuse disorders are among the most commonly reported disorders associated with pathological gamblers. To provide an illustration of this relationship, one can see the overall results of a Canadian study, with multiple national and international studies reporting similar findings (figure 3.1). As can be observed, there is a linear trend such that non-gamblers report least often engaging in these behaviors while problem gamblers are much more likely to engage in using all potentially addictive substances. It is important to note that these adolescents were all under the legal age to purchase alcohol and cigarettes and to gamble.

In another study with 2,300 adolescents ranging in age from 12 through 19, similar results were found. The evidence revealed that 8% of the youth who were non-gamblers were at risk for a substance use problem and appeared to be the group least at risk. Approximately 15% of youth who were identified as social gamblers (gamblers not experiencing major gambling-related problems), 32% of youth who were experiencing a number of gambling-related problems but who failed to reach the criteria designated as problem

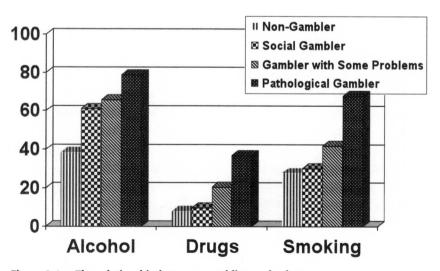

Figure 3.1.   The relationship between gambling and substance use.

gambling, and 51% of youth with pathological gambling disorders were at risk for a substance use problem.

As will be discussed in chapter 6, many of these other co-occurring problems and disorders will need to be directly treated or minimized simultaneously before the individual's gambling problems can be successfully addressed. The duration and type of intervention necessary to help individuals experiencing gambling problems may well be based not merely on the type and severity of the gambling problem but also related to the accompanying mental health or addictive disorders.

SOCIAL-ENVIRONMENTAL FACTORS

Environmental factors including accessibility and availability of gambling activities, the enforcement of regulatory restrictions prohibiting minors from gambling, parental attitudes, and peer relationships are just a few of the factors shown to have an impact. As discussed earlier with respect to the biopsychosocial model, problem gambling may be viewed from an ecological perspective and the interrelationship that exists between the individual and his/her environment is paramount.

Accessibility and availability of gambling venues and opportunities are clearly correlated with the frequency of gambling behaviors among children, adolescents, and adults. While there may be some social adaptation (that is, once availability and accessibility have been present for an extended period of time, people tend to ignore it as the novelty wears away), some activities not only seem to maintain themselves but actually increase (e.g., Internet use). This has often been referred to as the "inoculation effect" and has been advocated as an explanation for the general stability of prevalence rates of problem gambling in spite of the increased availability and proliferation of gambling venues. However, while the rates are relatively stable, the overall population has grown, resulting in more problem gamblers in absolute terms. In particular, this will be the first generation of youth who will spend their entire lives in a liberal gambling environment. Will this have an impact on them? What are the short-term harms?

ADVERTISING

There is a wide body of evidence suggesting that youth are particularly susceptible to advertisements in general and appear to be a favorite target of advertising executives for a wide diversity of products. Given their attentiveness and susceptibility to advertising, the question remains as to whether youth are particularly attracted to and influenced by the current gambling advertisements. While these advertisements may be targeting adults, their appeal to underage youth has certainly been apparent. For example, adolescents repeatedly complain about the multitude of Internet pop-up messages advertising online gambling sites. They also readily recall advertisements on the radio, television, and billboards. As such, the advertising and glamorization of gambling remains of great concern.

State and national lottery corporations have adopted a wide diversity of lottery tickets, predicated on familiar games for children and adolescents, to promote their products. Whether using licensed trademarks and pictures from games such as Monopoly, Battleship, and Twister, popular movies (e.g., *Indiana Jones*), or sporting events (most professional baseball, basketball, hockey, and football teams in the United States and other countries license their logos for use on lottery scratch tickets because they are attractive to adolescents and young adults), their appeal is undeniable. These scratch tickets are in full view of everyone on check-out counters in local convenience stores. With names such as "lucky money," "cash-for-life," or "scratch n'sniff" scratch tickets, these opportunities to win expensive guitars, motorcycles, cars, boats, stereos, and videogame stations are exceedingly popular among youth. The State of Virginia had an advertising campaign linked with NASCAR racing (a highly popular sport for adolescent and young adult males), several states have used Betty Boop (a cartoon character) with their lottery providing Betty Boop leather jackets to winners, while other promotions have included the opportunity to win tickets for upcoming Olympic events. A broad range of marketing strategies are typically used for the promotion of gambling opportunities to the public. Television and radio commercials, billboards, point-of-sale advertisements, sponsorship deals, and promotional products have all been successfully used to increase sales. Such advertisements are more apt to focus on the fun and entertainment aspect of gambling while simultaneously suggesting the possibility of "winning big" with little or no mention of the potentially negative consequences associated with gambling. Odds and probabilities of "winning" can be somewhat misleading. For example, the largest number of the prizes to be won on many lottery tickets remains a "free" ticket for another chance at winning a prize.

Adolescents typically report that advertisements portray gambling as a rewarding and exciting activity that leads to an improved and happier lifestyle. The central message of these advertisements, that gambling is a thrilling and worry-free activity, is more likely to be accepted and adopted by children and adolescents. In one study examining the impact of advertising on adolescents' gambling behavior, 47% of adolescent males and 38% of adolescent females reported that the gambling advertisements prompted them to want to gamble. In addition, problem gamblers reported being much more likely to gamble after viewing an advertisement, compared with social and recreational gamblers or non-gamblers. More recent concerns have also focused on Internet gambling-related advertisements, many of which incorporate sexually provocative females or avatars targeting young males. Such advertisements incorporate suggestive messaging pairing gambling with having a young attractive female companion. In one such advertisement for a poker website, there is a picture of a young man with two young ladies. One is rather plain looking without much makeup and the other, vibrant and attractive. The caption under the woman without makeup reads "Your girlfriend before Texas Hold'em" while the other says "Your girlfriend after Texas Hold'em."

Celebrity endorsements of Internet wagering by Ben Affleck, James Woods, Jason Alexander, and Neil Patrick Harris, free sign-up bonuses, and other incentives are frequently displayed as computer pop-up messages or on banners via the Internet. Responsible codes of advertising, where existent, have been relegated to general principles and recommended guidelines with little or no enforcement depending on the jurisdiction.

Gambling on Internet Websites

The rise of Internet gambling raises some new concerns and challenges related to the enforcement of age restrictions and prohibitions. The ability to gamble in an anonymous manner, with such ease of accessibility never before seen, raises the possibility of unrestricted and excessive gambling for adolescents. While electronic gambling machines (e.g., slots, VLTs, pokies) were once reported to be the "crack cocaine" of gambling, Internet gambling given its potentially habitual nature is now being referred to by some as the "new crack."

There is little doubt that youth as well as adults use the Internet for a multitude of purposes, be they educational, work-related, to acquire information, to do one's banking, for entertainment, and for socialization with others. A recent national study in Canada suggests that 99% of youth ages 9-17 reported using the Internet, 94% have Internet access at home, with 61% reporting having high-speed access, and 37% indicating that they have their own Internet connections. These numbers are growing daily. Internationally, access via high-speed WiFi networks has grown exponentially with high concentrations of usage. As the price of laptops and computers and high-speed access has decreased, accessibility and usage have increased dramatically. Internet cafes, restaurants, transportation terminals, along with a growing number of commuter trains and public places are now offering free WiFi Internet access. As well, a number of airlines are offering Internet service at reasonably modest costs while flying. At one point, Richard Branson, owner of Virgin Airlines, was thinking of hosting a mini-casino on several transatlantic flights. While some public venues still require a fee for Internet use, a growing number of venues are offering such services free to the public in return for being subjected to multiple advertisements. Today, access is readily available while travelling by car or train, in hotels, via smart phones and wireless Tablets.

There remains strong evidence that a large percentage of children and adolescents play games on the Internet with many youth indicating no household rules on Internet use and frequently little or no adult supervision. Will underage youth and young adults find this a popular avenue to access gambling venues? A recent U.S. national study conducted by the Annenberg Foundation and another conducted by the National Collegiate Athletic Association revealed that gambling via the Internet was the fastest growing form of gambling among young people. Exposure to Internet gambling sites has been widely reported by children and adolescents, with few of these sites maintaining and enforcing strict age controls. One teenager remarked that he was signing onto an Internet gambling site while doing his school homework. When the message asked him his date of birth, he inadvertently put in his actual date of birth which would have precluded him from accessing the site since it had a required minimum age of 18 years. To his astonishment, he received a message back from the site which read, "Are you certain this is your date of birth?" While the Internet has enormous social, educational, and economic benefits, it also has the potential to be a source of gambling problems for underage youth.

Given that a number of individual, situational, and environmental risk/protective factors have been found to be correlated to youth problem gambling behaviors, it is important to note that the causal links have not yet been established. Availability, accessibility, and structural features of specific games (e.g., schedules of reinforcement, speed of the game, colors and sounds associated with arousal levels) most likely combine with an individual's psychological and personality characteristics in various ways to create a rather complex pattern of risk.

PROTECTIVE FACTORS

Based on Richard Jessor's original model of a general theory of adolescent risk behaviors, which conceptualizes the interactive nature of risk and protective factors as a way of predicting the likelihood of acquiring or maintaining particular risky behaviors, the research team at the International Centre for Youth Gambling Problems and High-Risk Behaviors has expanded the theoretical model to include excessive adolescent gambling. In several studies examining protective factors (those factors which may inhibit or minimize the risk of acquiring a problem), we found that poor family interrelationships and lack of school connectedness (the inability to relate to one's school and peers, or the lack of desire to participate in extracurricular activities) were symptomatic of adolescent problem gambling. Family cohesion and spending overall family time together played a significant role as a protective factor in minimizing teen problem gambling (this has also been shown to be a general protective factor for a number of mental health and substance use disorders). Obviously, this refers to spending positive family time in socially acceptable, non-gambling activities. Conversely, participating, condoning, and/or encouraging gambling by parents is viewed as a significant potential risk factor. As previously noted, parents will occasionally, without thinking of the negative consequences, purchase a lottery ticket for their child as a holiday gift. Addressing the issue of gambling directly, as is done with substance abuse, will be important. Active participation in school activities was similarly found to be a protective factor.

The importance of the notion of "resilience," that is, the ability to do well in spite of adverse circumstances, has been widely explored in the field of mental health as an important protective factor. Enhancing resilience has long been considered a valuable cornerstone in protecting youth from a wide variety of mental health problems. The results of a number of studies conducted at the McGill University Centre during the last few years have revealed that adolescents perceived to be "vulnerable" (high risk/low protective factors) had a mean gambling severity index nine times greater than a "resilient" group (high risk/high protective factors), eight times larger than the "fortunate" group (low risk/low protective factor), and thirteen times greater than the "ideal" group (low risk/high protective factors). Given these findings, we concluded that those youth identified as vulnerable were at greatest risk for experiencing gambling problems. Interestingly, the results revealed that all (100% of youth identified as pathological gamblers and 87% of those identified as at risk for exhibiting a number of clinical problems but not reaching clinical criteria for pathological gambling) were identified as being vulnerable on the resilient measure. This is in contrast to the finding that only approximately 4% of youth identified as resilient showed some gambling-related problems and none were pathological gamblers, despite their reporting high levels of risk exposure. These findings were strongly supported by evidence revealing poor coping and adaptive behaviors among adolescent pathological gamblers. Taken together, these findings would suggest that those youth with good coping skills and who appear to be resilient when faced with difficulties and adversities seem less vulnerable to problem gambling and other mental health issues. These issues will be further explored when prevention issues are addressed in chapter 5.

FUTURE DIRECTIONS

Our current knowledge and understanding about adolescent problem gambling still remain limited as to the combinations of risk and protective factors which interact in rather complex ways to increase the likelihood of specific individuals engaging in problem gambling. It is exceedingly difficult to predict merely from the warning signs or the risk factors which individuals will likely develop a significant gambling problem once they begin to gamble. The biopsychosocial model has added greatly to our understanding and conceptualization of the problem. There is little doubt that adolescents are gambling at increasing rates and that they represent a high-risk vulnerable population for gambling-related problems. While this may be a "hidden addiction," its consequences for the individual, his/her family, and society are indeed severe.

It is important to remember that problem gamblers are not a homogeneous group. They differ by gender, age, types of gambling activities in which they engage, and the severity of their problems.

Poker players, sports gamblers, horse race gamblers, and casino gamblers, while having some common underlying behaviors, can be very different. Ultimately, individuals have to assume some personal responsibility for their gambling. The individual, the gambling industry, our educational institutions, parents, and governments certainly all have an important role and responsibility in helping individuals with this disorder. We need to continue to monitor the gambling behaviors of our youth as accessibility to gambling venues continues to increase and as technological advances bring gambling opportunities into our homes.

REFERENCES

Abbott, M., Volberg, R., Bellringer, M., and Reith, G. (2004). A Review of Research on Aspects of Problem Gambling. Report prepared for the Responsibility in Gambling Trust, U.K.

Australian Productivity Commission. (1999). Australia's Gambling Industries. Australian Government.

Australian Productivity Commission. (2010). Gambling, Report No. 50. Canberra.

Bergevin, T., Derevensky, J., Gupta, R., and Kaufman, F. (2006). Adolescent gambling: Understanding the role of stress and coping. *Journal of Gambling Studies, 22*(2), 195–208.

Black, D. W., and Moyer, T. (1998). Clinical features and psychiatric commodity of subjects with pathological gambling behavior. *Psychiatric Services, 49,* 1434–39.

Black, D. W., Moyer, T., and Schlosser, S. (2003). Quality of life and family history in pathological gambling. *Journal of Nervous and Mental Disease, 191,* 124–6.

Blaszczynski, A. P., and Nower, L. (2002). A pathways model of problem and pathological gambling. *Addiction, 97*(5), 487–99.

Blaszczynski, A., and Steel, Z. (1988). Personality disorders among pathological gamblers. *Journal of Gambling Studies, 11,* 195–220.

Comings, D. E. (1998). The molecular genetics of pathological gambling. *CNS Spectrum, 3*(2), 20–37.

Comings, D. E., and Blum, K. (2000). Reward deficiency syndrome: genetic aspects of behavioral disorders. *Progress in Brain Research, 126,* 325–41.

Comings, D. F., Rosenthal, R. J., Lesieur, H. R., et al. (1996). A study of the dopamine D2 receptor gene in pathological gambling. *Pharmacogenetics, 6*, 223–34.

Comings, D., Gade-Andavolu, R., Gonzalez, N., Wu, S., Muhleman, D., Chen, C., et al. (2001). The additive effect of neurotransmitter genes in pathological gambling. *Clinical Genetics, 60*(2), 107–16.

Delfabbro, P. (2009). *Australasian gambling review, Fourth edition covering 1992-2008.* Adelaide: Independent Gambling Authority.

Derevensky, J. (2008). Gambling behaviors and adolescent substance use disorders. In Y. Kaminer and O. G. Buckstein (Eds.). *Adolescent substance abuse: Psychiatric comorbidity and high risk behaviors.* New York: Haworth Press, 403–33.

Derevensky, J., and Gupta, R. (Eds.). (2004). *Gambling problems in youth: Theoretical and applied perspectives.* New York: Kluwer Academic/Plenum Publishers.

Derevensky, J., and Gupta, R. (2007). Internet gambling amongst adolescents: A growing concern. *International Journal of Mental Health and Addictions, 5*(2), 93–101.

Derevensky, J., and Gupta, R. (2007). Adolescent gambling: Current knowledge, myths, assessment strategies and public policy implications. In G. Smith, D. Hodgins, and R. Williams (Eds.) *Research and measurement issues in gambling.* New York: Elsevier, Inc., 437–63.

Derevensky, J., Gupta, R., and Baboushkin, H. (2007). Underlying cognitions in children's gambling behaviour: Can they be modified? *International Gambling Studies, 7*(3), 281–98.

Derevensky, J., Gupta, R., and Della-Cioppa, G. (1996). A developmental perspective of gambling behaviour in children and adolescents. *Journal of Gambling Studies, 12*(1), 49–66.

Derevensky, J., Gupta, R., and Della-Cioppa, G. (2002). A developmental perspective on gambling behavior in children and adolescents. In J. Moratta, J. Cornelieus, and W. Eadington (Eds.), *The downside: Problem and pathological gambling.* Nevada: University of Nevada Press, 411–28.

Derevensky, J., Pratt, L., Hardoon, K., and Gupta, R. (2007). The relationship between gambling problems and impulsivity among adolescents: Some preliminary data and thoughts. *Journal of Addiction Medicine, 1*(3), 165–72.

Derevensky, J., Sklar, A., Gupta, R., and Messerlian, C. (2010). An empirical study examining the impact of gambling advertisements on adolescent gambling attitudes and behaviors. *International Journal of Mental Health and Addiction, 8,* 21–34.

Dickson, L., Derevensky, J., and Gupta, R. (2004). Youth gambling problems: A harm reduction prevention model. *Addiction Research and Theory, 12*(4), 305–16.

Dickson, L., Derevensky, J., and Gupta, R. (2008). Youth gambling problems: An examination of risk and protective factors. *International Gambling Studies, 8*(1), 25–47.

Ellenbogen, S., Derevensky, J., and Gupta, R.. (2007). Gender differences among adolescents with gambling related problems. *Journal of Gambling Studies, 23,* 133–43.

Ellenbogen, S., Jacobs, D., Derevensky, J., Gupta, R., and Paskus, T. (2008). Gambling behavior among college athletes. *Journal of Applied Sports Psychology, 20,* 349–62.

Engel, G. L. (1977). The need for a new medical model: A challenge for biomedicine. *Science, 196*(4286), 129–36.

Faregh, N., and Derevensky, J. (2011). Gambling behavior among adolescents with Attention Deficit Hyperactivity Disorder. *Journal of Gambling Studies, 27,* 243–56.

Felsher, J., Derevensky, J., and Gupta, R. (2010). Young adults with gambling problems: The impact of childhood maltreatment. *International Journal of Mental Health and Addiction, 8,* 545–56.

Fisher, S. (1993). Gambling and pathological gambling in adolescents. *Journal of Gambling Studies, 9,* 277–88.

Galambos, N. L., and Tilton-Weaver, L.C. (1998). Multiple risk behavior in adolescents and young adults. *Health Review, 10,* 9–20.

Gillespie, M., Derevensky, J., and Gupta, R. (2007). The utility of outcome expectancies in the prediction of adolescent gambling behavior. *Journal of Gambling Issues, 19,* 69–85.

Griffiths, M. (1990). The cognitive psychology of gambling. *Journal of Gambling Studies, 6,* 31–42.

Griffiths, M. (1995). Technological addictions. *Clinical Psychology Forum, 76,* 14–19.

Griffiths, M. (2008). Convergence of gambling and computer game playing: Implications. *E-Commerce, Law and Policy, 10*(2), 12–13.

Griffiths, M., King, D., and Delfabbro, P. (2009). Adolescent gambling-like experiences: Are they a cause for concern? *Education and Health, 27,* 27–30.

Gupta, R., and Derevensky, J. (1996). The relationship between gambling and video game playing behavior in children and adolescents. *Journal of Gambling Studies, 12(4)*, 375–94.

Gupta, R., and Derevensky, J. (1997). Familial and social influences on juvenile gambling behavior. *Journal of Gambling Studies, 13(3)*, 179–92.

Gupta, R. and Derevensky, J. (1998). Adolescent gambling behavior: A prevalence study and examination of the correlates associated with problem gambling. *Journal of Gambling Studies, 14*, 319–45.

Gupta, R., and Derevensky, J. (1998). An empirical examination of Jacobs' General Theory of Addictions: Do adolescent gamblers fit the theory? *Journal of Gambling Studies, 14*, 17–49.

Gupta, R., and Derevensky, J. (2008). Gambling practices among youth: Etiology, prevention and treatment. In C. A. Essau (Ed.), *Adolescent addiction: Epidemiology, assessment and treatment*. London, UK: Elsevier, 207–30.

Gupta, R., Derevensky, J., and Ellenbogen, S. (2006). Personality characteristics and risk-taking tendencies among adolescent gamblers. *Canadian Journal of Behavioural Science, 38(2)*, 201–13.

Hardoon, K., Gupta, R. and Derevensky, J. (2004). Psychosocial variables associated with adolescent gambling: A model for problem gambling. *Psychology of Addictive Behaviors, 18(2)*, 170–79.

Huang, J-H., Jacobs, D., Derevensky, J., Gupta, R., and Paskus, T. (2007). Gambling and health risk behaviors among U.S. college student athletes: Findings from a national study. *Journal of Adolescent Health, 40(5)*, 390–97.

Huang, J-H., Jacobs, D., Derevensky, J., Gupta, R., Paskus, T., and Petr, T. (2007). Pathological gambling amongst college athletes. *Journal of American College Health, 56(2)*, 93–9.

Huang, J-H., Jacobs, D., and Derevensky, J. (2011). DSM-based problem gambling: Increasing the odds of heavy drinking in a national sample of U.S. athletes. *Journal of Psychiatric Research, 45*, 302–8.

Jacobs, D. R., Marston, A. R., Singer, R. D., Widaman, K., Little, T., and Veizades, J. (1989). Children of problem gamblers. *Journal of Gambling Behavior, 5*, 261–7.

Jessor, R. (Ed.). (1998). *New perspectives on adolescent risk behavior*. Cambridge, UK: Cambridge University Press.

Kaminer, Y., Burleson, J., and Jadamec, A. (2002). Gambling behavior in adolescent substance abuse. *Substance Abuse, 23*, 191–8.

Kaminer, Y., and Haberek, R. (2004). Pathological gambling and substance abuse. *Journal of the American Academy of Child and Adolescent Psychiatry, 43,* 1326–7.

Lesieur, H. R., and Klein, R. (1987). Pathological gambling among high school students. *Addictive Behaviors, 12,* 129–35.

Lussier, I., Derevensky, J., Gupta, R., Bergevin, T., and Ellenbogen, S. (2007).Youth gambling behaviors: An examination of the role of resilience. *Psychology of Addictive Behaviors, 21,* 165–73.

Lussier, I., Derevensky, J., and Gupta, R. (2009). Youth gambling problems: An international perspective. In A. Browne-Miller (Ed.), *The Praeger International collection on addictions. Volume IV.* CT: Praeger, 259–80.

Magoon, M., Gupta, R., and Derevensky, J. (2005). Juvenile delinquency and adolescent gambling: Implications for the juvenile justice system. *Criminal Justice and Behavior, 32(6),* 690–713.

Magoon, M., Gupta, R., and Derevensky, J. (2007). Gambling among youth in detention centers. *Journal for Juvenile Justice and Detention Services, 21,* 17–30.

McCormick, J., Delfabbro, P., and Denson, L. (2011). Pathological gambling: Understanding the role of early trauma and psychological vulnerability. Paper presented at the 8th conference on prevalence, prevention, treatment and responsible gambling, Reykjavik, Iceland

Messerlian, C., and Derevensky, J. (2006). Social marketing campaigns for youth gambling prevention: Lessons learned from youth. *International Journal of Mental Health, 4,* 294–306.

Monaghan, S., Derevensky, J., and Sklar, A. (2008). Impact of gambling advertisements on children and adolescents: Policy recommendations to minimize harm. *International Gambling Studies, 22,* 252–74.

Monaghan, S., and Derevensky, J. (2008). An appraisal of the impact of the depiction of gambling in society on youth. *International Journal of Mental Health and Addiction, 6,* 1557–74.

National Research Council (1999). *Pathological gambling: A critical review.* Washington, DC: National Academy Press.

Nower, L., and Blaszczynski, A. (2004). A pathways approach to treating youth gamblers, In J. Derevensky and R. Gupta (Eds.), *Gambling problems in youth: Theoretical and applied perspectives.* New York: Kluwer Academic//Plenum Publishers.

Nower, L., Gupta, R., Blaszczynski, A., and Derevensky, J. (2004). Suicidality ideation and depression among youth gamblers: A preliminary examination of three studies. *International Gambling Studies, 4(1),* 69–80.

Pagani, L., Derevensky, J., and Japel, C. (2009). Predicting gambling behavior in sixth grade from kindergarten. *Archives of Pediatric and Adolescent Medicine, 163*(3), 238–43.

Pagani, L., Derevensky, J., and Japel, C. (2010). Does early childhood emotional distress predict later gambling behavior? *Canadian Journal of Psychiatry, 55,* 159-165.

Petry, N. M. (2005). *Pathological gambling: Etiology, comorbidity, and treatment.* Washington, DC: American Psychological Association Press.

Potenza, M. (2006). Should addictive disorders include non-substance-related conditions? *Addiction, 101*(suppl 1), 142–51.

Potenza, M. N. (2001). The neurobiology of pathological gambling. *Seminars in Clinical Neuropsychiatry 6,* 217–26.

Potenza, M. N., Fiellin, D. A., Heninger, G. R., Rounsaville, C. M., and Mazure, C. M. (2002). Gambling: An addictive behavior with health and primary care implications. *Journal of General Internal Medicine, 17,* 721–32.

Potenza, M. N., Kosten, T. R., and Rounsaville, B. J. (2001). Pathological gambling. *Journal of the American Medical Association, 286*(2), 141–4.

Potenza, M. N., Steinberg, M. A., McLaughlin, S. D., Wu, R., Rounsaville, B. J., and O'Malley, S. S. (2000). Illegal behaviors in problem gambling: Analysis of data from a gambling helpline. *Journal of the American Academy of Psychiatry and the Law, 28,* 389–403.

Potenza, M. N., and Wexler, B. E. (2000). Magnetic resonance imaging used to study urges in pathological gamblers. *Report on Problem Gambling, 1,* 45–46.

Potenza, M., Xian, H., Shah, K., Scherrer, J., and Eisen, S. A. (2005). Shared genetic contributions to pathological gambling and major depression in men. *Archives of General Psychiatry, 62*(9), 1015–21.

Powell, G. J., Hardoon, K., Derevensky, J., and Gupta, R. (1999). Gambling and risk taking behavior of University students. *Substance Use and Misuse, 34*(8), 1167–84.

Romer, D. (2010). Internet gambling grows among male youth ages 18 to 22. Gambling also increases in high school age female youth. Unpublished report. Retrieved from http://www.annenbergpublicpolicycenter .org/Downloads/Releases/ACI/Card%20Playing%202010%20Release%20 final.pdf.

Shaffer, H., LaBrie, R., and LaPlante, D. (2004). Laying the foundation for quantifying regional exposure to social phenomena: Considering the case of legalized gambling as a public health toxin. *Psychology of Addictive Behaviors, 18,* 40–48.

Shead, N.W., Derevensky, J., and Gupta, R. (2010). Risk and protective factors associated with youth problem gambling. *International Journal of Adolescent Medicine and Health, 22*(1), 39–58.

Sklar, A., Gupta, R., and Derevensky, J. (2010). Binge gambling behaviors reported by youth in a residential drug treatment setting: A qualitative investigation. *International Journal of Adolescent Medicine and Health, 22*(1), 153–62.

Sklar, A., and Derevensky, J. (2010). Way to play: Analyzing gambling ads for their appeal to underage youth. *Canadian Journal of Communication, 35*(4), 533–54.

Slutske, W. (2006). Natural recovery and treatment-seeking in pathological gambling: Results of two U.S. national surveys. *American Journal of Psychiatry, 163*(2), 297–302.

Slutske, W., Caspi, A., Moffitt, T., and Poulton, R. (2005). Personality and problem gambling: A prospective study of a birth cohort of young adults. *Archives of General Psychiatry, 62*(7), 769–75.

Slutske, W., Eisen, S., Xian, H., True, W., Lyons, M., Goldberg, J., and Tsuang, M. (2001). A twin study of the association between pathological gambling and antisocial personality disorder. *Journal of Abnormal Psychology, 110*(2), 297–308.

Slutske, W. S., Eisen, S., True, W. R., Lyons, M. J., Goldberg, J., and Tsuang, M. (2000). Common genetic vulnerability for pathological gambling and alcohol dependence in men. *Archives of General Psychiatry, 57*, 666–73.

Slutske, W. S., Zhu, G., Meier, M. H., and Martin, N. G. (2010). Genetic and environmental influences on disordered gambling in men and women. *Archives of General Psychiatry, 67*(6), 624–30.

Steinberg, M. (1997). *Connecticut high school problem gambling surveys, 1989 and 1996.* Guilford, CT: Connecticut Council on Problem Gambling.

Ste-Marie, C., Gupta, R., and Derevensky, J. (2002). Anxiety and social stress related to adolescent gambling behavior. *International Gambling Studies, 2*(1), 123–41.

Ste-Marie, C., Gupta, R., and Derevensky, J. (2006). Anxiety and social stress related to adolescent gambling behavior and substance use. *Journal of Child and Adolescent Substance Abuse, 16*(4), 55–74.

Stinchfield, R. (2000). Gambling and correlates of gambling among Minnesota public school students. *Journal of Gambling Studies, 16*, 153–73.

Vitaro, F., Arseneault, L., and Tremblay, R. (1999). Impulsivity predicts problem gambling in low SES adolescent males. *Addiction, 94*(4), 565–75.

Vitaro, F., Brendgen, M., Ladouceur, R., and Tremblay, R. E. (2001). Gambling, delinquency, and drug use during adolescence: mutual influences and common risk factors. *Journal of Gambling Studies, 17*(3), 171–90.

Vitaro, F., Ladouceur, R., and Bujold, A. (1996). Predictive and concurrent correlates of gambling in early adolescent boys. *Journal of Early Adolescence, 16,* 211–28.

Vitaro, F., Wanner, B., Ladouceur, R., Brendgen, M., and Trembay, R. E. (2004). Trajectories of gambling during adolescence. *Journal of Gambling Studies, 20,* 47–69.

Volberg, R., Gupta, R., Griffiths, M., Olason, D., and Delfabbro, P. (2010). An international perspective on youth gambling prevalence studies. *International Journal of Adolescent Medicine and Health, 22,* 3–38.

Welte, J., Barnes, G., Wieczorek, W., Tidwell, M., and Parker, J. (2002). Gambling participation in the U.S. Results from a national survey. *Journal of Gambling Studies, 18*(4), 313–37.

Welte, J., Barnesa, G., Wieczorek, W., Tidwell, M., and Parker, J. (2004). Risk factors for pathological gambling. *Addictive Behaviors, 29*(2), 323–35.

Welte, J. W., Barnes, G. M., Tidwell, M. O., and Hoffman, J. H. (2011). Gambling and problem gambling across the lifespan. *Journal of Gambling Studies, 27,* 49–61.

Winters, K. C., and Anderson, N. (2000). Gambling involvement and drug use among adolescents. *Journal of Gambling Studies, 16,* 175–98.

4

MEASURING AND ASSESSING ADOLESCENT PROBLEM GAMBLING

Despite advances in our understanding of the underlying causes, etiology, and correlates associated with problem gambling in the last decade, new screening instruments assessing and diagnosing adolescent problem gambling have not kept up with other developments in the field. The measurement of problem gambling and the issues surrounding assessment of youth remain extremely important to help identify those in need of professional help and support. The importance also lies in ensuring that the expansion and proliferation of gambling will not result in increased personal and social problems. At the very least, measuring gambling prevalence rates may help to influence and impact public policy, and is influential in providing valuable information to our legislators. There has been some concern among a number of legislators that the global prevalence estimates may be grossly overstating the extent to which adolescents gamble and are experiencing gambling-related problems. Yet, study after study suggests fairly consistent prevalence rates of adolescent gambling and problem gambling. While adolescent problem gamblers are still relatively few in number compared to the general population, even when compared with adolescents who report gambling, they do appear to have higher rates of problem gambling than adults. The population of adolescents experiencing problem gambling among the general population remains highly skewed and is depicted in figure 4.1.

Figure 4.1. Spectrum of gambling problems.

The development of instruments used to assess problem gambling in general, and for adolescents in particular, has not been without controversy. Such instruments and screening measures have varied over the years since the American Psychiatric Association first identified pathological gambling as a clinically relevant mental health disorder in the third edition of their *Diagnostic and Statistical Manual of Mental Disorders* (DSM-III) in 1980. The DSM provides a common language and standard criteria for the classification of a wide diversity of mental health disorders and is widely used throughout North America and in varying degrees around the world by clinicians, researchers, drug regulation agencies, health insurance companies, pharmaceutical companies, and governmental policy makers as a benchmark of the criteria associated with different mental disorders.

Over the years, the DSM has attracted controversy and criticism as well as praise. While it articulates and identifies a large number of common mental health disorders, there has been concern that some disorders have not been adequately recognized while others may have been inaccurately categorized. Since its inception in 1952, the DSM has undergone several revisions with another revision expected shortly. With each revision, there has been a gradual increase in the number of documented mental health disorders, a reclassification of some, and a removal of others. The last major revision, DSM-IV, was published in 1994, although a "text revision" was produced in 2000.

The DSM-IV identifies and classifies pathological gambling as an impulse control disorder (impulsive behavior without any withdrawal effects) rather than an addictive disorder in spite of its many similarities and commonalities with substance abuse disorders. The fact that pathological gambling has not been viewed as an addictive behavior or addictive disorder has been troublesome to many in the field because some clinicians, policy makers, and insurance providers have tended to minimize its actual impact and importance on the individual's mental health. The fifth edition (DSM-5) is currently in consultation, planning, and preparation, and is scheduled for release in 2013. In this new edition, the term "pathological gambling" will most likely be changed to "disordered gambling" and will fit into a new overall classification scheme designated as "Addiction and Related Disorders." While we will only officially know the outcome when it is published, conventional wisdom suggesting some commonalities with other addictions, in particular other behavioral addictions, seems to suggest that its move closer to the "addictions" classification is welcome. In addition to the psychological underpinnings of the reclassification, there are some significant financial considerations given insurance companies (typically in the United States) are more likely to reimburse individuals and policy holders for treatment of an addiction rather than an impulse control disorder.

At the same time, on an international level, the World Health Organization has an alternative classification scheme that is used quite broadly outside North America. In their 1990 edition, the International Classification of Diseases (ICD) first recognized pathological gambling within a categorization identified as "Habit and Impulse Disorders" (ICD-10).

Given the widespread usage of the DSM-IV in North America and the fact that most of the measures used to assess both adult and adolescent gambling problems have been derived from the DSM criteria, it is worthwhile to explore the specific criteria used to assess pathological gambling. The following are the diagnostic criteria for pathological gambling as it currently exists within the DSM-IV. It is essential that both criteria A and B must be met in order for an assessment to be considered valid. As such, a clinical diagnosis of pathological gambling includes:

A. Persistent and recurrent maladaptive gambling behavior as indicated by *five* (or more) of the following diagnostic criteria:
  1. is preoccupied with gambling (e.g., preoccupied with reliving past gambling experiences, handicapping or planning the next venture, or thinking of ways to get money with which to gamble)
  2. needs to gamble with increasing amounts of money in order to achieve the desired excitement
  3. has repeated unsuccessful efforts to control, cut back, or stop gambling
  4. is restless or irritable when attempting to cut down or stop gambling
  5. gambles as a way of escaping from problems or of relieving a dysphoric mood (e.g. feelings of helplessness, guilt, anxiety, depression)
  6. after losing money gambling, often returns another day to get even ("chasing" one's losses)
  7. lies to family members, therapist, or others to conceal the extent of involvement with gambling
  8. has committed illegal acts such as forgery, fraud, theft, or embezzlement to finance gambling
  9. has jeopardized or lost a significant relationship, job, or educational or career opportunity because of gambling
  10. relies on others to provide money to relieve a desperate financial situation caused by gambling
B. The gambling behavior is not better accounted for by a Manic Episode.

While no final decisions have been made for the inclusion of items identifying pathological or disordered gambling in the DSM-5, because the working group is still accepting recommendations and is apt to make modifications, the proposed changes to these diagnostic criteria would eliminate item number 8—the item relating to illegal acts. The potential removal of this item has resulted in significant discussion among clinicians and treatment providers. While the working group contends that the removal of this item and reducing the criteria will not substantially change the overall population prevalence rates of pathological gambling, in a 2008 study examining the gambling behavior among 20,000 college student athletes in the United States, a number of researchers reported that the prevalence rate would in fact be reduced if the proposed revision is approved. The lower the prevalence rate, the less likely legislators, policy makers, and insurance companies are to be concerned with any mental health issue.

In spite of the fact that the DSM criteria were established as a clinical diagnostic tool, it became quite apparent early on that screening devices were much needed to help identify potentially problematic gambling behaviors and to help mental and public health officials monitor changes in the problem gambling prevalence rate as new forms of gambling were being introduced and gambling was rapidly expanding. As a result, a number of easily administered standardized screens for adults quickly became popular after the American Psychiatric Association formally recognized pathological gambling as a mental health disorder in 1980. These screening instruments were developed to parallel the established criteria in the original DSM-III and have been widely used and reported in prevalence studies attempting to identify the number of individuals with gambling problems. At the same time, it became apparent that underage youth were not only gambling but also experiencing gambling-related problems. As such, a number of clinicians and researchers suggested that the established adult criteria would need to be modified if these scales were to be appropriate for adolescents.

Most adolescent gambling screens currently used today to help identify problem gambling have been adapted and modified from adult screening instruments. Nevertheless, they generally continue to incorporate similar adult criteria while modifying the questions to make them more age and developmentally appropriate. The most commonly used of these screening instruments include the Diagnostic and Statistical Manual–Juvenile (DSM-IV-J) and its subsequent revision the Diagnostic and Statistical Manual–Multiple Response–Juvenile (DSM-IV-MR-J), the South Oaks Gambling Screen–Revised for Adolescents (SOGS-RA), the Massachusetts Gambling Screen (MAGS), the Gamblers Anonymous 20 Questions (GA20) (this scale is primarily for adults and was developed by former pathological gamblers and has on occasion been used with older adolescents and young adults), and the most recently developed instrument–the Canadian Adolescent Gambling Inventory (CAGI) (although there have been very few studies testing the efficacy of this instrument given it has only recently been released).

Similar to adult screening instruments (the DSM-IV criteria remains the best estimate and is considered the gold standard) there exist common constructs, themes, and items underlying most of the adolescent screening instruments. These screens typically incorporate items that assess the psychological, behavioral, and negative financial and social consequences associated with excessive gambling. Examples include stealing money to support one's gambling habit, occupational and/or school-related problems, disrupted familial and peer relationships, attempts at recouping losses, lying or deception about one's gambling problems, the need to increase the frequency and amount wagered, a preoccupation with gambling, and criticism from others concerning one's gambling behavior. These commonly assessed behaviors and constructs are typical of both adolescents and adults experiencing gambling problems and are generally found in most of the current instruments.

Differences in overall prevalence rates of problem gambling as well as divergent findings may be related to a number of issues as has previously been discussed: ease of accessibility, availability of both regulated and unregulated gambling opportunities, the types of gambling offered, the minimum legal gambling age, ethnic and cultural differences (certain cultural groups may be more prone to gambling in general and problem gambling than others, and some religious groups are vehemently opposed to gambling), the population studied, methods used to ascertain the findings (e.g., face-to-face interviews, the completion of instruments through anonymous classroom surveys, online surveys, telephone surveys) and gender distributions (males tend to gamble more frequently than females, wager higher stakes, and exhibit more gambling problems, thus an equal representation of males and females is necessary for an overall accurate prevalence rate). Variability in the actual screening instruments and the techniques incorporated for scoring of these screens is common.

The following instruments are the most commonly used screening measures for identifying problem gambling and for self-assessing the severity of adolescent gambling problems.

THE DSM-IV-J AND DSM-IV-MR-J

The DSM-IV-J, originally developed in 1992, and the DSM-IV-MR-J, a modified version of the original scale revised in 2000, are among the most widely used adolescent screening instruments. Based on the adult DSM criteria, the scales include twelve items, assessing nine of the ten DSM-IV diagnostic criteria related to adolescent pathological gambling. The DSM-IV-J, a self-administered questionnaire, represented the first adaptation of DSM-IV criteria for youth. This scale was subsequently modified by the author, Sue Fisher, and resulted in the creation of the DSM-IV-MR-J scale. What differentiates these scales is that in the DSM-IV-MR-J there are multiple response options (MR) which allow for gradations of responses to ensure that a specific behavior occurs sufficiently frequently before being considered a problem (see table 4.1; all tables appear in the chapter appendix). This modification represented an important step and improvement in helping to minimize the over-identification of adolescent problem gamblers.

The language and readability in this scale was simplified and gambling-related details less relevant for youth were omitted (e.g., embezzlement, losing employment). Given the nine categories, the potential scores range between 0 and 9, and a score of 4 or more out of the 9 categories is considered indicative of a significant and severe gambling problem. The DSM-IV-J is not identical with the DSM-IV-MR-J in that an item measuring the criteria for loss of control, that is, making repeatedly unsuccessful efforts to control, to cut back, or to stop one's gambling was omitted. Furthermore, while the DSM-IV-J assesses financial bailouts (someone helping the individual financially to relieve their immediate debt), the DSM-IV-MR-J does not. In spite of the fact that the DSM-IV-J and DSM-IV-MR-J use somewhat different criteria, performance scores by most adolescents have been shown to be quite similar. However, neither scale measures all ten of the adult DSM-IV criteria. In a number of empirical studies, researchers at the International Centre for Youth Gambling Problems and High-Risk Behaviors have concluded that both the DSM-IV-J and the DSM-IV-MR-J represent a reliable, valid, and conservative measure of adolescent problem gambling.

SOUTH OAKS GAMBLING SCREEN AND THE SOUTH OAKS GAMBLING SCREEN– REVISED FOR ADOLESCENTS (SOGS-RA)

Originally developed by Henry Lesieur and Sheila Blume for adults, the South Oaks Gambling Screen (often referred to as the SOGS) quickly grew in popularity, both as a measure for prevalence of pathological gambling and as a reliable screening instrument for identifying potential problem gamblers. The South Oaks Gambling Screen for adults, based upon the DSM-III, consists of twenty items to identify individuals who may be experiencing serious gambling and pathological gambling problems. This continues to be the most widely used screening scale for adults internationally and is available online in multiple languages. A research team from the University of Minnesota revised the original criteria to make it more age and developmentally appropriate for adolescents. The revised instrument, the South Oaks Gambling Screen–Revised for Adolescents (SOGS-RA), remains an internationally used screening measure for identifying adolescent problem gamblers. This self-report screen, like the DSM-IV-J and DSM-IV-MR-J, continues to be widely used in clinical practice, research, and prevalence studies.

The clinical research team that developed this revised instrument adapted the original screen by changing the lifetime time frame used for adults (e.g., Have you ever . . . in your lifetime?) to one encompassing a 12-month time period. Their belief was that because adolescents have more limited life experience than adults and tend to be more concerned with immediate consequences, using a past year framework (e.g., Have you ever . . . during the past year?) was deemed to be more reliable and age appropriate. This time framework is typically used by a number of screens including the DSM-IV-MR-J. Other revisions included modifying the wording of several items and alternative response options to more accurately reflect actual adolescent gambling behavior and to ensure that adolescents had little difficulty in reading and understanding the meaning of each of the items. Two of the original SOGS items were viewed as inappropriate for adolescents and were subsequently deleted from the original scale. Only one item related to borrowing money, rather than the original nine items, was retained. The final SOGS-RA consists of twelve simply worded questions to which adolescents respond. The actual screen and scoring of items can be found in table 4.2.

While two different scoring procedures have typically been used for the SOGS-RA, neither system has undergone extensive analyses as to their ability to accurately classify and predict problem gambling. The "broad criteria" scoring scheme is based on a combination of an individual's gambling frequency and the total SOGS-RA score. Using this scoring system, the classification scheme for the identification of a problem gambler makes the assumption that an individual must be gambling weekly at a minimum and has obtained a SOGS-RA score of at least 2. As well, the scale's authors contend that adolescents can be broadly identified as problem gamblers if they are gambling (for money) on a daily basis totally independent of the number of items endorsed on the SOGS-RA. Others have argued that if there are no negative social and psychological costs associated with daily gambling, then to identify these individuals as problem or pathological gamblers is inaccurate, unrealistic, and unjustified. In this scoring framework, the frequency of gambling as compared to the intensity of gambling (i.e., the length of time gambling or the amounts of money wagered) and the negative consequences associated with the individual's gambling are most important. While some would argue that gambling daily can be done in small intervals without much money or time lost (for example, if someone purchases a lottery ticket daily for $0.50 or $1.00), there is some indication that possibly even this criterion has been found to be a good predictor of problem gambling. In this vein, it is interesting to examine adolescents' perceptions of what constitutes gambling. In a number of internationally reported investigations, it is not unusual for adolescents to indicate they do not gamble, yet they report purchasing lottery tickets frequently, playing poker for money with friends, occasionally playing bingo for money, wagering on school performance, or betting on games of skill. Yet, many youth do not view these activities as "gambling." Rather, they tend to view more traditional forms of gambling—wagering on professional or college sports, casino and table games, slot machines, and horse racing—as "gambling."

In contrast to the broad criteria, a narrower set of criteria has also been established. This revised scoring is based on the number of endorsed items on the SOGS-RA, independent of merely noting the frequency of gambling, in response to concerns about overidentification of adolescent problem gamblers. This established measure, that is, the number of items needed to be endorsed to be identified or diagnosed as a problem or pathological gambler, is sometimes referred to as the "cut score." If on the SOGS-RA an adolescent endorses four or more items on the scale, the developers of this instrument viewed this behavior as indicative of problem gambling. Individuals who endorse two or three items are deemed not to have reached the clinical criteria and are frequently referred to as being "at-risk" for a gambling problem, given the notion that gambling problems are progressive in nature and there remains a distinct likelihood that the individual's problems may eventually escalate. Those youth who gamble and endorse either none or one item do not appear to be at serious risk for a gambling problem, at least for the moment. As such, these individuals are typically referred to as occasional, recreational, or social gamblers. The narrow criteria cut score of 4 has faced some criticism, so that a number of clinicians have argued that using a minimum criteria score of 4 yields "unreasonable estimates of problem and at-risk gambling" and suggest raising the cut score to 5 or more to reflect the same score and criteria used with the adult SOGS.

Other problems and discrepant findings have resulted from people modifying the questions and/or changing the narrow criteria to identify problem gamblers, thereby not allowing for direct comparisons between prevalence studies. The higher the cut score used, the fewer the number of people identified. If one's intent is to identify individuals with a gambling problem, then individuals scoring high on any of the screens should always be assessed clinically. However, if we are merely trying to determine the incidence and/or prevalence rates, then keeping the same criteria for comparative purposes remains crucial. While some public health workers would like to change the screens used for identifying pathological and problem gambling, differences in comparability remain problematic.

MASSACHUSETTS GAMBLING SCREEN (MAGS)

The Massachusetts Gambling Screen (MAGS) is a 40-item screening instrument designed to measure gambling problems among the general population and was not developed exclusively for use with adolescents but has nevertheless been used in a number of adolescent studies. Similar to the DSM-IV-MR-J and the SOGS-RA, the MAGS inquires about gambling behavior using a past year time framework. The MAGS classifies respondents into three possible basic categories: (a) non-pathological gambling, (b) transitional gambling (sometimes referred to as at-risk gambling), and (c) pathological gambling. The cut scores are derived using a specific weighted scoring equation. The brevity and ease of administration of the MAGS is one of its strongest assets. However, one limitation is that the scoring was derived based on a small number of high school students and may not be truly representative of a general adolescent population. In comparison with other instruments, the MAGS is reported to be more conservative and identifies many fewer adolescents as exhibiting problem gambling behavior. As such, there is a concern that the scale may significantly underestimate problem gambling rates. The MAGS items and scoring criteria can be observed in table 4.3.

CANADIAN ADOLESCENT GAMBLING INVENTORY (CAGI)

The Canadian Adolescent Gambling Inventory (CAGI) is the most recently developed adolescent instrument and is currently undergoing validation testing in a number of research studies. Unlike the other instruments frequently used to assess gambling problems among adolescents, the CAGI is not an adaptation of an adult instrument but followed an instrument development process defining the specific behaviors of interest and concern for adolescents. In developing the CAGI, the goal was to develop a scale specifically for adolescents that is representative of a continuum of gambling severity, ranging from low-level gambling to highly problematic gambling. Rather than merely assessing items that tap into high problem gambling severity exclusively, it includes several subscales, measuring multiple domains of gambling problem severity. The CAGI primarily measures two main elements of youth gambling: the gambling behavior itself, and gambling problem severity (including preoccupation and assorted negative consequences associated with problem gambling). Unlike most other adolescent screens, the CAGI incorporates a past three month time frame (rather than past year) and assesses behaviors in five distinct areas: (a) types of gambling activities in which young people engage, (b) frequency of participation for each gambling activity, (c) time spent gambling in each activity, (d) money spent gambling, and (e) an overall problem gambling severity index. The CAGI, available in both English and French versions, assesses 19 potentially different types of gambling activities in which adolescents typically engage. The remaining 24 items, divided into five subscales, focus on the consequences resulting from gambling and these are assessed according to their impact in diverse areas of an adolescent's life. Of the five subscales, three refer to consequences experienced by adolescents: psychological, social, and financial. A fourth subscale addresses issues concerning loss of control of gambling, while the fifth subscale represents an overall composite score reflective of the degree of severity of gambling problems. This newly released instrument, while representing a potential advancement in the field, has to undergo rigorous testing and comparability with other existing instruments before its acceptance as a reliable and valid measure of adolescent problem gambling.

SOME GENERAL COMMENTS CONCERNING THE ASSESSMENT OF ADOLESCENT PROBLEM GAMBLING

Those in the field of gambling studies have yet to agree on what is often referred to as the "gold standard" instrument for the assessment of adult gambling problems. This is even more contentious when examining adolescent problem gambling behaviors. Differences in prevalence rates have sometimes been shown to occur when one asks individuals directly about their gambling behaviors (some are embarrassed and attempt to answer the questions as they think the interviewer would like). Other assessments are done more anonymously over the telephone (there is no way to ascertain whether a parent is nearby, which may influence the adolescent's responses), and some are done in schools through anonymous surveys, although this obviously omits dropouts from responding. Other concerns relate to the availability and accessibility of gambling opportunities, cultural influences, and gender distributions.

In spite of all the limitations and the variability of results found in adolescent prevalence studies, there is little doubt that adolescents represent a distinctly vulnerable group from a public health perspective. In some earlier reported studies (excluding the use of the CAGI as it was only recently released), researchers have reported overall strong concordance and agreement among the various instruments. Whether the results differ by a small percentage does not diminish the importance and need to provide awareness and educational prevention programs. Our screening efforts can help raise awareness among adolescents that there is a problem, raise awareness amongst educators that there is a need for educational and prevention programs, and similarly raise awareness among parents that gambling is not an innocuous behavior with few negative consequences. Individuals completing any of the scales who score within the problem or pathological gambling range would be well advised to seek help to discuss curtailing their gambling.

APPENDIX: GAMBLING ASSESSMENTS

Table 4.1. DSM-IV-MR-J Criteria and Test Questions to Identify Adolescent Problem Gambling

Dimension of Problem Gambling	Adolescent Criteria	Adolescent Test Questions	Response			
1. Preoccupation	Preoccupied with gambling (e.g., thinking about gambling or planning next venture)	In the past year how often have you found yourself thinking about gambling or planning to gamble?	Never	Once or twice	Sometimes	Often
2. Tolerance	Needs to gamble with increasing amounts of money in order to achieve the desired excitement	During the course of the past year have you needed to gamble with more and more money to get the amount of excitement you want?		Yes	No	
3. Loss of control	Often spent much more money on gambling than planned	In the past year have you ever spent much more than you planned to on gambling?	Never	Once or twice	Sometimes	Often
4. Withdrawal	Restlessness or irritability when attempting to cut down or stop gambling	In the past year have you felt bad or fed up when trying to cut down or stop gambling?	Never	Once or twice	Sometimes	Often
5. Escape	Gambles as a way of escaping from problems or relieving dysphoric mood (e.g., feelings of helplessness, guilt, anxiety, depression)	In the past year how often have you gambled to help you to escape from problems or when you are feeling bad?	Never	Once or twice	Sometimes	Often
6. Chasing	After losing money gambling, often returns another day in order to get even ("chasing" one's losses)	In the past year, after losing money gambling, have you returned another day to try and win back money you lost?	Never	Less than half the time	More than half the time	Every time
7. Lies	Lies to family about gambling behavior	In the past year has your gambling ever led to lies to your family?	Never	Once or twice	Sometimes	Often

Item Number	Description	Question	Never	Once or twice	Sometimes	Often
8. Illegal acts	Committed unsocial or illegal acts, such as gambling with school dinner or fare money, stealing from the home or stealing from outside of the home	In the past year have you ever taken money from the following without permission to spend on gambling: School dinner money or fare money? Money from your family? Money from outside the family?	Never	Once or twice	Sometimes	Often
9. Risked job, education, or relationship	Has had arguments with family, friends, or others or truanted from school because of gambling	In the past year has your gambling ever led to: Arguments with family or friends or others? Missing school?	Never	Once or twice	Sometimes	Often
10. Bail out	N/A	N/A	N/A	N/A	N/A	N/A

MR = multiple response; J = juvenile.

Scoring System of DSM-IV-MR-J

Item Number	Endorsement
1	"Often"
2	"Yes"
3	"Often"
4	"Sometimes" OR "Often"
5	"Sometimes" OR "Often"
6	"More than half the time" OR "Every time"
7	"Once or twice" OR "Sometimes" OR "Often"
8	"Once or twice" OR "Sometimes" OR "Often"
9	"Once or twice" OR "Sometimes" OR "Often"
10	N/A

DSM-IV-MR-J was developed for use with adolescents who have gambled in the past year. The items on the scale are scored as follows, based on the responses provided. A respondent who scores four (4) "Yes" answers is classified as a "Problem Gambler."

From Fisher, S. E. (2000). Developing the DSM-IV criteria to identify adolescent problem gambling in non-clinical populations. *Journal of Gambling Studies,*16 (2/3), 253-73.

Table 4.2. SOGS-RA (South Oaks Gambling Screen: Revised for Adolescents)

1. How often have you gone back another day to try and win back money you lost gambling?	Every time Most of the time Some of the time Never
2. When you were betting, have you ever told others you were winning money when you were not?	Yes No
3. Has your betting money ever caused any problems for you such as arguments with family and friends, or problems at school or work?	Yes No
4. Have you ever gambled more than you had planned to?	Yes No
5. Has anyone criticized your betting, or told you that you had a gambling problem whether you thought it true or not?	Yes No
6. Have you ever felt bad about the amount of money you bet, or about what happens when you bet money?	Yes No
7. Have you ever felt like you would like to stop betting, but didn't think you could?	Yes No
8. Have you ever hidden from family or friends any betting slips, IOUs, lottery tickets, money that you won, or any signs of gambling?	Yes No
9. Have you had money arguments with family or friends that centered on gambling?	Yes No
10. Have you borrowed money to bet and not paid it back?	Yes No
11. Have you ever skipped or been absent from school or work due to betting activities?	Yes No
12. Have you borrowed money or stolen something in order to bet or to cover gambling activities?	Yes No

Scoring Rules for SOGS-RA

#1: "Every time" OR "Most of the time" = 1
#1: "Some of the time" OR "Never" = 0
#2-12: "Yes" = 1, "No" = 0

Level	Calculation of Narrow Rates	Calculation of Broad Rates
0	No past year gambling	No past year gambling
1	SOGS-RA score of 1	Gambling less than daily and SOGS-RA score = 0, OR less than weekly gambling and SOGS-RA score 1
2	SOGS-RA score of 2 or 3	At least weekly gambling and SOGS-RA score 1, OR gambling less than weekly and SOGS-RA score 2
3	SOGS-RA score of 4	At least weekly gambling + SOGS-RA score 2, OR daily gambling

From Winters, K.C., Stinchfield, R.D., and Fulkerson, J. (1993). Toward the development of an adolescent problem severity scale. *Journal of Gambling Studies, 9*, 63-84.

Table 4.3. Massachusetts Gambling Screen (MAGS)

DIRECTIONS: *Please circle the response that best represents your answer.*

1.	Have you ever gambled (for example, bet money on the lottery, bingo, sporting events, casino games, cards, racing, or other games of chance)?	YES	NO
2.	Have you ever experienced social, psychological, or financial pressure to start gambling or increase how much you gamble?	YES	NO
3.	How much do you usually gamble compared with most other people?	Less · About the Same	More
4.	Do you feel that the amount or frequency of your gambling is "normal"?	YES	NO
5.	Do friends or relatives think of you as a "normal" gambler?	YES	NO
6.	Do you ever feel pressure to gamble when you do not gamble?	YES	NO

If you never have gambled, please skip to question #29 now.

7.	Do you ever feel guilty about your gambling?	YES	NO
8.	Does any member of your family ever worry or complain about your gambling?	YES	NO
9.	Have you ever thought that you should reduce or stop gambling?	YES	NO
10.	Are you always able to stop gambling when you want?	YES	NO
11.	Has your gambling ever created problems between you and any member of your family or friends?	YES	NO
12.	Have you ever gotten into trouble at work or school because of your gambling?	YES	NO
13.	Have you ever neglected your obligations (e.g., family, work, or school) for two or more days in a row because you were gambling?	YES	NO
14.	Have you ever gone to anyone for help about your gambling?	YES	NO
15.	Have you ever been arrested for a gambling-related activity?	YES	NO
16.	Have you been preoccupied with thinking of ways to get money for gambling or reliving past gambling experience (for example, handicapping) during the past 12 months?	YES	NO
17.	During the past 12 months, have you gambled in increasingly larger amounts of money to experience the desired level of excitement?	YES	NO
18.	Did you find during the past 12 months that the same amount of gambling had less effect on you than before?	YES	NO
19.	Has stopping gambling or cutting down how much you gamble made you feel restless or irritable during the past 12 months?	YES	NO
20.	Have you gambled during the past 12 months to make the uncomfortable feelings that come from stopping gambling (for example, restlessness, or irritability) go away or to keep from having them?	YES	NO
21.	Have you gambled as a way of escaping from problems or relieving feelings of helplessness, guilt, anxiety, or depression during the past 12 months?	YES	NO
22.	After losing money gambling, have you returned to gambling on another day to win back your lost money?	YES	NO
23.	Have you lied to family members or others to conceal the extent of involvement in gambling?	YES	NO
24.	Have you committed any illegal acts (such as forgery, fraud, theft, embezzlement, etc.) during the past 12 months to finance your gambling?	YES	NO

Table 4.3. (*Continued*)

25. During the past 12 months, have you jeopardized or lost a significant relationship, job, or educational or career opportunity because of your gambling?	YES	NO
26. Have you relied on others (for example, family, friends, or work) to provide you with money to resolve a desperate financial situation caused by your gambling?	YES	NO
27. During the past 12 months, have you made efforts unsuccessfully to limit, reduce, or stop gambling?	YES	NO
28. How old were you when you placed your first bet?		
29. What is your sex?		
30. What is your age as of your last birthday?		

31. How honest were your responses to each of the questions on this survey?	Not at all honest	Somewhat dishonest	Somewhat honest	Very honest

Scoring Rules for the Massachusetts Gambling Screen (MAGS)

- On the Scoring Guide (next page), indicate the respondent's survey answers by circling the appropriate response option for each of the specified questions. The question numbers on the Scoring Guide refer to the question numbers on the MAGS survey. Not all of the MAGS survey items are used on the Scoring Guide.
- For each question, write the selected value on the corresponding line.
- Add the seven (7) scores for the MAGS items. Enter the sum on the Subtotal line. Next, subtract the value .62. Enter the resulting value on the TOTAL 1 line. To classify the respondent according to MAGS criteria, refer to the MAGS Classification Key and select the category that corresponds to the value on the TOTAL 1 line.
- Add the twelve (12) scores for the DSM-IV items. Enter the sum on the TOTAL 2 line. To classify the respondent according to the DSM-IV criteria, refer to the DSM-IV Classification Key and select the category that corresponds to the value on the TOTAL 2 line.

Massachusetts Gambling Screen (MAGS) Scoring Guide

To classify according to the MAGS:

Question 6:	no = 0	yes = 0.63	_____
Question 8:	no = 0	yes = 0.91	_____
Question 10:	yes = 0	no = 0.56	_____
Question 11:	no = 0	yes = 0.93	_____
Question 12:	no = 0	yes = 1.51	_____
Question 13:	no = 0	yes = 1.53	_____
Question 15:	no = 0	yes = 1.63	_____
		Subtotal	_____
		Subtract	0.62
		Total 1	_____

To classify according to DSM-IV:

Question 16:	no = 0	yes = 1	_____
Question 17:	no = 0	yes = 0.5	_____
Question 18:	no = 0	yes = 0.5	_____
Question 19:	no = 0	yes = 0.	_____
Question 20:	no = 0	yes = 0.5	_____
Question 21:	no = 0	yes = 1	_____
Question 22:	no = 0	yes = 1	_____
Question 23:	no = 0	yes = 1	_____
Question 24:	no = 0	yes = 1	_____
Question 25:	no = 0	yes = 1	_____

Question 26:	no = 0	yes = 1	_____
Question 27:	no = 0	yes = 1	_____
		Total 2	_____

MAGS Classification Key
If the value on the Total 1 line is a negative number, the respondent is classified as: Nonpathological.

If the value on the Total 1 line is between 0 and 2 (including 0 and 2), the respondent is classified as In Transition.

If the value on the Total 1 line is greater than 2, the respondent is classified as Pathological.

DSM-IV Classification Key
If the value on the Total 2 line is less than 5, the respondent is classified as Nonpathological.

If the value on the Total 2 line is 5 or greater, the respondent is classified as Pathological.

From Shaffer, H.J., LaBrie, R., Scanlan, K.M., and Cummings, T.N. (1994). Pathological gambling among adolescents: Massachusetts Gambling Screen (MAGS). *Journal of Gambling Studies*, 10(4), 339-62.

REFERENCES

American Psychiatric Association. (1980). *Diagnostic and statistical manual of mental disorders(DSM-III)* (3rd ed.). Washington, DC.

American Psychiatric Association. (1994). *Diagnostic and statistical manual of mental disorders (DSM-IV)* (4th ed.). Washington, DC: American Psychiatric Association.

Boudreau, B., and Poulin, C. (2007). The South Oaks Gambling Screen–Revised Adolescent (SOGS-RA) revisited: A cut-point analysis. *Journal of Gambling Studies*, 23, 299–308.

Derevensky, J., and Gillespie, M. (2005). Gambling in Canada. *International Journal of Mental Health and Addiction*, 3(1), 3–14.

Derevensky, J., and Gupta, R. (2000). Prevalence estimates of adolescent gambling: A comparison of the SOGS-RA, DSM-IV-J, and the G.A. 20 Questions. *Journal of Gambling Studies*, 16 (2/3), 227–51.

Derevensky, J., and Gupta, R. (2004). The measurement of youth gambling problems: Current instruments, methodological issues and future directions. In J. Derevensky and R. Gupta (Eds.), *Gambling problems in youth: Theoretical and applied perspectives*. New York: Kluwer Academic/Plenum Publishers, 121–44.

Derevensky, J., and Gupta, R. (2006). Measuring gambling problems amongst adolescents: Current status and future directions. *International Gambling Studies*, 6(2), 201–15.

Derevensky, J., Gupta, R., and Winters, K. (2003). Prevalence rates of youth gambling problems: Are the current rates inflated? *Journal of Gambling Studies, 19*(4), 405–25.

Fisher, S. E. (1992). Measuring pathological gambling in children: The case of fruit machines in the UK. *Journal of Gambling Studies, 8,* 263–85.

Fisher S. (2000). Developing the DSM-IV-MR-J criteria to identify adolescent problem gambling in non-clinical populations. *Journal of Gambling Studies, 16,* 253–73.

Govoni R, Rupcich, N., and Frisch, G.R.(1996). Gambling behavior of adolescent gamblers. *Journal of Gambling Studies, 12,* 305–17.

Gupta, R., and Derevensky, J. (2011). Understanding the etiology of youth problem gambling. In J. Derevensky, D. Shek and J. Merrick (Eds.), *Youth gambling problems: The hidden addiction.* Berlin: De Gruyter.

Hardoon, K., Derevensky, J., and Gupta, R. (2003). Empirical vs. perceived measures of gambling severity: Why adolescents don't present themselves for treatment. *Addictive Behaviors, 28,* 933–46.

Jacques C., and Ladouceur, R. (2003). DSM-IV-J criteria: A scoring error that may be modifying the estimates of pathological gambling among youths. *Journal of Gambling Studies, 19*(4), 427–31.

Langhinrichsen-Rohling, J., Rohling, M. L., Rohde, P., and Seeley, J. R. (2004). The SOGS-RA vs. the MAGS-7: Prevalence estimates and classification congruence. *Journal of Gambling Studies, 20*(3): 259–81.

Lesieur, H. R., and Blume, S. B. (1987). The South Oaks Gambling Screen (SOGS): A new instrument for the identification of pathological gamblers. *American Journal of Psychiatry, 144,* 1184–8.

Lesieur, H. R., and Blume, S. B. (1993). Revising the South Oaks Gambling Screen in different settings. *Journal of Gambling Studies, 9,* 213–23.

National Research Council. (1999). *Pathological gambling: A critical review.* Washington, DC: National Academy Press.

Olason, D. T., Sigurdardottir, K. J., and Smari, J. (2006). Prevalence estimates of gambling participation and problem gambling among 16-18 year old students in Iceland: A comparison of the SOGS-RA and DSM-IV-MR-J. *Journal of Gambling Studies, 22*(1), 23–39.

Shaffer, H. J., LaBrie, R., Scanlon, K. M., and Cummings, T. N.(1994). Pathological gambling among adolescents: Massachusetts Gambling Screen (MAGS). *Journal of Gambling Studies, 10,* 339–62.

Stinchfield, R.(2001). Reliability, validity, and classification accuracy of the South Oaks Gambling Screen (SOGS). *Addictive Behaviors, 27,* 1–19.

Temcheff, C., Derevensky, J., and Paskus, T. (2011). Pathological and disordered gambling: A comparison of the DSM-IV and DSM-V criteria. *International Gambling Studies, 11*, 213–20.

Volberg, R. (2002). The epidemiology of pathological gambling *Psychiatric Annals, 32*(3), 171–8.

Volberg, R., Gupta, R., Griffiths, M., Olason, D., and Delfabbro, P. (2010). An international perspective on youth gambling prevalence studies. *International Journal of Adolescent Medicine and Health, 22*, 3–38.

Welte J. W., Barnes, G. M., Tidwell, M. O., and Hoffman, J. H.(2008). The prevalence of problem gambling among U.S. adolescents and young adults: Results from a national survey. *Journal of Gambling Studies, 24*, 119–33.

Wiebe J., Wynne, H., Stinchfield, R., and Tremblay, J. (2005).Measuring problem gambling in adolescent populations: Phase I report. Canadian Centre on Substance Abuse.

Wiebe J., Wynne, H., Stinchfield, R., and Tremblay, J. (2007). The Canadian Adolescent Gambling Inventory (CAGI): Phase II Final Report. Canadian Centre on Substance Abuse. http://www. gamblingresearch.org.

World Health Organization. (1990). *International classification of diseases (ICD).* Geneva: World Health Organization.

5

PREVENTING ADOLESCENT PROBLEM GAMBLING

In spite of our increased knowledge about some of the risk and pro-tective factors and correlates associated with youth gambling and the deleterious impact of problem gambling experienced by some adolescents, there have been very few systematic attempts at edu-cating today's youth about the risks and warning signs associated with excessive gambling. The normalization of gambling whereby our governments and the industry have presented gambling as a socially acceptable and benign form of entertainment is worrisome. While most individuals actually gamble in a responsible manner and few experience serious problems, a number of youth go on to have quite severe gambling-related problems. What begins as a fun activ-ity can escalate fairly quickly. Whether these problems are short-lived or extend over time, the residual consequences associated with problem gambling can take a significant toll on the individual.

While primary prevention programs are typically available for today's youth concerning issues related to substance use and abuse, drinking and driving, sex education, bullying (including cyber-bully-ing), smoking, eating disorders, and other mental health issues, only a limited number of programs exist for the prevention of gambling problems. Few if any television shows or documentaries have ad-dressed this issue, nor have prevention programs been systemati-cally implemented in most schools. Instead, school administrators and parents have tended to work on a crisis model, intervening only when a significant problem arises. This may well be a result of the perception that adolescents do not have gambling problems, that the consequences of youth gambling are inconsequential, and the fact that it may be a "hidden addiction" despite the large numbers of youth gambling.

The vast majority of primary prevention programs currently available that are intended to prevent gambling problems have focused on youth, with others starting to target particularly high-risk and vulnerable groups (e.g., elderly/seniors, minorities, individuals with lower income, and those experiencing other impulse and addictive disorders). The Massachusetts Council on Compulsive Gambling has an excellent resource and compendium of programs designed to help prevent gambling problems. Other programs, such as self-exclusion programs, are designed for individuals already experiencing gambling problems and will be discussed later in this chapter. However, it should be noted that the vast majority of self-exclusion programs and other harm-minimization prevention programs do not target adolescents because they are typically under the legal age for gambling on regulated gambling activities.

While our conceptual knowledge and understanding concerning adolescent gambling behavior in general, and specifically problem gambling, has grown considerably in the past two decades, its social impact continues to lag far behind. The lack of scientific knowledge is compounded by a lack of youth and parental awareness about the risks and hazards associated with gambling. A number of research studies have revealed that both adults and youth do not think that gambling among teenagers is of significant concern in spite of the existing prevalence rates and multiple problems associated with adolescent problem gambling. In a recent national Canadian study, when asked to identify potentially problematic adolescent behaviors, more than 50% of parents identified a wide range of behaviors of concern (drug use [87 %], alcohol use [82%], drinking and driving [81%], unsafe sexual activity [81%], violence in schools and bullying [75%], smoking [73%], obesity and eating disorders [66%], excessive online Internet use [66%], negative body image [64%], excessive videogame playing [64%], and depression [60%]). It was interesting to note that only 40% of parents identified adolescent gambling as a potential problem, the only activity in which less than half of all parents were concerned. Similar findings were found in a recent follow-up study including high school teachers where gambling problems among teenagers were perceived to be the least problematic behavior among thirteen potentially problematic adolescent behaviors.

PREVENTION PROGRAMS

Most existing primary prevention programs are considered universal programs, focusing on all individuals rather than merely focusing on individuals who are considered at high risk for developing a gambling problem. Such universal programs are typically designed to minimize and/or prevent a diversity of mental disorders and antisocial and risk-taking behaviors. These programs have traditionally fallen under the general category of "primary prevention." Multiple studies have shown that adolescents, as a group, remain at high risk and are prone to engage in a wide range of risky behaviors including substance and tobacco use, unprotected sex, eating disorders, violence, drinking and driving, and excessive gambling, among others.

Understanding the severity of the consequences associated with youth problem gambling can be difficult in light of the generally accepted perception that youth have little readily available money, that accessibility to gambling venues is typically limited and prohibited to underage minors, and the widespread belief that few adolescents have significant gambling or gambling-related problems. In spite of these general perceptions, there is a growing body of evidence that youth often begin gambling early, much earlier than engaging in any other form of potentially addictive behaviors, including substance use (alcohol or drug use) and cigarette smoking. Interviews with adult pathological and problem gamblers further suggest they report beginning gambling for money during their childhood, often as young as nine or ten years of age. Independent of our existing sanctions, legal prohibitions, and age restrictions, adolescents readily report having managed to gamble on most forms of legalized, regulated, and unregulated gambling activities.

While our current knowledge of the efficacy of prevention of youth gambling problems is really in its infancy, there is a growing and substantial body of research focused on the prevention of adolescent alcohol and substance abuse. Substance abuse prevention has a long and rich history of research, development, implementation, and evaluation. As a result, this information has served as a foundation for our understanding of the types of programs that have been successful. The basic principles found in these programs have helped shape many of the current initiatives designed to minimize problem gambling among adolescents.

In the general field of prevention, several alternative types of programs have been proposed. These are often conceptualized based on the targeted individuals. For some, a more global approach is advocated, whereas for others the targeted population may be more refined and limited. Some of the decisions going into which group(s) should be targeted are based on financial and human resources, accessibility of specific groups, the severity of the problem, and the time necessary to address the problems. Prevention programs can be best viewed as either (a) primary prevention (aimed toward individuals who are not currently exhibiting any problems), (b) secondary prevention (including a framework that focuses on screening individuals for a specific gambling problem as well as those individuals who are thought to be at risk for developing a gambling problem [i.e., endorsing a number of criteria on the scales discussed in chapter 4 but not reaching the clinical criteria for pathological gambling]), and (c) tertiary prevention (helping those individuals currently exhibiting significant gambling-related problems who are identified as pathological gamblers on a gambling screen).

Currently, many of the concerns with respect to prevention have focused on primary prevention, given our inability to accurately predict future problem gamblers and given that almost anyone might be potentially vulnerable to developing a gambling problem. Similar to the field of substance abuse, the vast bulk of resources have been allocated to primary prevention initiatives with the goal of preventing or postponing the initial use of a particular substance. A similar trend encompasses the field of problem gambling.

ABSTINENCE VERSUS THE HARM REDUCTION APPROACH

There are two global paradigms under which specific prevention approaches can be grouped. These are either an abstinence approach where one takes the perspective that all underage youth refrain from gambling entirely or a harm reduction approach (the terms "harm reduction" and "harm minimization" have often been used interchangeably) where while gambling may not be condoned it is understood that individuals will probably gamble but not necessarily excessively. While these two approaches are not completely mutually exclusive, they are predicated on different short-term goals. For many, the idea of gambling, whether it be children, adolescents, or adults, is appalling. While the vast majority of individuals view gambling as a socially acceptable form of entertainment, there are individuals and certain cultural and religious groups who are vehemently opposed to gambling in any form. These individuals would undoubtedly argue for an abstinence approach. In contrast, many individuals argue for a more moderate approach. This may include prohibiting underage youth from gambling. These individuals would likely suggest educating adolescents about the warning signs associated with problem gambling and would be supportive of programs designed to teach adolescents/children to better understand laws of probability through a mathematics curriculum.

Harm reduction or harm minimization strategies primarily seek to help individuals without demanding total abstinence. Such programs are based on the assumption that individuals who gamble do so responsibly, not exceeding limits, and typically not getting into any major difficulties. Gambling can range from someone purchasing a lottery ticket occasionally to travelling to major destination casino resorts in order to gamble. Included in a harm minimization approach would be secondary prevention strategies, based on the assumption that individuals cannot be prevented from engaging in particular risky behaviors. The best analogy for gambling might be consuming alcohol. If one is of legal age and does it responsibly (e.g., not getting inebriated, bingeing, drinking and driving), then this behavior is generally viewed as acceptable (although in some cultures it may be prohibited). Gambling can be viewed in much the same way. If one does it occasionally, within one's financial means, and does not gamble excessively (both in terms of time and money), then the negative consequences associated with gambling are likely minimal. Tertiary prevention strategies are primarily those designed to help ameliorate and provide assistance for those in need of immediate help through direct intervention (these strategies are discussed in the next chapter).

While the negative consequences resulting from excessive gambling are evident (e.g., financial difficulties, depression, suicide ideation and attempts, health problems, academic issues, criminal behavior, familial disruptions, peer difficulties, interpersonal problems), it still remains unclear as to whether the social costs associated with legalized gambling outweigh their benefits.

Almost universally, underage youth are prohibited access to government regulated forms of gambling and venues (different jurisdictions have different regulations as to the age permitted to gamble and/or gamble on certain types of activities). While these laws are necessary, there is evidence indicating that early gambling experiences primarily occur with non-regulated games (e.g., playing cards for money among peers, placing wagers on sports events, betting on games of skill, or parents and family members allowing children to have scratch lottery tickets or purchasing them as holiday and birthday gifts). The fact that parents report being aware of their children's gambling, both within and outside their home, and fail to directly address this issue represents a form of tacit approval. This highlights both the paradox and the confusion as to which primary prevention approach should be used—abstinence or harm reduction. If one were to advocate an abstinence approach, is it realistic to expect youth to stop gambling when between 70% and 80% of children and adolescents report having gambled during the past twelve months? Similar to adults, one could rightfully argue that it is unrealistic to expect youth to stop gambling completely especially given it is exceedingly difficult to regulate access to gambling activities organized by peers (e.g., card betting, sports betting, wagering on personal games of skill). Not only do children report receiving lottery tickets as gifts, parents readily admit purchasing them for their underage children. In contrast, many underage youth are not given alcohol or tobacco products, at the very least, until they reach the age of majority. In fact, one of the primary reasons many casino operators require individuals to be 21 years of age has nothing to do with the belief that younger individuals cannot gamble responsibly but rather that the drinking of alcohol is prohibited in public places until the age of 21 (other jurisdictions sometimes have age restrictions of 18 or 19 as the minimum legal age for cigarette purchases, alcohol consumption, and casino gambling).

There is ample evidence highlighting that age at onset of gambling behavior represents a significant risk factor associated with problem gambling, with the younger the age of initiation being associated with the development of gambling-related problems. Thus, delaying the age of onset of gambling experiences would be one strategy in a successful prevention paradigm. While this argument would support an abstinence approach, other mitigating factors would suggest its limitations. This hypothesis assumes that all forms of gambling are equally risky. Some gambling critics have argued that electronic forms of gambling, be they electronic gambling machines or wagering on Internet gambling sites, are the most potentially problematic. Others have suggested that the "least harmful" gambling would be bingo and the lottery, primarily because the games require minimal amounts to be wagered and take considerable time to play.

The International Centre for Youth Gambling Problems and High-Risk Behaviors has maintained that a harm reduction approach makes more intuitive sense on many levels. This is not to suggest that advocating for underage minors to gamble is preferred. Rather, the pressures and acceptance to gamble negates a total abstinence approach. Included under the principles of harm minimization is the promotion of responsible behavior, teaching and informing youth about the facts and risks associated with gambling, modifying erroneous thoughts, misperceptions, and beliefs, and enhancing the skills necessary to foster their ability to maintain control when gambling. If these skills are encouraged and reinforced for youth throughout their formative years, it is more than likely that the adolescents may be less vulnerable to the risks of a gambling problem once they become of legal age to gamble on regulated gambling activities. The harm minimization approach is not without its critics who have argued that permitting young people to gamble will only encourage them to engage in this behavior. However, given that there are multiple socially acceptable risk behaviors (e.g., alcohol consumption and gambling) where involvement in such activities can be viewed on a continuum ranging from no problems to significant psychological, social, physical, and financial harm to one's self and others, the utility of the harm reduction approach as a means to prevent problem behavior has received wide support and acceptance.

There is also ample reason to believe that an individual's involvement in many potentially risky behaviors may be approached in a responsible manner. For example, the majority of youth who drink alcohol, gamble, or smoke marijuana do not do so excessively nor do they develop an addiction. Rather, their behaviors are done moderately. Youth may engage in these behaviors occasionally, on weekends, rather than during the school week and typically establish and set fairly reasonable limits. Yet we do know that these limits may be intermittently disrespected. Empirical evidence focused on understanding the patterns of use and personal and social control mechanisms associated with different substances also points to the possibility of achieving controlled involvement in risky behaviors, free from excessive problematic involvement. There are also indications from studies that substance users can and do make rational choices, weighing the perceived positive benefits versus risks associated with drug or alcohol use. Surprisingly, in one of the centre's studies that anticipated that problem gamblers would perceive only the benefits and not the risks associated with gambling, adolescent problem gamblers were found to be able to discern both the benefits and risks associated with problem gambling. If problem gamblers did see the risks as well as the benefits associated with gambling, how can their problem gambling behaviors be explained? Do the perceived benefits far outweigh any perceived risk? It appears that problem gamblers either do not recognize themselves as problem gamblers and/or that they view the risks associated with gambling coming much later (they likely assume that by the time the consequences become problematic, they will have stopped gambling).

The research on the risk and protective factors associated with gambling problems offers an important reminder that in spite of these risk and protective factors, gambling problems are operating within a complex person-environment-situation pyramid (this is often referred to as the "biopsychosocial model"). Thus, it has been argued that the continuum of harm is associated with a number of different risk-based profiles and that harm reduction as a strategy may be a useful way to prevent normal adolescent gambling behavior from becoming increasingly problematic.

HARM REDUCTION PREVENTION PROGRAMS

Harm reduction prevention programs have the potential for lowering the overall prevalence rate of problem gambling. To date, universal harm reduction programs have generally been primarily integrated in the form of school-based drug, alcohol, and smoking awareness education and prevention programs. A greater variety of strategies are employed when considering selective prevention, given the variety of at-risk populations that certain programs may target (e.g., street youth at high risk for drug and alcohol abuse, individuals with antisocial, conduct, delinquent, and/or behavioral disorders, or entire schools at high risk for a multiplicity of problems due to sociocultural factors).

Such universal harm reduction prevention programs are intended to modify inappropriate attitudes toward risky behaviors, enhance positive decision making, educate youth about both short-term and long-term risks associated with excessive gambling, and facilitate their understanding of the construct of tolerance (a process in which individuals continuously need to increase the amount and frequency of their wagers in order to achieve the same level of excitement). A basic premise underlying such an approach is that once the individual's awareness and knowledge increases about a potentially risky activity such as gambling and they have developed efficient decision-making and coping skills, they can make appropriate decisions about whether they need to avoid gambling entirely or more carefully monitor their gambling.

THE IMPORTANCE OF RESILIENCE

There exists in the psychological literature a long history of research suggesting that resilient youth typically have competent problem solving skills (the ability to think abstractly and to generate and implement solutions to problems). Being resilient is thought to be extremely important in order to minimize mental health disorders. Resilient individuals have specific coping strategies when faced with adversity, attempt to problem solve using socially acceptable strategies, and do not use substances on a long-term basis to cope with problems. In addition to having effective problem solving skills, there is ample evidence that they are socially competent (encompassing the qualities of flexibility, effective communications, empathy, and concern for others), autonomous (can maintain self-control), and have a sense of purpose (are motivated, realistic yet optimistic). Much of the field of prevention, in particular work by the Substance Abuse and Mental Health Services Administration in Washington, DC, has prompted our realization that in order to best prevent substance abuse or addictive behaviors of all types we need to enhance and promote those attributes thought to buffer and protect individuals from harm through the enhancement of protective attributes. These protective factors, built into many of the current prevention programs, are designed to enhance an individual's resilience in the face of adversity. This can be done by reducing stressors that have prompted the individual to initially engage in these behaviors. Unfortunately, we all face some sort of adversity on a fairly regular basis, with most being minor inconveniences. Such adversities can be identified as either "major" (examples might include the death of a parent or close family member, parental divorce, being repeatedly bullied at school) or more "minor" hassles (having a fight with a best friend, a teacher or parent reprimanding a student about not completing homework).

Protective and risk factors have been shown to interact in such a way that protective factors may reduce the strength of specific stressors. For example, the effects of positive school experiences have been shown to moderate and lessen the negative impact of family conflict, which in turn decreases the association between family conflict and several adolescent problem behaviors (e.g., pathological gambling, alcohol and substance abuse, suicide, and delinquency). If prevention programs can enhance one's resilience, problem solving, and adaptive coping, then they are likely to mitigate the probability that adolescents will gamble excessively as an avoidance mechanism (remembering that when youth gamble on certain activities, such as electronic gambling machines, they go into a dissociative state where they become unaware of time and the "outside world").

CURRENT GAMBLING PREVENTION PROGRAMS

The past decade has witnessed an increase in the number of prevention programs attempting to reduce the incidence of problem gambling. The development of these programs is the result of a considerable infusion of money, primarily from governments, which has directly benefited from the revenues of the very gambling venues which may be the cause of the problem in the first place. Of those prevention programs that are currently in use (although implementation is quite sporadic), most developed for youth have few underlying science-based principles, fail to account for essential risk and protective factors, and have not been systematically evaluated. However, advances are being made continually to rectify this situation. The majority of these new programs can best be described as primary and/or universal preventive efforts with the overall goal of reducing the incidence of problem gambling (a harm minimization versus abstinence approach). Several programs have explicitly identified risk factors associated with the development of problem gambling. A number of these programs are predicated on increasing one's understanding of the mathematical laws of probability (the basic assumption being that if one understands the laws of probability, the individual will either refrain from gambling or do so more responsibly), while others are focused on deconstructing the myth that there is considerable skill involved in random activities (e.g., slots, roulette).

COMMONALITIES AND DIFFERENCES AMONG PROGRAMS

Prevention programs designed to reduce the incidence of gambling problems for youth have typically aimed at raising awareness concerning issues related to problem gambling. Most of these programs conceptualize gambling as an addiction, foster a harm reduction framework, and while some may try to advocate abstinence until one has the cognitive intellectual capacity necessary to set and maintain limits, typically emphasize responsible gambling.

Since the objective of the majority of current programs is to raise awareness, most present information relevant to gambling and problem gambling, discuss motivations to gamble, articulate the warning signs associated with problem gambling, identify the consequences of excessive gambling, and try to provide information on where individuals can get help with a gambling problem. Several curriculums go a little further than merely presenting factual information and dispelling erroneous beliefs. These programs encourage the development of interpersonal skills, provide activities which foster and promote effective coping mechanisms, promote techniques and methods to help enhance one's self-esteem, and provide useful insights into how to resist peer pressure.

A growing number of gambling prevention programs have been developed. Some of these current programs include Don't Bet on It—a South Australian program for children ages 6 to 9 years; Gambling: Minimizing Health Risks, in Queensland, Australia, for children in levels 5 and 6; Facing the Odds, in Louisiana for children in grades 5 through 8; Wanna Bet, in Minnesota for children in grades 3 through 8; Gambling: A Stacked Deck, in Alberta; and the Harvard/Massachusetts Council's Mathematics Curriculum for High School Students.

For the past twenty years, the International Centre for Youth Gambling Problems and High-Risk Behaviors at McGill University has tried to incorporate the knowledge acquired from examining the risk and protective factors associated with youth gambling and gambling problems into prevention initiatives. This work has led to a better understanding of the components necessary to include in youth prevention programs. At the same time, the importance of providing a diversity of strategies for teachers, prevention specialists, and parents seems warranted. While most of these programs are school-based, a number of them have been used in after-school programs and on some occasions parents have elected to review them with their children. In spite of some evidence which suggests that single trial inoculations are ineffective for long-term gains in behavior changes, the centre has adopted a multi-level approach, with some efforts being directly student-based, others requiring some teacher intervention, and still others requiring more direct instruction and discussion. This multifaceted approach is designed to appeal to educators who may be unfamiliar with the issue of teen gambling and/or gambling problems as well as those with a limited time in which to administer a curriculum.

The centre's prevention programs are also intended to address a number of different audiences: children and adolescents, teachers, parents, physicians, lawyers, and even judges. All of the centre's programs have been evaluated for their short-term gains (insufficient funding has been available for long-term follow-up) and they have generally been found to be beneficial in improving knowledge, increasing awareness of the warning signs for problem gambling, modifying inappropriate attitudes, and correcting false cognitions, understandings, and erroneous beliefs (e.g., probabilities, skill versus luck, strategies, superstitions, independence of events) with the intention of ultimately reducing gambling behavior and helping prevent excessive pathological gambling behavior disorders. While it is not the intent here to exhaustively describe the specific goals for each of these prevention initiatives (see www.youthgambling.com for a more detailed description of each of the products), the more general goals of the programs are to enhance problem-solving skills, increase feelings of self-confidence, improve coping skills, provide tools to resist peer pressure and social temptations, and facilitate good decision making while simultaneously addressing the issues associated with teen gambling. Many of these programs are currently being used in the United States, Canada, Europe, Australia, New Zealand, and Singapore.

The following activities have been developed for use in primary and secondary schools:

The *Amazing Chateau* (grades 4–7) and *Hooked City* (grades 7–12)

These award-winning interactive educational computer software games are designed for youth from the ages of 9 to 17. The games are played individually, with each game taking approximately sixty minutes to complete. Both games have been developed to capture the imagination of youth, provide them with some facts about gambling, dispel myths, and foster good decision making while incorporating a problem solving approach. Children can complete a self assessment of their gambling and print valuable information. The games enable the students to maintain records of success while reinforcing a wide variety of concepts and misconceptions related to youth gambling issues. Players can stop and start whenever they like. In the *Amazing Chateau,* players try to acquire some special crystals while answering skill-testing questions. Special attention is paid to increasing children's knowledge about gambling, challenging inappropriate attitudes toward gambling, and increasing decision-making skills. Within *Hooked City,* the adventure begins with players being transported through dark and intriguing settings while trying to free their friend Tom. Unfortunately, their friend Tom has fallen into the trap of Mr. Hook, a dark character who is intent on having the players make highly questionable decisions and choices. The evil Mr. Hook wants to get Tom addicted to gambling, which is imprisoning poor Tom. Fortunately, the players also meet Zack, a personable individual, who will guide the players into making the correct choices which will help them ultimately free Tom and avoid falling into Mr. Hook's devious grasp. Players' performance is reinforced throughout the game based on their accurate knowledge of gambling questions and perceptions. If they perform well, they receive a clue which helps them solve the puzzle to free Tom. As in the *Amazing Chateau,* the players in *Hooked City* are exposed to many of the myths surrounding gambling and the risk signs of problem gambling. As well, they are introduced to a problem gambler who successfully sought treatment. Students are urged to complete a gambling screen to assess the severity of their gambling behaviors and are provided feedback and suggestions based on their performance. Both programs come with a comprehensive manual for teachers. Ultimately, these programs were developed to help children adopt a healthier lifestyle and more positive attitudes and behaviors toward gambling.

Youth Awareness and Prevention Workshops (Levels 1 and 2)

These PowerPoint workshops were developed for children in late elementary, junior high, and senior high school. Each package includes a CD-ROM containing the PowerPoint presentation as well as an instructor's manual. Included in each manual is background information on the subject of youth gambling, identification of the goal(s) of each slide, and suggested questions to help promote discussion. These workshops are designed to help educate children about the potential hazards associated with problem gambling, The workshops, using age-appropriate examples, help clarify misperceptions, challenge erroneous beliefs, dispel myths associated with gambling, and provide students with the opportunity to discuss concerns. Both workshops were evaluated on over 7,000 school-aged children and adolescents and have been shown to be effective in achieving their goals. While intended to be completed in one sitting, they can and have been done over several days.

Clean Break

This award-winning docudrama is approximately 28 minutes in length and was developed for typical high school students. With support from the Canadian Ministry of Justice, a special emphasis was placed on providing examples that would be particularly appealing to delinquent youth. The production, using MTV fast-paced video and audio technology, follows a pathological gambler who describes his lifelong gambling addiction. Ultimately, in a moment of desperation, he attempts suicide by jumping off a bridge. While not readily apparent to the audience until the final moments of the video, his unsuccessful suicide attempt resulted in him now being a paraplegic confined to a wheelchair. The title of the docudrama, *Clean Break*, came from his powerful statement that he prefers being confined to a wheelchair than being plagued by a gambling addiction. He is now a "happy man" since he has made a "clean break" from the throes of this devastating addiction. Interspersed throughout the DVD are scenes using professional actors and examples of adolescent problem gambling behaviors based upon the centre's clinical experiences working with youth having gambling problems. This hard-hitting award-winning docudrama is accompanied by an examiner's manual and a PowerPoint presentation for follow-up discussions. Unlike other documentaries, it is fast-paced and uses the newest technology to help retain the interest of its audience. *Clean Break* has been viewed by tens of thousands of youth. The special music used throughout the video was written by a rock band exclusively for this project.

Know Limits

Issues around gambling, drug and alcohol use, tobacco, and other high-risk behaviors are presented in a team game format. Incorporating elements of Charades, Taboo, and Word Scramble, information is disseminated in a fun and enjoyable game format for high school students. Like other prevention initiatives, this game is designed to help clarify misperceptions, challenge erroneous beliefs, and dispel myths associated with gambling and other addictive behaviors. Trivia questions related to music and entertainment are interspersed among the questions, which were tested by professionals and hundreds of students.

PUBLIC AWARENESS CAMPAIGNS AND SAFE GAMBLING MESSAGES

Other prevention initiatives have been used to target individuals who frequently come into contact with adolescents and adolescent problem gamblers. For example, the centre has developed two successful public service announcements (PSAs) targeting Internet wagering and poker playing. The PSAs were developed to raise parental awareness that children's gambling, which starts off innocently, may in fact become a significant problem. Using no verbal language, these attention-grabbing PSAs are 30 seconds in length and have a clear message: "Talk with your children." Having no verbiage in these PSAs provides an opportunity to use these initiatives for multiple cultural and linguistic groups. Also, the tag line "Talk with your children" is easily translated without reshooting the entire PSA. Two versions of each PSA are currently available. One uses predominantly North American adolescents while the other incorporates Asian teenagers in each PSA.

More recently, several prevention and awareness programs have been developed for physicians, *Youth Gambling Problems: Practical Information for Health Professionals*, and for those in the legal profession, *Youth Gambling Problems: Practical Information for Professionals in the Criminal Justice System.* These programs are designed to raise awareness among physicians and individuals in the legal profession (lawyers and judges) about the extent of youth gambling, provide strategies to best identify youth gambling problems, and show ways in which professionals can help individuals and their families. Each of these programs includes a DVD with pertinent information on youth gambling problems incorporating interviews with the leading international experts in the field. As well, the package includes a CD-ROM containing relevant seminal research papers, posters, and screening instruments, all of which can be downloaded and printed.

While these programs have been directly targeted to children and adolescents, a number of other relevant public awareness programs have been developed in many jurisdictions. There is evidence that a large percentage of adults are aware of the problems associated with excessive gambling. In a number of surveys, adults have acknowledged that gambling problems appear to be worsening within their communities, with many able to accurately describe the impacts of gambling including the effects on the psychological health of the individuals, the financial consequences, and the impact on families. However, what is most important is not merely their awareness of the problem but whether they are able to recognize the onset and existence of problem gambling (remembering that this is often referred to as the "hidden addiction") in specific individuals or themselves. As a result, a number of public awareness campaigns using catchy slogans have been developed, such as "Keep it a game," "Have fun but play it safe," "Bet with your head, not above it," "Gambling is for adults, not children." While some are appealing, it is not possible to know whether such slogans work.

Public awareness campaigns have evolved for all forms of gambling, be it the lottery, electronic gambling machines, land-based casinos, harness racing, or even Internet gambling. As previously discussed, parents often purchase lottery tickets for their underaged children as holiday or birthday gifts or for special occasions. One successful campaign initiated by the International Centre for Youth Gambling Problems and High-Risk Behaviors in collaboration with the U.S. National Council on Problem Gambling has been targeting adults during the Christmas holiday period urging them not to purchase lottery tickets for children as gifts. This highly successful program, incorporating a variety of adult-oriented slogans, has been adopted by lottery corporations throughout Canada, the United States, and Europe, with Asia and Australasia similarly being targeted. The message has to be clear —the earlier one starts gambling the more likely one *may* become a problem gambler (delaying the onset of gambling reduces the risks for problem gambling), and that gambling is for adults, not children. Most people would not purchase alcohol for their underaged children yet perceive that lottery tickets are a relatively benign form of gambling with few negative consequences. A number of researchers have even suggested that the purchasing of lottery tickets may be a "gateway" into other forms of gambling. While most people think of purchasing a lottery ticket as relatively harmless, there have been instances where individuals have spent their food and rent money gambling. Recently, the former finance director of the Valley Forge Convention and Visitors Bureau was found guilty and sent to prison for embezzling more than $700,000 from the organization, which was used to continually purchase lottery tickets.

Other successful campaigns have been developed to help lottery corporations themselves try to refrain from making tickets particularly attractive to children. In several studies, adolescents' report that familiarity with the games promoted on scratch tickets, the prizes to be won, as well as the number of games on each of the scratch cards can be particularly enticing. Developed by several researchers in the United Kingdom, in collaboration with an international advisory panel, a procedure referred to as GAM-GaRD identifies how risky a proposed (or established) game is likely to be for a vulnerable player by studying the specific characteristics of the game. Its basic premise is that by examining the structural and situational characteristics that constitute the fundamental features of the game, they can predict which games or scratch cards will be more enticing to problem gamblers. GAM-GaRD displays the results in three bands analogous to a traffic light; low risk (green), medium risk (yellow), and high risk (red). A classification of red does not necessarily mean that a game should be entirely discarded but indicates that there are elements that need modifying, or require additional responsible gaming features (e.g., limit the availability or spending limit of a game). Once the outcome becomes known, the gambling operator can elect to modify these features and promote a safer product. A number of lottery corporations use this procedure to help shape which products might be feasible. However, it remains an important discussion question of why many corporations are still using licensed games particularly attractive to youth.

PREVENTION PROGRAMS TARGETING ADULTS

In many land-based gambling venues, new warning signs, pamphlets, and posters are being implemented in high traffic areas including places where individuals acquire money (e.g., automatic teller machines [ATMs]), washrooms, casino hotel check-in desks, and throughout the actual venue. In some casinos in Canada, there are actual centers within the casinos themselves where individuals can learn the laws of probability, how electronic gambling machines actually work, and where counselors are available for immediate discussion. While intuitively these programs appear beneficial, their effectiveness has not been empirically tested. Some have argued that there is a real need to consider images and messages that will actively engage people's cognitive, emotional, and motivational faculties. Merely providing factual information with catchy slogans may be insufficient in preventing problem gambling. Most individuals are aware of the odds and laws of probabilities and are indeed cognizant that gambling can result in problems but think it will not happen to them. However, once engaged in gambling, they tend to forget the odds and get caught up in the excitement of the game.

Providing information at gambling venues has been traditionally viewed as a responsible gambling measure. This information has typically focused on providing the payout rates to individuals. There is actually some evidence suggesting that providing all the payout rates and the odds of winning can be confusing. Where else can one observe huge neon signs in casino venues advertising that their slot machines pay out the highest rates of return (e.g., 98%). While this is based on millions of spins of the slot machine, in essence the casinos are advertising to the individual that for every dollar they insert and play, they will get $0.98 back. On the next spin it will be 98% of 0.98 (approximately $0.96) and, by the end of the day or evening, many people walk away with nothing. It is no wonder these machines are referred to as one-armed bandits. Their speed of play, intermittent reinforcements, and the lights and sounds associated with the machines keep many people glued. There have actually been instances where people have refused to leave "their" machine during a fire. Merely understanding the odds can also result in the gambler's fallacy that they can readjust their wagering to accommodate the probabilities during the actual play. Seeing nine red numbers come up on a roulette wheel doesn't increase the odds of the ball landing on a black number on the next spin of the wheel.

KEEPING TRACK OF AN INDIVIDUAL'S PLAYING BEHAVIOR

There is some evidence that helping individuals keep track of their playing behavior may be a useful strategy to help non-problem gamblers maintain their gambling at a safe level. This may take the form of using smart card or biometric technology on electronic gambling machines. The technology permits the individual to set pre-established expenditure limits for each session (daily, weekly, or monthly). It also enables the individual to establish the time period of a particular session. Once these limits have been reached, the machine automatically refuses to allow the player to continue. Preliminary research in pilot projects has suggested that this may be a helpful resource for some individuals. Tracking these behaviors, whether through a smart card, an App on a cell phone, or other device can be a useful strategy for most people. We also know that problem gamblers tend to over-exaggerate their wins and minimize their losses. Mainlining and keeping track of monies won or lost per session, cumulative amounts won or lost, and the amount of time spent gambling may be useful feedback for the individual concerning their gambling behavior. Some Internet gambling providers have also included a host of these features into their software. Other strategies currently being employed in certain jurisdictions on electronic gambling machines include displaying a visible clock on the machine such that players can monitor the time spent playing, monetary amounts being displayed rather than number of credits, limits on the amount of money one can insert into a bill acceptor (devices on a machine that allow individuals to insert bills rather than coins into the machines), and automatic cash payouts after either a predetermined time or amount won. In a growing number of jurisdictions, the electronic gambling machines now have warning signs or messages on their screens. Many of these machines currently have the ability to play multiple games simultaneously, with operators having the ability to modify the machines electronically from a central location.

THE IMPORTANCE OF DEVELOPING RESPONSIBLE ADVERTISING POLICIES AND GUIDELINES

Although there is only a limited amount of information available concerning the specific impact of gambling advertisements on gambling behavior, there is little doubt that most individuals are bombarded by advertisements enticing them to "live the dream" or visit a destination casino. Never in any of these advertisements promoting gambling is there a true balance between the benefits and problems associated with gambling. Rather, in some research conducted at the International Centre for Youth Gambling Problems and High-Risk Behaviors, adolescents report that these advertisements depict individuals who are always winning, happy, and excited. Youth report being bombarded through the Internet with pop-up messages enticing them to gamble and offers of sign-up bonuses with a growing number of gaming operators using social media advertising to invite individuals to gamble money or to play on their free sites.

There is little doubt that direct marketing and advertising are effective with individuals becoming very sensitive to the availability and diversity of new gambling products and venues. Adolescents who report having a good knowledge and recall of popular gambling commercials are familiar with the slogans of land-based casinos or lotteries and easily remember the expressions of those who have won. In a study examining lottery playing among adolescents, while adolescents recall the tickets being advertised, only the problem gamblers were more likely enticed to purchase the tickets.

One of the concerns for problem gamblers is to avoid situations or triggers prompting gambling (more thoroughly described in chapter 6). Many teenagers in treatment report that this is now impossible due to the widespread advertising using traditional media (radio, television, newspapers, billboards) and through Internet pop-up messages and social media. Exposure to such advertisements likely entices problem gamblers to continue gambling. Similar bans on cigarettes and alcohol advertising are in place in many jurisdictions and have been proposed for gambling. While there is no available evidence to suggest which triggers or advertisements are most likely to impact problem gamblers, we nevertheless need some monitoring of such advertising practices. A number of international jurisdictions have established regulated guidelines and prohibitions for advertising that is deceptive, misrepresents the probability of winning, gives the impression that gambling is a "reasonable" strategy to increase one's financial wealth, and targets minors, disadvantaged, or low income groups. Limitations on the extent and nature of advertising are one form of prevention. However, limiting direct mailing of advertisements by land-based casinos to individuals on self-exclusion lists remains essential.

LIMITING INDUCEMENTS FOR PROBLEM GAMBLERS

Everyone likes something for free. Many gambling venues offer their patrons some form of inducement to gamble or even enter their establishment. It is not unusual in Las Vegas for adults to be enticed into a casino by being offered a free spin on a slot machine and an opportunity to win a variety of prizes. In many jurisdictions, inexpensive meals are provided (some casinos in Las Vegas offer a "day pass" to their buffets such that an individual can eat breakfast, lunch, and dinner for a specified low price). This is all in an effort to keep people within their casino. Patrons who gamble large sums of money are "comped" (provided free meals, tickets to shows, rooms, etc.), others are provided free coffee in some venues, and in others free alcoholic drinks are provided as long as the individual is gambling. Loyalty cards are huge incentives to keep individuals playing. These cards when inserted into a slot machine earn points which are exchangeable for gifts. A gambler once remarked that these cards are like an IV hooked to the machine. Individuals who gamble extensively are provided limousines, free airline tickets, and in some cases refunded a certain percentage of losses. While many of these perks and loyalty schemes are indeed attractive to the average player, the problem gambler is much more interested in the "gambling" than in either eating or attending shows. One young man told me that when he was in a local casino, he had two young ladies with him in the expensive dining room where all food and alcohol were complimentary and all he could think about was getting back to the Blackjack table. Enticements and invitations to gamble are certainly another form of trigger for individuals with gambling problems and need to be addressed and limited for problem gamblers.

ACCESSING GAMBLING VENUES FOR INDIVIDUALS WITH GAMBLING PROBLEMS

Preventing individuals with gambling problems from accessing gambling venues has been a primary way of helping prevent further problems. Self-exclusion programs have probably been the number one way of restricting individuals with severe gambling problems from accessing specific *types* of venues. This has been typically done in casinos. Individuals with a gambling problem (in fact, any individual of legal age) can elect to be included on self-exclusion lists barring themselves from the gambling venue. If they manage to re-enter the venue, in principle, these individuals will be escorted out of the premises by the security staff. All that is necessary is that they complete an application and provide a picture. Using this program, an individual can establish a set period for their exclusion (different jurisdictions have different regulations, with bans generally ranging from three months to lifetime). In some venues, before re-entry is permitted, after the time limit, the individual must meet with a counselor. In other locations, the exclusion is merely based on time. Part of the problem for the problem gambler is that this denial of entry may be restricted to a specific venue, state, or type of venue. For example, barring oneself from gambling at Caesar's Palace in Las Vegas may have no impact on Caesar's properties in other states or countries. Barring oneself from a casino may still allow entry into harness racing tracks, gambling with a bookmaker, playing electronic gambling machines, engaging in online gambling, etc. There is considerable evidence that problem gamblers report gambling in multiple venues, manage to gamble in venues in spite of their being placed on self-exclusion lists, and often evade security. New systems are being developed including the use of facial recognition software and cameras to minimize some of these problems, while others argue for the importance of requiring a passport for entry. Within some jurisdictions, once on a self-exclusion list, entry into the venue can result in criminal charges.

In a rather unique situation, the government of Singapore has instituted a third-party self-exclusion program. Within this system, an individual with detailed knowledge of the problem gambler (e.g., typically a spouse, child, employer, or therapist) can provide a recommendation to an oversight committee that they examine evidence which might decree that an individual should be prohibited from gambling at the two licensed casinos in spite of the individual's wishes. While too early to know the effectiveness of the program, this may be expanded into other jurisdictions. It is also important to note that in the Singapore casinos one must present a passport before gaining entry, thus providing another layer of security prohibiting banned individuals from casino entry.

OTHER PREVENTION INITIATIVES

Other typical programs include the use of a state run, provincially run, or national "hot line." These hot lines, which receive calls from problem gamblers, vary greatly in the services provided, with some giving immediate help by discussing issues with the client, others referring them to treatment providers, and others taking the information and having a counselor return the individual's call. These calls are typically made when the problem gambler is in a desperate phase and are most often used as a stopgap measure to try to de-escalate a crisis. Hot-line workers generally have some training in crisis intervention.

Through legislation, a number of jurisdictions also restrict access to money at gambling venues. Some jurisdictions permit credit to gamblers while others do not. There is no question that problem gamblers are more likely to borrow money in order to gamble. The availability of credit facilities, ATMs, and loan sharks (individuals who loan people money with exorbitant interest charges) likely exacerbates the problem gambler's losses. Individuals with gambling problems typically take winnings and continue to gamble. In certain jurisdictions, the ATMs must be off the casino floor in order to give the gambler a "cooling off period" before accessing additional funds. In other jurisdictions, the individual must have the money in the bank before funds can be withdrawn (as opposed to using a line of credit). In an Australian study, it was revealed that almost 60% of gamblers with severe gambling problems "often" or "always" used ATM machines at gambling venues with only 4% of non-problem gamblers reporting doing so. Some compromised situations have been implemented such that ATMs have been placed in more remote locations within the gambling venues, limits are set on the amounts of money that can be withdrawn in a single day, there is a limit on the number of withdrawals, and responsible gambling messages have been placed near or within the terminals themselves.

Restricting financial access is an important issue which necessitates the inclusion of responsible social policies. The following example illustrates the perseverance of some problem gamblers to continually acquire money with which to gamble. One client in our treatment program, a young man age 19, entered a casino with his sister. On entering the casino he had $500 and gave his sister half to hold with the explicit instructions that no matter what happened or how much he asked she was not to give him the remaining $250. After losing his initial $250, he went to his sister and asked for the balance of his money. When she refused, he argued with her that it was *his* money and she must return it. After a heated argument, he grabbed her purse while knocking her to the floor, took out the remaining money, and proceeded to gamble it all. On the way home, he screamed at his sister for giving him the balance of the money.

Other strategies may include the closing of casinos or electronic gaming machine establishments during certain hours. While some jurisdictions have employed this strategy, Internet gambling sites operate 24 hours per day, seven days per week. As such, this has minimized the potential for this strategy to be effective. There is evidence from both adolescents and adults that when the time is drawing close to when they must stop gambling they tend to increase the frequency and amounts of money wagered. Given that the odds are always against them, this generally results in greater losses. The existing evidence would suggest that while casino or electronic game shutdowns during certain periods may have some influence on problem gamblers' behaviors, this policy in general will not significantly impact their gambling. The actual timing of the shutdown may be more important and play a more influential role in influencing their behavior and expenditures.

With respect to modifications of the games themselves, a number of innovative strategies have been attempted to help minimize harm. In addition to the use of the smart card and biometric technologies previously discussed, the notion of forced breaks in gambling after a large win has been advocated. The underlying rationale for this approach is that by forcing the individual to cash out his winnings before replaying the machine, he is forced to rethink his decision to continue to play. There has been some evidence to support this approach although a number of studies have pointed to the fact that many gamblers typically pause after a large win. The key determinant would likely be the duration between the gambling episodes. Thus, if the individual was forced to discontinue playing for a significantly long period of time he/she might leave. The problem remains that they might just go play another machine unless there was some form of smart card technology associated with it.

INTERNET GAMBLING: AN OPPORTUNITY FOR INNOVATIVE PROTECTION STRATEGIES

While a more in-depth discussion is provided in chapter 7, which focuses on responsible social policies, a brief discussion is merited because a number of harm prevention initiatives have begun to be employed on Internet gambling sites. It is likely that mobile gambling operators will also attempt to employ many of these strategies. Please note that some of these prevention strategies are voluntary and others are prescribed by legislation. A number of groups have been quite instrumental in setting standards and codes of practice for Internet gambling operators, given the general lack of regulation in the online gambling industry. These organizations have allowed online gambling operators to increase their credibility by voluntarily following an established framework and code of conduct and to engage in regular training of employees. Internet gambling operators have the potential capability to monitor player behavior more effectively and efficiently than in any other gambling environment. Their ability to establish controls to help problem gamblers remains crucial. Typically, many sites have self-exclusion policies and enable players to establish time and money limits.

Two further developments are ongoing with respect to the prevention of gambling problems among Internet gamblers. The first includes computer-based software which can block Internet gambling sites. This is similar to much of the software used in schools to block pornographic material. Some jurisdictions, for example British Columbia and Nova Scotia, allow free downloads of this Internet gambling blocking software. One unintended benefit of the availability of this software was that parents actually began to see the need to discuss gambling as an issue with their adolescents. We will likely see an increased number of software programs of this nature as more jurisdictions adopt, license, and/or regulate Internet wagering, especially in North America. A second and more recent development is the advances in the informatics and algorithms that are designed to identify specific gambling patterns typical of problem gamblers. Imagine if by observing an individual's early playing behavior, we can target these individuals for messages encouraging them to avail themselves of some of the responsible gaming prevention tools. Few other opportunities are available to researchers to track every single bet. Yet, accessing data from the Internet does actually permit this because every single wager is recorded. Several researchers from the Harvard Medical School have been examining this information as a way of developing a more sophisticated database enabling Internet gambling providers to notify players of aberrant playing patterns.

NEW DIRECTIONS

Helping individuals to establish and maintain both time and money limits remains important and is the hallmark of a responsible gambling program. There is little doubt that while our knowledge concerning youth with gambling problems has steadily increased during the past two decades, our need to incorporate such knowledge into a risk-protection-resilience prevention model requires further elaboration. Viewing risk and protective factors in light of some of the new findings will ultimately provide strategies to specify program goals, enable us to better establish outcome evaluation criteria, and help determine the best type of program for certain individuals.

Findings from the field of adolescent alcohol and substance abuse suggest that no one universal approach to prevention appears to be uniformly successful. As such, a combination of strategies seems to work best toward the goal of nurturing resilience and serves to protect youth against undesirable substances and behaviors. Ultimately, such strategies will likely include information dissemination, prevention education, providing alternative activities in lieu of the particular addictive behavior, problem identification and referral, community-based processes (training community members and agencies in substance use and gambling education and prevention), and activities thought to reduce risk factors and enhance protective factors. As well, our practices will need to be adapted for youth of different cultural and ethnic backgrounds, ages, and developmental stages. It is important to understand the venues in which such programs will occur. For example, if teachers remain reluctant to use one type of program, then alternative approaches may be necessary. Finally, the social acceptability and availability of types of gambling experiences has been constantly evolving. We will certainly need to modify our prevention approaches based on these changes while using advancing technologies and social media to our advantage.

REFERENCES

Barnes, G. M., Welte, J. W., Hoffman, J. H., and Dintcheff, B. A. (1999). Gambling and alcohol use among youth: Influences of demographic, socialization, and individual factors. *Addictive Behaviors, 24*(6), 749–67.

Brounstein, P. J., Zweig, J. M., and Gardner, S. E. (1999). *Understanding substance abuse prevention: Toward the 21st century—A primer on effective programs.* Substance Abuse and Mental Health Services Administration, Center for Substance Abuse Prevention, Division of Knowledge Development and Evaluation.

Byrne, A., Dickson, L., Derevensky, J., Gupta, R., and Lussier, I. (2005). An examination of social marketing campaigns for the prevention of youth problem gambling. *Journal of Health Communication, 10*, 681–700.

Campbell, C., Derevensky, J., Meerkamper , E., and Cutajar, J. (in press). The influence of cultural background on parental perceptions of adolescent gambling behaviour: A Canadian study. *International Journal of Mental Health and Addictions.*

Campbell, C., Derevensky, J., Meerkamper, E., and Cutajar, J. (2011). Parents' perceptions of adolescent gambling: A Canadian national study. *Journal of Gambling Issues, 25*, 36–53.

Curriculum Services Canada (CSC). Don't Bet on It–A Youth Problem Gambling Prevention Program. http://curriculum.org/resources/dont-bet-on-it-8211-a-youth-problem-gambling-prevention-program.

Delfabbro, P. (2009). *Australasian gambling review, Fourth edition covering 1992-2008.* Adelaide: Independent Gambling Authority.

Derevensky, J., and Gupta, R. (2007). Internet gambling amongst adolescents: A growing concern. *International Journal of Mental Health and Addictions,* 5(2), 93–101.

Derevensky, J., Gupta, R., Dickson, L., Hardoon, K., and Deguire, A. E. (2003). Understanding youth gambling problems: A conceptual framework. In D. Romer (Ed.), *Reducing adolescent risk: Toward an integrated approach.* California: Sage Publications, 239–46.

Derevensky, J., Gupta, R., and Dickson, L. (2004). Adolescent gambling problems: Prevention and treatment implications. In J. E. Grant and M. N. Potenza (Eds.) *Understanding and treating pathological gambling.* Washington, DC: APPI Press, 159–68.

Derevensky, J., Gupta, R., Dickson, L., and Deguire, A. E. (2004). Prevention efforts toward reducing gambling problems. In J. Derevensky and R. Gupta (Eds.) *Gambling problems in youth: Theoretical and applied perspectives.* New York: Kluwer Academic/Plenum Publishers, 211–30.

Derevensky, J., Sklar, A., Gupta, R., and Messerlian, C., Laroche, M. and Mansour, S. (2007). The effects of gambling advertisements on child and adolescent gambling attitudes and behaviors (Les effets de la publicité sur les attitudes et les comportements de jeu des enfants et des adolescents). *Fonds de recherché en santé du Québec (FRSQ),* Quebec, 68 pp.

Derevensky, J., Sklar, A., Gupta, R., and Messerlian, C. (2010). An empirical study examining the impact of gambling advertisements on adolescent gambling attitudes and behaviors. *International Journal of Mental Health and Addiction,* 8, 21–34.

Derevensky, J., St-Pierre, R., Temcheff, C., and Gupta, R. (2011). Beliefs and attitudes of teachers with respect to youth gambling. Poster presented at the Canadian Psychological Association annual conference, Toronto, June.

Dickson, L., Derevensky, J., and Gupta, R. (2002). The prevention of youth gambling problems: A conceptual model. *Journal of Gambling Studies,* 18(2), 97–160.

Dickson, L., Derevensky, J., and Gupta, R. (2004). Harm reduction for the prevention of youth gambling problems: Lessons learned from adolescent high-risk prevention programs. *Journal of Adolescent Research, 19*(2), 233–63.

Dickson, L., and Derevensky, J. (2006). Preventing adolescent problem gambling: Implications for school psychology. *Canadian Journal of School Psychology, 21*(1/2), 59–72.

Dickson, L., Derevensky, J., and Gupta, R. (2008). Youth gambling problems: An examination of risk and protective factors. *International Gambling Studies, 8*(1), 25–47.

Durlak, J. A. (1997). Primary prevention programs in schools. *Advances in Clinical Child Psychology, 19*, 283–318.

Faregh, N., and Derevensky, J. (2011). Prevention of impulse control disorders. In J. E. Grant and M. N. Potenza (Eds.). *Understanding impulse control disorders*. New York: Oxford University Press, 499–515.

Felsher, J., Derevensky, J. and Gupta, R. (2004). Lottery playing amongst youth: Implications for prevention and social policy. *Journal of Gambling Studies, 20*(2), 127–53.

Felsher, J., Derevensky, J. and Gupta, R. (2004). Lottery participation by youth with gambling problems: Are lottery tickets a gateway to other gambling venues? *International Gambling Studies, 4*(2), 109–26.

Ferland, F., Ladouceur, R., and Vitaro, F. (2001). Prevention of problem gambling: Modifying misconception and increasing knowledge. *Journal of Gambling Studies, 18*, 19–30.

Gaboury, A., and Ladouceur, R. (1993). Evaluation of a prevention program for pathological gambling among adolescents. *The Journal of Primary Prevention, 14*, 21–28.

GAM-GaRD. http://www.gamgard.com.

Gillespie, M., Derevensky, J., and Gupta, R. (2007). The utility of outcome expectancies in the prediction of adolescent gambling behavior. *Journal of Gambling Issues, 19*, 69–85.

Gillespie, M., Gupta, R., Derevensky, J., Pratt, L., and Vallerand, R. (2005). Adolescent Problem Gambling: Evaluating Perceived Risks and Benefits (Le jeu problématique chez les adolescents: perceptions des risques et des bénéfices). Report prepared for the Fonds de recherché en santé du Québec (FRSQ), Québec, 36 pp.

Gupta, R., and Derevensky, J. (1998). Adolescent gambling behavior: A prevalence study and examination of the correlates associated with problem gambling. *Journal of Gambling Studies, 14*, 319–45.

Gupta, R., and Derevensky, J. (1998). An empirical examination of Jacobs' General Theory of Addictions: Do adolescent gamblers fit the theory? *Journal of Gambling Studies, 14*(1), 17–49.

Gupta, R., and Derevensky, J. (2008). Gambling practices among youth: Etiology, prevention and treatment. In C. A. Essau (Ed.), *Adolescent addiction: Epidemiology, assessment and treatment.* London, UK: Elsevier, 207–30.

Hardoon, K., Derevensky, J., and Gupta, R. (2003). Empirical vs. perceived measures of gambling severity: Why adolescents don't present themselves for treatment. *Addictive Behaviors, 28,* 933–46.

Lussier, I., Derevensky, J., and Gupta, R. (2009). Youth gambling prevention and resilience education: A harm reduction approach. *The Praeger International collection on addictions. Volume IV.* CT: Praeger, 339–50.

Lussier, I., Derevensky, J., Gupta, R., Bergevin, T., and Ellenbogen, S. (2007). Youth gambling behaviors: An examination of the role of resilience. *Psychology of Addictive Behaviors, 21,* 165–73.

Messerlian, C., Byrne, A., and Derevensky, J. (2004). Gambling, youth and the Internet: Should we be concerned? *The Canadian Child and Adolescent Psychiatry Review, 13*(1), 3–6.

Messerlian, C., and Derevensky, J. (2005). Youth gambling: A public health perspective. *Journal of Gambling Issues, 14,* 97–116.

Messerlian, C., and Derevensky, J. (2006). Social marketing campaigns for youth gambling prevention: Lessons learned from youth. *International Journal of Mental Health, 4,* 294–306.

Messerlian, C., and Derevensky, J. (2007). Evaluating the role of social marketing campaigns to prevent youth gambling problems: A qualitative study. *Canadian Journal of Public Health, 98,* 101–4.

Messerlian, C., Derevensky, J., and Gupta, R. (2004). A public health perspective for youth gambling: A prevention and harm minimization framework. *International Gambling Studies, 4*(2), 147–60.

Messerlian, C., Gillespie, M., and Derevensky, J. (2007). Beyond drugs and alcohol: Including gambling in our high-risk behavior framework. *Paediatrics and Child Health, 12*(3), 199–204.

Monaghan, S., and Derevensky, J. (2008). An appraisal of the impact of the depiction of gambling in society on youth. *International Journal of Mental Health and Addiction, 6,* 1557–74.

Monaghan, S., and Derevensky, J. (2008). A critical review of the Internet gambling literature: Some policy recommendations. Report submitted to Nova Scotia Gaming Corporation.

Najavits, L. M., Grymala, L. D., and George, B. (2003). Can advertising increase awareness of problem gambling: A statewide survey of impact. *Psychology of Addictive Behaviors, 17,* 324–7.

North American Training Institute. Kids don't gamble . . . Wanna Bet? A curriculum for Grades 3-8. https://nati.org/products/index .aspx?mode=descandid=28.

Productivity Commission. (1999). Australia's gambling industries. Report No. 10. Canberra: AusInfo.

Shaffer, H. J., LaBrie, R., Scanlon, K. M. and Cummings, T. N. (1994). Pathological gambling among adolescents: Massachusetts Gambling Screen (MAGS). *Journal of Gambling Studies, 10,* 339–62.

Stewart, S.H, Kushner, M.G. (2003). Recent research on the comorbidity of alcoholism and pathological gambling. *Alcoholism Clinical and Experimental Research, 27*(2), 285–91.

Stinchfield R. (2001). A comparison of gambling among Minnesota public school students in 1992, 1995 and 1998. *Journal of Gambling Studies, 17*(4), 273–96.

Stockwell, T., Gruenewald, P. J., Toumbourou, J. W. (2005). *Preventing harmful substance use: The evidence base for policy and practice.* New York: John Wiley and Sons.

St-Pierre, R., Derevensky, J., Gupta, R. and Martin, I. (2011). Preventing lottery ticket sales to minors: Factors influencing retailers' compliance behavior. *International Gambling Studies, 11,* 173–92.

Turchi, R. M., and Derevensky, J. (2006). Youth gambling: Not a safe bet. *Current Opinions in Pediatrics, 18*(4), 454–8.

Turner, N. E., Macdonald J., and Somerset M. (2008). Life skills, mathematical reasoning and critical thinking: a curriculum for the prevention of problem gambling. *Journal of Gambling Studies, 24*(3), 367–80.

van Hamel, A., Derevensky, J., Dickson, L., and Gupta, R. (2007). Adolescent gambling and coping within a generalized high-risk behaviour framework. *Journal of Gambling Studies, 23(4),* 377–93.

Welte, J. B., Barnes, G. M., Wieczorek, W F., Tidwell, M. C., and Parker, J. (2001). Alcohol and gambling pathology among U.S. adults: prevalence, demographic patterns and comorbidity. *Journal of Studies on Alcohol and Drugs, 62*(5), 706–12.

Williams, R. J., Connolly, D., Wood, R.T., Currie, S., and Davis, R. M. (2004). Program findings that inform curriculum development for the prevention of problem gambling. *Gambling Research, 16,* 47–69.

Williams, R. J., Simpson, R. I., and West, B. (2007). Prevention of problem gambling. In G. Smith, D. C. Hodgins, and R. J. Williams (Eds.), *Research and measurement issues in gambling studies.* New York: Academic Press.

Williams, R. J., Wood, R. T., and Currie, S. (2010). *"Stacked Deck": An effective high school curriculum to prevent problem gambling.* Lethbridge: Author.

Winters, K. C., Stinchfield, R., and Fulkerson, J. (1993). Patterns and characteristics of adolescent gambling. *Journal of Gambling Studies, 9*(4), 371–86.

Wynne, H., Smith, G., and Jacobs, D. (1996). Adolescent gambling and problem gambling in Alberta. Alberta Alcohol and Drug Abuse Commission.

Young, M., Tyler, B., and Lee, W. (2007). Destination-style gambling – A review of the literature concerning the reduction of problem gambling and related social harm through the consolidation of gambling supply structures. Report prepared for the Department of Justice, Victoria Government.

6

HELPING ADOLESCENTS WITH GAMBLING PROBLEMS

The current treatment programs for helping adolescents and young adults with gambling problems have in general been based on a multiplicity of theoretical approaches that parallel those used for adults. Each of these approaches is reflective of its basic assumed underlying cause and perceived etiology associated with a gambling problem. Different theoretical approaches assume different underlying causes. Given the small number of individuals seeking help for problem gambling and the limited number of investigations examining the effectiveness of different treatment options, there currently remains no proven scientific evidence as to what in fact constitutes the best approach for treating individuals. The empirical support for effective treatments is often referred to as "Best Practices."

As previously noted in other chapters, there is a growing consensus that problem and pathological gamblers are not a homogeneous group. As such, individuals not only have different game preferences (some people have argued that treatment and help should be oriented toward specific forms of gambling) but their reasons for gambling differ, the extent and severity of their gambling problems vary, and motivation for seeking help differs, so specific cultural factors need to be taken into account when helping individuals with a gambling problem. There is also increasing evidence that a large percentage of individuals will eventually stop their excessive and problematic gambling by themselves through what psychologists refer to as "natural recovery," without any formal, structured intervention or professional treatment. While some individuals may relapse and return to gambling at some point, this relapse may or may not be short-lived. Of critical importance for problem gamblers is that they become aware that help is often available and that it can be effective in supporting the individual not only for their gambling problems but also to help resolve other associated emotional and/or mental health issues that may be the underlying cause for their excessive gambling. While the current evidence suggests that less than 10% of adults with gambling problems seek formal types of treatment and that even fewer adolescents and young people are likely to seek traditional forms of treatment or help, it is important to address this problem as quickly as possible. As discussed earlier, financial concerns are only one of many problems associated with gambling. Unless the cycle of problem gambling can be stopped fairly quickly, the short-term negative consequences can easily result in major long-term consequences (e.g., dropping out of school, disrupted relationships, legal issues, mental health problems).

The current treatment programs have incorporated a rather narrow focus depending on the therapist's theoretical orientation of the underlying causes of the gambling problem, his or her background work in the field of addictions, and whether he believes in "controlled gambling" versus abstinence. While the biomedical model has dominated the treatment community in the United States (where gambling is viewed as a disease), a cognitive-behavioral model (entailing erroneous thinking and inaccurate beliefs about the amount of skill required to win) or social learning theory (modeling of parents, peers, or significant others that gets reinforced) has been dominant in other countries. There is ample evidence to suggest that while adolescent pathological gamblers may engage in multiple types of gambling activities, differences in therapeutic approaches need to take into account the individual's culture, gender, and age. It remains absolutely essential to better understand the underlying reasons prompting an individual's desire to gamble. While on the surface most individuals typically report gambling to win back money lost, it is often the thrill, excitement, adrenaline rush, and enjoyment that keeps problem gamblers continuing their gambling in spite of repeated losses. Attempting to recoup losses, often called "chasing," only results in greater debt.

A number of clinical observations when working with adolescent problem gamblers have shed light on the psychology of individuals seeking help. First, therapists typically never see individuals walking into their offices who are winning a lot of money and desire to stop. If they are winning, they are on top of the world, view themselves as clever and intelligent gamblers, and think their luck will never stop. Second, most adolescents with a gambling problem are typically in denial, often pointing to friends who have a "much more severe problem." Third, most adolescents, like their adult counterparts, seek help when they have hit rock bottom and feel they can no longer recover their lost funds, their lies have caught up with them, and they are at a loss as to how to get out of their predicament. Finally, many adolescents are brought into treatment facilities by a close family member (most often their parents), boyfriend/girlfriend, or peer who is aware that their gambling and associated behaviors are out of control.

The recognition that one's gambling is problematic is often difficult to accept by youth. The "I don't really think I have a problem but my parents do" or "I can stop at any time" thinking is pervasive. Outside my office is a poster with the DSM-IV-MR-J criteria for pathological gambling and on the bottom it reads "if you have answered yes to four or more questions you may have a gambling problem." One teenager walked into my office having read the poster and indicated that he answered yes to all the questions but that he didn't think he had a gambling problem in spite of the fact that his parents, girlfriend, and friends thought he had a serious problem.

Many of the current treatment facilities are often located in substance abuse clinics and our experience is that adolescents report not wanting to be seen entering one of these clinics because their initial perception is that a gambling problem is "not as severe as someone with a drug problem." Teenagers, in general, are both reluctant to admit having a problem and to seek professional help for most problems.

Given the lack of empirically based strategies and the complexities of working with adolescents with gambling problems, a wide diversity of approaches are currently being used. Some clinicians have argued that it is really important to match the individual's personality with the type of help offered. This may be more difficult than it appears because many therapists and treatment providers have their own orientation toward working with problem gamblers. Having a good match and rapport between the individual seeking help and the treatment provider is essential. In some cultures, the gender of the treatment provider may be critical while for others the age of the therapist and ability to relate to adolescent problems may be perceived as the most essential attribute of the treatment provider.

A brief description of each of the more popular treatment approaches is provided. It is important to note that many treatment providers may use a combination of approaches, based on individual needs and expectations and their own orientation.

PSYCHODYNAMIC/PSYCHOANALYTIC APPROACHES TO PROBLEM GAMBLING

Our early history and understanding of problem gambling viewed this behavior as a form of impulsive act that ultimately resulted in maladaptive behavior with multiple negative consequences. The impulsive drive motivating the gambler was believed to emanate from a wide diversity of underlying reasons. One of the earliest notions about the underlying reasons prompting excessive gambling stemmed from a Freudian psychodynamic or psychoanalytic perspective (while there are fine distinctions between these approaches, the terms are used interchangeably). From this perspective, impulsive gambling behavior is believed to be primarily associated with an individual's desire to achieve pleasure and gratification. As such, the act of gambling in and of itself is perpetuated because it results in some form of pleasurable gratification. However, the act of gambling is thought to ultimately result in the individual's feeling guilt about their behavior and subsequently, unconsciously, desiring some form of punishment. Psychoanalytic therapists would argue that repeated excessive gambling generally results in financial losses, thereby relieving some of the individual's guilt. The acting-out behavior (excessive gambling) is also thought to be symbolic and representative of a rebellion against one or both parents (you may recall Freud's concerns with the Oedipus complex).

In order to help the individual resolve a gambling problem, the therapist needs to primarily focus on helping the individual understand the origins and unconscious decisions and desires which underlie the gambling. Ultimately, the goal is to help resolve any of the deep-rooted underlying conflicts that prompted the individual to initially begin gambling. The psychodynamic approach encompasses traditional Freudian theory and involves a long and protracted process to deal with unresolved conflicts and issues before the individual sees the necessity to stop gambling. While it has a long historical precedence, this approach has not been popular because of the length of time necessary for helping the individual. In particular, young people often fail to see the relevance of this approach and typically seek more immediate solutions to their problem. Unlike most other treatment methodologies, the therapist using this approach must be well schooled in psychoanalytic principles and techniques. As a result, this approach is typically only practiced by certified psychoanalysts or psychiatrists.

BEHAVIORAL THERAPIES

In contrast to the psychodynamic approach, behavioral approaches, which began to appear in the 1960s, conceptualized excessive gambling in terms of learned patterns of reinforcements. The behaviors that are reinforced and associated with gambling are thought to be on both an emotional level (e.g., feelings of excitement, entertainment, exhilaration) or can be related to the financial gains associated with winning money (there is a strong body of evidence that an early "big win" is often considered a risk factor for problem gambling). From a behaviorist's perspective, understanding one's gambling behavior is predicated on an examination of an individual's overall behavioral and functional patterns. For the behavioral practitioner, it is necessary to understand the antecedents of the behavior (factors preceding the behavior, and those triggers or events that prompt the individual to continue gambling), the actual overt act of gambling (examining the types and frequencies of gambling in which the individual engages, increased preoccupation with gambling, thinking about losses, loss of control, the use of gambling as a means of coping with anxiety, depression, stress, or feelings related to abuse), and ultimately the consequences associated with the gambling behavior (more specifically, the patterns of reinforcement, which can be emotional or pleasurable and may be derived from winning money, or the enjoyment, exhilaration, and excitement associated with the gambling activity). Individual variation in terms of all these factors coexists along with important cultural and environmental factors. What we also know about gambling behavior is that both positive and negative reinforcements occur in an intermittent, often random manner. Because these patterns of behavior occur intermittently (e.g., wins are interspersed with losses), these behaviors are more easily acquired but more difficult to stop. Gambling, whether winning or losing, by its very nature typically occurs intermittently. No person wins all the time nor do individuals typically lose all the time. If a person lost whenever they gambled, they would be more prone and likely to discontinue this behavior rather quickly (the exception to this rule may be the lottery where for a relatively small amount of money you have the opportunity to win a huge prize). Winning occasionally or intermittently frequently keeps the individual motivated to stay in the game, hoping that their winning will be repeated.

Typical behavioral therapies attempt to modify the individual's pattern of gambling by intervening in one or more of the components related to their behavior. For example, by eliminating or removing the antecedents or stimuli (sometimes referred to as "triggers") prompting the gambling, it is more likely that the behavior may be minimized or stopped. For older adolescents and young adults, this might mean avoiding a place where gambling machines are located, not reading the odds of sporting events in the local newspaper, or avoiding going to casinos or other venues where gambling occurs. Specific attempts are made to help the individual focus on developing alternative strategies (e.g., avoidance) to deal with the antecedent events wherever possible. If an adolescent has friends who are gambling, we often recommend they meet with their friends *after* their friends are finished gambling.

Some behavioral therapies attempt to modify the reinforcement patterns associated with the gambling by incorporating what is referred to as "aversive conditioning." By doing so, negative, unpleasurable associations are coupled with gambling thereby likely resulting in the individual wanting to discontinue gambling. If pleasurable feelings accompany gambling then individuals are more likely to want to continue and maintain this activity. Conversely, if an individual is overcome with negative emotions and feelings, he will often do whatever possible to avoid the situation. Still other behavioral therapies, especially cognitive-behavioral therapies, are much more focused on restructuring gambling-specific erroneous, irrational thoughts and beliefs. Having the individual grasp and understand the concepts of randomness, understand erroneous beliefs (the notion that random events cannot be accurately predicted), be aware of inaccurate assumptions, and correct false perceptions become the central focus of the intervention.

While many individuals can accurately explain the concept of randomness associated with gambling, this knowledge tends to be suppressed when gambling. Where else can you find bright intelligent people who, when they enter a casino or gambling environment, leave all their intelligence outside the door? The reality remains that all gambling activities within a regulated operation favor the "house" (operator), otherwise casinos would not offer the game. The gambling industry wants people to keep playing and enjoy themselves. The basic premise is that the longer an individual plays and has fun, the more likely he is to lose and return.

Do gambling operators promote and foster an illusion of control? Take for example the game of roulette. In almost every modern casino on the side of the roulette wheel sitting on the table is an electronic board which indicates the last 14 to 20 numbers that have won. If you ask a croupier the purpose of this electronic board, they are very likely to tell you that it is intended to help players select the next "winning" number. Many people use this information to help guide their playing. If one takes the numbers that are odd or even or red and black, we know that approximately 50% of the time they will be one or the other (the exception being that most roulette tables also have one or two numbers [0 or 00] in green). While the probability of picking a high or low number or red versus black is typically 50%, these percentages are based on hundreds of spins of the wheel. Yet, individuals watch this pattern of winning numbers and after a long string of red winning numbers they understand the concept that half the time it should be black and half the time red. As such, individuals are prone to place their next wager on a black number. Unfortunately, the little white ball spinning around the wheel cannot remember where it landed last. Psychologists like to refer to this as the "law of independence of events." In spite of the overall probabilities, each spin of the wheel is completely different and independent from each other and the two are unrelated. Yet, individuals are more likely to have a cognitive, perceptual distortion and inaccurately believe they can more accurately predict the outcome of where the ball will land.

A further example also illustrates how casinos are oriented to provide consumers with a cognitive distortion. In some casinos, on top of a slot machine, a bold neon sign is displayed that reads "our slots have the highest payout rate," for example, 98%. While this sounds impressive (we tend to think of percentages out of 100%), it is overtly advertising to customers that for every dollar one puts into these machines they are going to pay out less. You never see signs indicating slot machines pay out in excess of 100% because if this were true the casino or gambling operator would lose money.

The dispelling of such cognitive distortions and erroneous beliefs has become the central focus of the cognitive-behavioral approach to helping individuals with a gambling problem. The belief that a win is imminent becomes a primary reason to continue gambling.

Another core perception is that the individual's excessive gambling emanates from his belief that he is able to predict, influence, or control the outcome of games of chance. Distorted cognitions and beliefs further become easily influenced and reinforced by one's gambling as wins are most often attributed to skill while losses are considered more random and bad luck. Males in particular tend to internalize their thoughts related to their gambling abilities and have a tendency to externalize their losses (e.g., bad luck, poor dealer, "I was distracted," "the person next to me doesn't know how to play and ruined my chances of winning"). When they are winning, it is never because of a good dealer but rather their exceptional skills and abilities. Females tend to internalize both wins and losses.

A popular and effective cognitive-behavioral therapeutic framework, often referred to as CBT, aims to facilitate the individual's awareness of their thoughts and the links between their thoughts, behaviors, and emotions. The therapeutic process is designed to help guide the individual to question the validity of his erroneous thoughts and provides information and feedback through education, logical discussions, and experimentation. Such a process is thought to ultimately lead to a change in thinking about gambling, a modification and reduction of their gambling behavior, and a more realistic perspective, thus enabling the individual to resist urges to gamble and manage their negative emotions and difficulties without resorting to gambling. Strategies to help improve communication, problem solving, reduce anxiety, and cope with adversity, and techniques for dealing with daily hassles and crises are also emphasized.

BRIEF TREATMENTS AND SELF-DIRECTED TREATMENTS

There has been a growing trend toward the use of briefer treatments and interventions for resolving many mental health issues, including gambling problems. Given that treatment services may not be readily available (this is particularly true for youth who may have limited financial resources to pay for help or that referral centers may not be easily accessible by public transportation), there is a growing group of clinical researchers who are experimenting with alternative approaches: home-based workbooks (with and without telephone counseling support), self-help manuals, telephone-based support systems, and online resources where individuals can seek help and support via e-mail-based or interactive chat lines in real time. These new approaches can enhance and facilitate the ease of accessibility of available services and can capitalize on young people's general acceptance of computer-based technology. Many of these approaches have limited face-to-face interactions with a treatment provider and they eliminate the need and burden associated with traveling to acquire help. A number of innovative self-help programs through workbooks have been developed for adults, with others currently under development for youth. While some exercises and curriculums have been developed for youth, these are far fewer in number.

In an interesting pilot project called "Talk It Out," the clinical team from the International Centre for Youth Gambling Problems and High-Risk Behaviors examined the efficacy of using an online interactive web-based service in real time, similar to the MSN Messenger chat line. This service provided adolescents and young adults with a brief intervention by trained clinical graduate students who provided help for adolescents and young adults with gambling problems while encouraging others to seek professional counseling services. Based on the positive responses received from those individuals who used this service, the pilot project was viewed as highly successful and may be a viable way of reaching out to youth in need of help. Using this new technology may well be an effective approach for some young people reluctant to engage in more traditional forms of therapy. Such services can be provided in a very cost-effective and efficient manner. There is some ongoing experimentation currently under way at the Center for Addiction and Mental Health Services in Toronto concerning the use of Apps as self-evaluation tools. Given adolescents' comfort with computers, smart phones, Tablets, and new technologies, such innovative intervention approaches seem promising. Other approaches have used list-serves and e-mail communications as a way of providing support for problem gamblers. Overall, these brief interventions have been shown to have had some success in helping adults and youth decrease their gambling behaviors. Given accessibility problems and greater transportation difficulties for young people, these approaches appear to have some distinct advantages. Further work on these strategies is required in order to evaluate their long-term success.

PHARMACOLOGICAL TREATMENT

The use of medication or pharmacological drug intervention has continued to gain in popularity as a way of helping suppress what some individuals call the biological urges that often accompany the need to gamble. Many problem gamblers talk of withdrawal symptoms when trying to stop their gambling similar to those experienced by individuals having a drug or alcohol addiction. This work has also been predicated on the research that has examined the similarities between a number of addictive behaviors (pathological gambling, alcohol and drug abuse) as well as on an examination of the concomitant similarities associated with a number of mental health disorders. Genetic and biological examinations of addictive behaviors have looked at neural pathways in the brains of addicted individuals. The central nervous system transmitter, dopamine, has been repeatedly shown to be the most strongly associated with the reward pathways within the brain. A number of other biological models have attempted to isolate those neural pathways which may be treated with medication, enabling problem gamblers to resist the urges to gamble. Some drugs, commonly referred to as SSRIs (selective serotonin reuptake inhibitors) have been somewhat effective for use with a number of adult problem gamblers. However, no clinical trials or interventions have been done with this category of drugs among adolescents. Much of this research is currently being carried out by Jon Grant at the University of Minnesota. While Grant advocates a psychopharmacological treatment approach for some individuals (that is, use of Naltrexone, for example), he strongly urges the inclusion of traditional forms of therapy in conjunction with medication. At present, there is no medication that has received regulatory approval for treating problem or pathological gamblers although there are a growing number of studies examining the effectiveness of a wide variety of medications.

SELF-HELP GROUPS

Probably the oldest and best known self-help group for problem gamblers is Gamblers Anonymous (GA). Originally founded in the 1950s in California, there are now chapters operating in at least 55 countries worldwide. Individuals follow a program referred to as the "12 step program." This program was modeled and adapted from the original Alcoholics Anonymous program to help individuals with excessive drinking problems. Within these self-help groups, a total abstinence approach to gambling is considered mandatory. The Gamblers Anonymous groups and their members provide a sense of common purpose, supporting and reinforcing each other to help maintain their gambling abstinence. Meetings are typically held frequently (often dependent on the size and population of the city), with support groups for family members also being available. Similar to Alcoholics Anonymous, members receive periodic pins celebrating their abstinence (one month, three months, etc.). It is also not unusual for members of Gamblers Anonymous to also be involved in other traditional forms of therapy simultaneously while trying to stop their gambling. Long-time members emphasize the importance of the support group structure, which has sponsors available to the problem gambler virtually 24 hours a day. Attendance at meetings has been shown to be an important predictor of success. As such, long-term members who attend meetings typically do well in the program. Our experience with adolescents and young adults has not always been positive. A major problem is that many of the members are generally older and these youth have difficulty in relating to the severe negative consequences associated with the older members' past gambling. Many of the older members report that their gambling ultimately resulted in family discord and dissolved marriages and loss of homes (youth report that they have not been married and still live at home), others report losing jobs and businesses (teens report that they do not work but rather are in school), and some report serious criminal offenses (teens typically do not get involved in embezzlement, forgery, etc.). Few jurisdictions have specific Gamblers Anonymous meetings exclusively for youth, although the premise is a good one. This is likely because the number of individuals attending would be extremely limited. While the program has great promise, getting teens to attend meetings at the same time, on the same day, has also often proved extremely difficult.

FAMILY THERAPY

A number of advances in family therapy intervention programs for the treatment of substance abuse disorders have been adapted for individuals with gambling problems. In these programs, members of the family who are non-gamblers or non-problem gamblers are typically instructed and trained to use behavioral principles to reinforce gambling abstinence for the individual experiencing gambling-related problems. Money management strategies are also provided to help monitor and control the expenditures of the gambler. An additional important component is trying to help the family understand the problem gambler's behavior. While traditionally used with adults, our experience has been that this approach represents an important adjunct when working with adolescents and young adults. In our therapeutic sessions, we encourage adolescents and young adults to bring in significant others, be they parents, siblings, girlfriends/boyfriends, close friends, or other relatives. Helping parents, siblings, and others important to the problem gambler understand the warning signs of problem gambling and the underlying need to gamble can be very enlightening and helpful. These individuals can provide a similar type of support as that found in Gamblers Anonymous while carefully monitoring the individual's behavior.

HELPING YOUTH WITH GAMBLING PROBLEMS

For over 15 years, our clinical team has been working with adolescents and young adults with excessive gambling problems. From both our clinical and research work at McGill University's Treatment Centre, we have long argued that a dynamic interactive approach needs to take into account the multiplicity of interacting factors when helping youth experiencing significant gambling problems. Support for Durand Jacobs' *General Theory of Addiction* for adolescent problem gamblers further suggests that adolescent problem and pathological gamblers generally exhibit evidence of some biological disposition (possibly hyperactivity, attention deficit disorder, depression, anxiety disorders). Youth problem gamblers, like their adult counterparts, when gambling are more prone to dissociation (e.g., losing track of time, feeling spaced out), demonstrate more erroneous beliefs and misperceptions when gambling, display more depressive behaviors, and are more likely to have higher rates of other addictive and mental health problems. As such, our experience suggests that merely treating the gambling problem in isolation from other pressing social, physiological, developmental, cognitive, and emotional difficulties may lead to short-term success but ultimately increases the likelihood of relapse and returning to levels of problem gambling.

THE STAGES OF CHANGE MODEL

Recent work suggests that Prochaska and DiClemente's *Transtheoretical Model of Intentional Behavior,* which was originally intended for adults, may be useful in helping to understand the treatment and natural recovery of pathological gamblers. More specifically, Carlo DiClemente and his colleagues have also suggested that the "stages of change" model represents a viable conceptual framework as an effective treatment program for adolescent pathological gamblers. This model examines the process of change from initiation to cessation of an individual's problematic gambling behavior. It suggests that patterns of behavior, in this case gambling, are not created, modified, or terminated in a single moment of time. Rather, the model describes various steps (stages) in the process in which individuals engage to successfully modify their behaviors. The change model presupposes a number of distinct stages and describes the motivations and the process of change over time, and further suggests that within each stage there are a number of specific tasks that must be accomplished and goals that must be achieved before the individual can move from one stage to the next.

During the initial stage, described as the "precontemplation stage," the individual may think of changing his patterns of gambling, but in reality he is not seriously considering stopping gambling or even reducing the frequency of his gambling. At this point, the individual has not "reached rock bottom" and is not truly desperate. Discussions of possibly stopping or reducing one's gambling are merely to appease others and there is no perceived serious underlying thought to stop or reduce one's gambling. The primary goal for the therapist during this stage is to create interest and discussion concerning the desire to change excessive gambling behavior. The precontemplation stage is followed by the "contemplation stage," where individuals are beginning to seriously consider changing and modifying their gambling behavior. This involves considerable self-reflection and understanding of the severity of one's problems and an acceptance and recognition of the negative consequences directly associated with excessive gambling. Contemplating change, stopping, or cutting back on gambling is a crucial advance in helping individuals with gambling problems. Eventually, individuals progress to the "preparation stage" where they are preparing to change their behavior. In addition to merely contemplating and thinking about changes in their behavior, the actual commitment and planning of this change process becomes realized. This stage would include an expressed commitment, with the individual, in conjunction with a therapist, deciding on a realistic plan and program of change. As a result, in the next ensuing stage, the "action stage," the individual actually begins to modify his behavior with the goal of establishing new behaviors to replace past gambling behavior (ideally, not replacing gambling with another addictive behavior). Adolescents can begin refocusing on socializing with friends and peers (not gambling-related), getting involved in sports activities, possibly dating, spending time at the movies, etc. Finally, according to the model, individuals who have successfully changed and modified their behavior will seek to move to the "maintenance stage," where their abstinence from gambling is sustained over time and integrated into a new lifestyle for the adolescent. This model has been applied and found to be highly useful in working with other addictive behaviors and may have important implications for young problem gamblers. While the stages within this change model make good clinical sense, there is currently little empirical support confirming its effectiveness and utility. While this process seems relatively simple for the individual attempting to stop gambling, this can be an arduous, painful process akin to losing one's best friend.

Adolescents in many ways are in fact no different from adults when it comes to their underlying reasons for gambling, although it has been argued that their brain maturation is not complete until approximately age 24. Yet, the developmental period of adolescence is marked by distinct beliefs and accompanied by biological, physical, and psychological changes. As such, working with adolescents has some distinct challenges.

There remains some controversy among clinicians and academics concerning whether abstinence or controlled gambling should be the desired outcome for individuals with severe gambling problems. Our clinical experience with adolescents and young adults suggests that abstinence remains a desired goal given that most individuals have difficulty not only in setting time and/or money limits but also in maintaining and adhering to these limits. In spite of the large percentage of adolescents and young adults preferring a controlled gambling approach ("Just teach me to gamble in moderation so I can enjoy myself"), our research and clinical experience suggests that while controlled gambling can be an intermediary goal, abstinence is necessary in order to prevent increased levels of gambling and relapse. For individuals to continue to enjoy gambling and still maintain a sufficient level of thrills and excitement (often referred to by problem gamblers as an "adrenaline rush") two things must happen: (a) they must continuously increase the size of their wagers, and (b) they must gamble more frequently. While controlled gambling in moderation represents a good beginning, our goal is ultimately to have youth with gambling problems resume a healthy lifestyle, ensure that no other risky behavior replace their gambling, and achieve abstinence.

Similar to other mental health issues, adolescents with gambling problems typically do not present themselves for treatment in the absence of some type of outside (most often parental or peer) pressure or influence. A number of reasons have been suggested for why they fail to seek help, including (a) fear of being identified, (b) self-perceptions of invincibility and invulnerability to future negative consequences, (c) negative views of therapy, (d) guilt associated with their gambling problems, (e) lack of recognition and acceptance that they have a gambling problem despite scoring high on gambling severity screens or associated gambling problems, (f) they are not ready to stop their gambling in spite of the negative consequences, and (g) their inherent belief in natural recovery and self-control.

Parents, friends, teachers, the court system, and the local "Help/ Referral Line" are the primary sources through which most treatment centers receive referrals. As part of the International Centre for Youth Gambling Problems and High-Risk Behaviors' outreach prevention and intervention programs, posters and brochures are distributed to schools, media campaigns are frequently initiated, and workshops are provided for school psychologists, guidance counselors, social workers, teachers, and directly to children and adolescents to raise awareness about issues related to youth gambling. As a result of this outreach work, we receive calls from adolescents and family members directly requesting assistance. The centre's website (www.youthgambling.com) also generates several inquiries for online help and assistance.

Research and clinical experience suggest that adolescent problem gamblers develop a social network consisting of other peers with gambling problems. This frequently results in adolescents who have sought help for a gambling problem often referring their friends for assistance. Once adolescents accept and realize that they have a serious gambling problem, they typically become more acutely aware of gambling problems among their friends. Eventually, some successfully convince their peers to seek help as well.

Since adolescents with gambling problems have limited access to discretionary funds for professional help and many initially seek treatment without parental knowledge, treatment is provided without cost. There is a growing trend in many jurisdictions to provide this type of help at no cost to the youth, with monies generated from gambling operators paying the bulk of costs for treatment either through voluntary contributions or mandatory levies.

The location of the treatment facility may play an important role in successfully attracting and working with young gamblers. Concerns about being seen entering an addiction treatment facility, mental health center, or hospital may discourage some youth from seeking treatment. Easy accessibility by public transportation is essential because most young clients do not own cars or have money for a taxi.

Before presenting an approach to working with adolescents and young adults with gambling problems, it should be noted that many adolescents decide to stop gambling and do so successfully on their own through natural recovery. While there is a growing body of evidence concerning this phenomenom in the substance abuse literature, psychologists are only beginning to understand this phenomenon with respect to problem gambling. As noted earlier, the prevalence rates of problem gambling among adolescents and young adults is considerably higher than the general adult population. This would seem to suggest that as these young people mature and assume adult responsibilities they very likely stop gambling excessively. Unfortunately, the negative consequences associated with their former excessive gambling often stay with them—disrupted and problematic family and peer relationships, poor school performance, higher dropout rates, associated mental health disorders, and criminal records among others. We also know that the relapse rate among individuals who have not received some form of support may be higher than those who have received traditional help. The good news is that in most communities help and support are available for individuals experiencing gambling problems.

THE MCGILL TREATMENT APPROACH

The McGill University treatment approach has been developed and is predicated on recent research findings and our clinical work with adolescents and young adult problem gamblers. The treatment philosophy is based on the assumption that sustained abstinence is ultimately necessary for youth to recover from gambling and gambling-related problems, to reduce the likelihood of relapse, and that for many individuals a wide variety of social and mental health issues may need to be simultaneously addressed (e.g., developing or re-establishing social networks, enhancing the individual's ability to cope with adversity, addressing issues related to cognitive distortions, helping individuals cope with attention-deficit hyperactive disorders, and general mental health issues associated with depression and anxiety). While controlled gambling (ability to respect self-imposed limits) is preferred by youth and can be an interim goal for adolescents, our experience has been that abstinence is eventually necessary. Accepting that adolescents set initial goals to decrease their gambling instead of becoming abstinent allows us time to develop strong working alliances before introducing the need for sustained abstinence.

Our clinical experience suggests that adolescents typically need to be closely monitored for at least one year after their formal treatment has ended. This monitoring can be done via telephone calls, e-mail, or interactive chat lines, and does not necessarily require the individual to physically attend a session. We encourage youth who may have relapsed and returned to gambling to return for help. Relapse is fairly typical for individuals over time and returning for help should not be negatively viewed or perceived as a weakness.

STEPS OF TREATMENT

While the stages described are those employed by the McGill Youth Treatment Centre, they are often typical of those used in many other treatment facilities.

1. Intake Interviews

Intake interviews can typically take place over several sessions. The primary goal associated with these sessions is for both the adolescent and treatment provider to get to know each other. Expectations are shared and a working relationship is established. During these initial sessions, the severity of the individual's gambling problem is ascertained. This would include a discussion focused on the frequency of gambling, the amounts of money wagered and lost, the types of gambling in which the individual participates, the typical duration of gambling episodes, triggers prompting the gambling, and the negative consequences realized as a result of the excessive gambling (e.g., family and/or peer problems, school or work performance, legal issues). Other mental health issues should also be discussed during these initial sessions where relevant. It is important to try to begin to articulate and help the adolescent understand the underlying reasons for gambling. While most adolescents report that the reason for continued gambling is to recoup their losses, this is most often not their primary underlying motivation for gambling. The two most highly endorsed reasons refer to the excitement and enjoyment associated with gambling. However, for some it provides a great diversion from their daily problems and represents an escape, albeit a temporary escape, from their daily routines or mental health or interpersonal issues.

Diagnosis

The intake procedure includes a semi-structured interview using the DSM-IV-MR-J or DSM-IV criteria, depending on the individual's age, for pathological gambling as well as the identification of relevant gambling behaviors (e.g., preferred activities, frequency, wagering patterns, history of gambling, accumulated losses, financial and legal issues). This gives the individual and the treatment provider a clearer picture of the individual's gambling patterns and the severity of associated problems.

Functional Assessment

The functional assessment represents a vital component when planning the treatment process. This assessment includes information gathering in a number of areas including triggers for problematic gambling, cognitions and thought processes, behaviors, emotions before and during gambling episodes, and consequences following gambling episodes. Identifying triggers, those elements in the environment that may prompt gambling (casinos, bars with electronic gambling machines, Internet pop-up messages, televised or radio advertisements, poker parties, televised sporting events, etc.), people (friends who gamble), activities (going to a party, excessive consumption of alcohol), or dysregulation of emotional states (e.g., anxiety, loneliness, sense of loss, depression) provides vital information for the treatment provider. While many individuals may be unaware of their specific triggers initially, they can be identified through discussions of prior experiences or by examining the individual's written journals (a component within the therapeutic process). Cognitive distortions that follow from exposure to triggers should also be identified and addressed (e.g., "If I gamble now, I will be more relaxed for the party tonight and I will have a better time"). Finally, the consequences following excessive, out-of-control, or bingeing gambling episodes are explored.

Assessing and Fostering Motivation for Change

While those individuals voluntarily seek help, many may be less than motivated to initially participate. A considerable number of youth attend treatment sessions as a result of parental pressure, mandatory referrals from the judicial system, or are strongly encouraged by people close to them (i.e., boyfriends, girlfriends) and may comply for fear of losing relationships. Others may see the necessity and fear that if a girlfriend or boyfriend finds out about their gambling they will leave them. Lying about their gambling is commonplace and few problem gamblers initially acknowledge their gambling is out of control despite the repeated losses, excessive amount of time gambling, and host of negative consequences.

Therapy for an addiction or mental health disorder can be a long and arduous process that demands significant effort and focus on the part of the problem gambler. For this reason, before beginning any type of intervention, it is important to assess the individual's readiness and motivation for change. It is not atypical or unusual for the problem gambler's motivation to fluctuate throughout treatment. Some essential therapeutic elements included in motivational interviewing with individuals experiencing gambling problems include (a) providing personalized and specific feedback relevant to the individual's situation (reality check), (b) shifting responsibility for treatment to the individual, (c) allowing individuals to engage in a "decisional balance" exercise where they can weigh the hypothetical costs and benefits of continuing versus quitting gambling, (d) providing several alternative options depending on the situation and giving objective advice, and (e) encouraging the individual's decision-making abilities. Of course, the provisions of a safe environment to share experiences as well as empathic listening are key components of any therapeutic relationship.

2. Therapy for Gambling Problems

General Therapeutic Environment

At the International Centre for Youth Gambling Problems and High-Risk Behaviors, a staff psychologist provides individual therapy and help for the problem gambler. On occasion, peers with similar gambling problems, family members, or significant others are requested to participate. Group therapy, while having many advantages, is often extremely difficult to coordinate due to differing timetables.

Therapy is typically provided weekly; however if the therapist deems more frequent sessions are required, appropriate accommodations are made on a short-term basis. The overall total number of sessions can vary significantly based on the individual's level of motivation, degree and length of gambling activity, severity of gambling, and other accompanying mental health issues. Typically, treatment lasts between 20 and 50 sessions.

For adolescents experiencing gambling problems, total honesty during each session is emphasized and a nonjudgmental relationship is formed. This is fundamental in terms of creating an environment in which the adolescent does not fear reactions of disappointment or condemnation if weekly personal goals are not successfully achieved.

Mutual respect is a top priority and adolescents are held to a high standard of personal responsibility. They are required to respect the treatment provider's time. This involves calling ahead to cancel and/or reschedule appointments, punctual attendance at sessions, and a commitment to complete assignments between sessions.

Goal Setting

Overarching goals for help are established at the outset of the meetings and are revised several times during the therapeutic process. Smaller, objective, and measurable weekly goals are also a crucial part of creating an environment where individuals can feel supported, motivated, and track progress through their healing process. It is important that goals be tailored to the individual's priorities and gambling severity and are dependent on whether the individual has accompanying mental health issues. In most cases, multiple goals are addressed simultaneously over many sessions, while tailoring the time allocated to each goal to meet the needs of the individual.

Environmental Changes and Triggers

Once triggers have been identified as part of the functional assessment, it becomes possible to proactively address them during the intervening process. For example, one of the most common triggers for gamblers is the handling of large sums of money (this is relative to their age). In this case, adolescents are helped to adopt strategies to minimize carrying such large sums of money and limit their access to cash withdrawals from bank machines. In one case, a parent who was financially supporting his son made daily deposits into his account rather than weekly deposits. Other examples of triggers include viewing gambling advertisements or landmarks, personal anxiety or depressed feelings, interpersonal difficulties, enticement by peers, stressful academic or work-related situations, and the need to acquire money quickly. Sometimes, merely having the awareness of one's triggers provides the individual with a better ability to deal with gambling urges. Individuals with a machine gambling addiction (e.g., slots, VLTs, pokies) are urged not to spend time in establishments housing these machines. While it is probably not possible to eliminate all triggers (e.g., pop-up messages, lottery tickets on checkout counters in convenience stores, billboard advertisements), it is possible to help individuals understand the importance of triggers in prompting them to gamble.

Understanding Motivations for Gambling

Most adolescents experiencing serious gambling problems continue gambling in the face of repeated losses and serious negative consequences because of their need to dissociate and escape from stressful situations. This can be school-, family-, or peer-related. Many youth with gambling problems report that when they are gambling they enter a "different world," a world without problems and stress. They report that while gambling, they feel invigorated and alive, they are admired and respected, time passes quickly, and all their problems are forgotten—be they psychological, financial, social, familial, academic, work-related, or legal. As such, for a large number of youth experiencing gambling problems their gambling becomes the ultimate escape, albeit for a short period of time. From their perspective, a good day for these youth is when their gambling money lasts all day—a bad day is when their money runs out in an hour.

Adolescents are asked to write a short essay on why it is they feel the need to gamble—"What gambling does for me." Gambling can be both positively and negatively reinforcing to players, providing intermittent pleasurable feelings or escape from negative situations or emotions. This is at least partly responsible for the fact that adolescents with gambling problems continue playing despite potentially serious negative long-term consequences. Writing about gambling is important for several reasons. First, it enables the treatment provider to have a better understanding of the individual's perceptions of the reasons underlying excessive gambling. More important, it enables the individual to articulate and better understand the underlying reasons for gambling. The following are excerpts from several writings by adolescents who have attended our treatment facility. The first highlights difficulties with interpersonal relationships and poor coping/adaptive skills, while the second illustrates an individual's gambling to alleviate a depressed state and psychological escape.

"I always had trouble making friends, and never had a girlfriend. Gambling has now become my best friend and my one true love. I can turn to her in good times and bad and she'll always be there for me." (Male, age 18)

"Gambling, well, it's strange to talk about the positive side because of how upside down it has turned my life, but I guess the pull of it is how it makes me feel so alive, so happy, and so much like I belong, but only when I am gambling. The low I feel after I realize what I did, and how much I have lost, is worse than anything I can explain. I guess I just need to feel good from time to time—it lets me escape the black hole that is my life." (Male, age 17)

Analysis of Gambling Episodes

Gaining awareness of psychological and emotional gambling triggers and the behavioral reactions to those triggers as well as the consequences that follow is important. This type of understanding and critical analysis can have an empowering impact on adolescents and ultimately may encourage them to make long-term changes in their behaviors. It is essential that the individual does not attribute the repeated losses to an external event (e.g., bad luck or, as one client noted, "my parents are on my back all the time and I was unable to concentrate and review all the statistics needed to pick the winning team"). Problem gamblers are in some ways like alcoholics. Many alcoholics have a favorite drink but if their favorite drink is removed they will inevitably switch to another. One youth who was an excessive blackjack player at a local casino remarked that individuals who gambled on electronic gambling machines (slots) were "stupid" because there was no skill involved. After we managed to keep him out of the casino he became a machine gambler until eventually he stopped gambling.

The importance of identifying and dealing with triggers has already been discussed. However, it is also essential to understand the times in an individual's day when he does not seem to have the urge to gamble. Identifying the circumstances, time of day, emotional state, activity levels, physical proximity to gambling venues, etc., is essential. This is becoming more difficult with the spread of Internet gambling and the use of smart phone technology that provides easy access and the capability to gamble 24 hours a day, seven days per week. Understanding the circumstances under which the urge to gamble is lessened or absent, helps to develop a set of guidelines by which the treatment provider can recreate similar situations at other times in the day. For example, we have noted that many of the young gamblers undergoing treatment often report that when actively engaged in playing sports with friends, bicycling, or some other form of physical activity (e.g., gym), they feel better and had their minds clear of their gambling desires both during and after the activity. As a result, for these youth, when helping them to structure and organize their week, attempts are made to include similar types of activities on a daily basis.

Establishing a Baseline of Gambling Behavior and
Encouraging a Decrease in Gambling

Once the motivations for gambling are understood and an analysis of gambling patterns has been made, efforts are focused on making changes to the individual's gambling behavior. In order to set goals and measure improvements, it is often useful and important to initially establish a baseline of gambling behavior. As such, during the intervention process we require adolescents to record their gambling behaviors daily in terms of frequency, duration, time of day, type of gambling activity, amount of money spent, losses, and wins. When establishing goals for a decrease in gambling participation, adolescents are guided to set reasonable goals for themselves. Some individuals elect to target multiple indices such as frequency, duration, and amount spent simultaneously, while others may focus on only one aspect of gambling (e.g., frequency or duration). For these individuals, we encourage a decrease in frequency or duration of each gambling episode versus initially focusing on amount wagered. Some meet their goals immediately at which point we generally support decisions to maintain this decrease for a short period before establishing new goals. Others struggle to meet their goals and as such the goals require modification and amendments. Establishing realistic goals is in itself rewarding and helps the problem gambler feel good about changes to his behavior.

Cognitive Therapy and Cognitive Distortions

It has been well established that individuals with gambling problems experience multiple cognitive distortions. They are prone to have an illusion of control, perceive that they can control the outcome of random events, underestimate the amount of money lost and overestimate the amount won, fail to utilize their knowledge of the laws of independence of events, and believe that if they persist at gambling they will likely win and recoup all money lost. Addressing these distortions remains an important goal. An analysis of gambling behavior typically reveals the rationalizations used to justify behavior. These rationalizations need to be directly addressed, as they represent distortions of reality. One such example is, "by gambling now, the urge will be out of my system and I'll be better able to focus on studying for my exam." In this case, the overarching goal is to ensure that the individual understands that the gambling will likely result in a bad mood if they were to lose money and subsequently create a new set of problems which will likely impede the individual's ability to focus on studying for an exam. We have worked with teenagers who report being so preoccupied that they dream of gambling. One adolescent reported dreaming about flashing colored lights. When asked about the dream, he reported it was a roulette wheel spinning in his head. Others report thinking about the poker hand they played, should have played, or would have played should the "right" cards have been dealt. Ultimately, the goal of addressing many of the cognitive distortions is to highlight how one's thinking can be self-deceptive, to provide examples and pertinent information about randomness, and to encourage a realization that gamblers are often incapable of controlling outcomes of random events and games, payout rates, etc.

In addition to examining constructs such as the illusion of control, laws of independence of events, and randomness, we have tried to incorporate specific examples for both sports gamblers and poker players. For sports gamblers, we discuss the results of several large studies conducted by the National Collegiate Athletic Association in the United States (approximately 20,000 college athletes in each study). The results of these studies suggest that there are a small but identifiable number of college athletes who report trying to manipulate the outcome of games as a result of their personal gambling losses. We challenge adolescents' perceptions of selecting winning teams, in spite of their extensive knowledge about the sport, if the outcome of the game may be altered by a player or coach.

The identification of specific cognitive distortions particular for each individual is customized, developed specifically for the individual, and forms a critical component of the therapeutic intervention. Erroneous thinking patterns are addressed throughout the therapeutic process. There is a growing body of evidence that such erroneous cognitions and beliefs can be altered and modified (similar to the strategies incorporated in several of our gambling prevention programs).

Establishing the Underlying Causes of Stress, Anxiety, Depression, and Other Mental Health Disorders

In light of research evidence and clinical findings, it has become apparent to most clinicians that it is essential to identify and address any underlying problem that may result in increased stress, anxiety, and depression. For some individuals, the financial losses and delinquent behaviors associated with their excessive gambling result in increased anxiety, stress, and/or depression. Yet for others, these mental health issues are the reason prompting their gambling. As most winnings and losses are intermittent, individuals experience both benefits and consequences associated with their playing behavior, often during the same gambling episode. Problem gamblers report gambling is like a rollercoaster, with many ups and downs. The metaphor is a good one, with the rollercoaster going on its track with the problem gambler unable to stop it, slow it down, or exert any control. Individuals who have attended our clinic have a wide diversity of other mental health issues: poor self-image, depression, anxiety disorders, attention deficit disorders, conduct disorders, suicide ideation, and social and interpersonal issues. Pharmacological treatment, in conjunction with traditional forms of therapy, can be done in collaboration with consulting psychiatrists and primary care physicians.

Evaluating and Improving Coping Abilities

Once underlying anxieties or affective states that contribute to the adolescents' desire to gamble have been identified, another important goal is to assist them to acquire new positive strategies. The importance of building resilience as an important protective factor in helping individuals refrain from excessive gambling cannot be overemphasized. Excessive gambling as a need to escape one's problems usually occurs more frequently among individuals who have poor coping and less resilient adaptive skills. Using gambling or other addictive activities to deal with daily stressors, anxiety, or depression represents a form of maladaptive coping. Recent research efforts have confirmed these clinical observations—adolescents who meet the criteria for pathological gambling demonstrate less effective coping skills and greater depression compared with their peers who do not have a gambling problem.

Given this information, building and expanding the individual's repertoire of coping abilities remains an important goal in enabling adolescents to be resilient in light of adversity. As adolescents begin to acquire more sophisticated adaptive strategies and their repertoire of coping responses expands, they are more apt to apply these skills in their daily lives. Examples of healthy coping skills and strategies include effective communication with others, the desire to seek responsible social supports, and the ability to differentially respond to situations based on potential risks and benefits. Also included in the discussions are role-playing exercises as a way to improve the individual's social skills (e.g., learning to communicate with peers, developing healthy friendships, being considerate of others, and developing trust).

Rebuilding Healthy Interpersonal Relationships

A common consequence of a serious gambling problem involves impaired and damaged relationships with friends, peers, and family members. Helping adolescents rebuild these crucial relationships constitutes an important therapeutic goal. Often through lies and possibly delinquent behaviors, friends and family members become alienated, leaving unresolved, hurt, or ambivalent feelings and problematic relationships. Once a youth has been identified as a liar or thief, it becomes difficult to regain the trust of others and to resume healthy relationships. This is one of the more difficult situations faced by problem gamblers. They have typically lied so many times in the past about having quit gambling, once they actually stop their gambling they want to be trusted almost immediately. This is in some ways analogous to the boy who cried wolf. How are parents, relatives, and friends able to trust someone who has repeatedly lied to them? While on an intellectual level problem gamblers understand the lack of trust by important people in their lives, they nevertheless have great difficulty being repeatedly questioned about their daily activities by parents or those close to them. We often remind youth that it took quite some time to destroy the trust and will likely take even longer to rebuild it. One parent asked his son to bring receipts for all expenses to help account for his money. This proved both embarrassing and difficult to ask friends for receipts when purchasing anything, no matter how small or insignificant. While he understood the underlying reason, he was quite humiliated having to ask his friend for a receipt for an ice cream. This type of situation requires some intervention on behalf of the treatment provider.

Family members, peers, and other important people in the adolescent's life can become essential supports to help ensure abstinence and can take an active role in preventing a relapse. Youth with gambling problems are likely to be happier and more apt to abstain from gambling if they feel they belong to a peer group and are supported by family and friends. As a result, the periodic inclusion of family members and friends in therapy sessions has proved to be very beneficial. Nevertheless, the process of rebuilding relationships can be long, arduous, and is often met with only partial success. While highly dependent on circumstances, some friends or family members may not be willing to forgive the problem gambler or reestablish contact independent of the individual's needs.

Restructuring Free Time

Adolescents struggling to overcome a gambling problem experience more positive outcomes when not faced with large amounts of unstructured time. Most adolescents in treatment are still in school and/or have a job, and as such their free time consists mainly of evenings and weekends. Others may have dropped out of school and may have a part-time job, while others are not working. For these youth, structuring their time becomes paramount as they initially find it exceedingly difficult to resist urges to gamble when they are bored. We frequently request adolescents to carry a notepad to keep track of their daily schedule. Spending time with friends, family, or in school- or work-related activities is extremely beneficial. Other suggested activities may involve participating in organized sports activities, engaging in a hobby, watching movies, and performing volunteer work. Success is measured on how well the individual achieves the agreed-upon weekly goals, with their gambling-related goals (reduction or abstinence) being one component of the program. If an individual fails to meet the goals surrounding their gambling behavior, they still may achieve success in other areas. This approach tends to keep adolescents from being totally discouraged, motivates them to attain a balanced lifestyle, and helps maintain their interest and attendance in treatment.

Fostering Effective Money Management Skills

Adolescents typically are not the greatest budgeters under optimal circumstances, and this is even more pronounced for youth with gambling problems. Goals need to involve educating youth as to the value of money. Many youth tend to lose perspective after wagering large sums of money. One teenager in our program valued everything in terms of a "blackjack hand." When asked how he would get to the casino, he responded "half a hand." Since he typically wagered $25 per hand, a taxi fare was approximately $12.50. Other adolescents report that they could never get a part-time job making minimum wage because they spent considerably more gambling in an hour than they could earn in a week. Building money management skills and helping individuals develop and maintain a sensible debt repayment plan is part of the recovery process. Having youth carry less money or in small denominations (large bills enhance their stature and self-image as the "big shot") is also important.

3. Preparation for Cessation of Treatment and Relapse Prevention

While abstinence improves the likelihood that relapse of gambling problems will not reoccur, occasional relapses (we tend to refer to them as "slips" with adolescents) throughout the treatment process can be expected. However, once gambling has ceased for an extended period of time (i.e., approximately 6 months), an effective relapse prevention program should help these individuals remain free of gambling.

Given that gambling treatment usually goes on over an extended period, it is important to phase out any intervention gradually. This allows the adolescent to become accustomed to having longer stretches without support during which he must take control of his behavior autonomously. Difficulties encountered during this phasing-out process provide useful information and can be dealt with while the adolescent is still actively engaged in therapy.

Relapse prevention post-termination includes continued access to their primary treatment provider for "booster" sessions, the existence of a good social support network, engagement in either school or work, the practice of a healthy lifestyle, and avoidance of powerful triggers. Youth are contacted periodically via telephone, text messages, or e-mail for one year post-treatment to ensure they are maintaining their abstinence and doing well in general, and additional support is offered when required.

There is little doubt that working with adolescent problem gamblers can be challenging. Whether supporting a friend or family member with a gambling problem, these stages provide an overall framework for helping the individual. While youth with gambling problems may not be in debt at the same level as many adults, they are nevertheless facing some profound problems. These difficulties can alter their entire life trajectory. Poor academic performance, disrupted relationships, and legal problems set the stage for lifelong difficulties. The earlier one addresses the issue of problem gambling the better. While many youth can stop on their own through natural recovery, others require a variety of support systems and professional help. Some adolescents have even entered our treatment facility having stopped gambling but requesting support and assistance to maintain their abstinence. Adolescents with serious gambling problems are well advised to seek help in resolving their problems.

The following text was written by a young pathological gambler attending our treatment program, one year post-treatment:

> Gambling is an extremely addictive activity which can get unbelievably out of control. It can lead to a very horrible reality, one in which just getting out of bed can seem unthinkable. Unfortunately, I have lived this reality. I was eighteen when I began to fight for my life back. My future did not look very good. I was severely depressed, anxious and overweight, I wanted to disappear. Thankfully, with the support of an amazing team I have managed to overcome my addiction, lose thirty pounds and continue my schooling. I feel like I am relearning how to live. This continues to be a very long and emotionally painful process, however it does get easier with time. My memories of the gambling, the lies and unhappiness are slowly fading away . . . becoming part of the past. However I will never forget my struggle or how easy it was to lose control. In my gambling years I have seen and experienced firsthand an incredible amount of heartache. I hope to never witness such avoidable pain again. Now at twenty years old, I am beginning a journey which holds an endless amount of opportunity. My dream to be a health care professional seems closer than ever. Please let my story be a source of hope for anyone in a similar situation. I understand how bad life can seem, I've been there, believe me. You are not alone. Get the help you need, be true to yourself and start your own journey. —Bianca

REFERENCES

American Psychiatric Association. (2000). *Diagnostic and statistical manual of mental disorders (DSM-IV)* (4th Edition). Washington, DC: American Psychiatric Association.

Australian Government Productivity Commission. (2010). Gambling Inquiry. Canberra.

Beck, A., Wright, F., Newman, C., and Liese, B. (Eds.). (2001). *Cognitive therapy of substance abuse.* New York: Guilford Press.

Black, D. (2004). An open-label trial of bupropion in the treatment of pathologic gambling. *Journal of Clinical Psychopharmacology, 24*(1), 108–10.

Black, D. W., and Moyer, T. (1998). Clinical features and psychiatric co-morbidity of subjects with pathological gambling behavior. *Psychiatric Services, 49,* 1434–39.

Blaszczynski, A. P. (1985). A winning bet: Treatment for compulsive gambling. *Psychology Today, 38,* 42–44, 46.

Blaszczynski, A. P. (Ed.). (1998). *Overcoming compulsive gambling: A self help guide using cognitive behavioural techniques.* London: Robinson Publishing Ltd.

Blaszczynski, A. P. (2005). Pathological gambling: A clinical guide to treatment. *Addiction, 100*(4), 565–66.

Blaszczynski, A. P., McConaghy, N., and Frankova, A. (1991). Control versus abstinence in the treatment of pathological gambling: A two to nine year follow-up. *British Journal of Addiction, 86,* 299–306.

Blaszczynski, A. P., and McConaghy, N. (1989). The medical model of gambling: Current short-comings. *Journal of Gambling Behavior, 5,* 42–52.

Blaszczynski, A. P., and Nower, L. (2002). A pathways model of problem and pathological gambling. *Addiction, 97*(5), 487–99.

Blaszczynski, A. P., and Silove, D. (1995). Cognitive and behavioral therapies for pathological gambling. *Journal of Gambling Studies, 11,* 195–220.

Breen, R., and Zuckerman, M. (1999). "Chasing" in gambling behavior: Personality and cognitive determinants. *Personality and Individual Differences, 27,* 1097–111.

Bujold, A., Ladouceur, R., Sylvain, C., and Boisvert, J. M. (1994). Treatment of pathological gamblers: An experimental study. *Journal of Behavioral Therapy and Experimental Psychiatry, 25,* 275–82.

Carlton, P. L., and Goldstein, L. (1987). Physiological determinants of pathological gambling. In T. Galski (Ed.), *Handbook on pathological gambling.* Springfield, IL: Charles C Thomas.

Cunningham, J. (2005). Little use of treatment among problem gamblers. *Psychiatric Services, 56,* 1024–25.

Custer, R., and Milt, H. (1985). *When luck runs out: Help for compulsive gamblers and their families.* New York: Facts on File.

DeCaria, C. M., Hollander, E., Grossman, R., Wong, C. M., Mosovich, S. A., and Cherkasky, S. (1996). Diagnosis, neurobiology, and treatment of pathological gambling. *Journal of Clinical Psychiatry, 57*(suppl 8), 80–84.

DiClemente, C. C., and Prochaska, J. O. (1982). Self-change and therapy change of smoking behavior: A comparison of processes of change in cessation and maintenance. *Addictive Behaviors, 7*(2), 133–42.

DiClemente, C. C., Story, M., and Murray, K. (2000). On a roll: The process of initiation and cessation of problem gambling among adolescents. *Journal of Gambling Studies, 16,* 289–313.

Garboury, A., and Ladouceur, R. (1989). Erroneous perceptions and gambling. *Journal of Social Behavior and Personality, 4,* 411–20.

Goorney, A. B. (1968). Treatment of compulsive gambling by aversion therapy. *British Journal of Psychiatry, 114,* 329–82.

Grant, J., Kim, S., Potenza, M., Blanco, C., Ibanez, A., Stevens, L., et al. (2003). Paroxetine treatment of pathological gambling: A multi-centre randomized controlled trial. *International Clinical Psychopharmacology, 18*(4), 243–49.

Grant, J. E., and Kim, S. W. (2002). Pharmacotherapy of pathological gambling. *Psychiatric Annals, 14*(3), 155–61.

Grant, J. E., and Kim, S. W. (2002). Effectiveness of pharmacotherapy for pathological gambling: A chart review. *Annals of Clinical Psychiatry, 14*(3), 155–61.

Grant, J. E., Kim, S. W., and Potenza, M. N. (2003). Advances in the pharmacological treatment of pathological gambling. *Journal of Gambling Studies, 19,* 85–109.

Grant, J. E., Potenza, J. D., Marc, N., Hollander, E., Cunningham-Williams, R., Nurminen, T., and Kallio, A. (2006). Multicenter investigation of the opioid antagonist nalmefene in the treatment of pathological gambling. *American Journal of Psychiatry, 163*(2), 303–12.

Grant, J. E., Kim, S. W., and Potenza, M. N. (2003). Advances in the pharmacological treatment of pathological gambling. *Journal of Gambling Studies, 19,* 85–109.

Grant, J. E., and Potenza, M. N. (2004). *Pathological gambling: A clinical guide to treatment.* Washington, DC: American Psychiatric Publishing Inc.

Grant, J. E., and Won Kim, S. (2002). Pharmacotherapy of pathological gambling. *Psychiatric Annals, 32,* 186–91.

Griffiths, M. (1993). Pathological gambling: Possible treatment using an audio feedback technique. *Journal of Gambling Studies, 9,* 295–97.

Griffiths, M. (1996). Pathological gambling and treatment. *British Journal of Clinical Psychology, 35,* 477–79.

Griffiths, M., and Macdonald, H. (1999). Counselling in the treatment of pathological gambling: An overview. *British Journal of Guidance and Counselling, 27*(2), 179–90.

Gupta, R., and Derevensky, J. (2000). Adolescents with gambling problems: From research to treatment. *Journal of Gambling Studies, 16,* 315–42.

Gupta, R., and Derevensky, J. (2008). A treatment approach for adolescents with gambling problems. In M. Zangeneh, A. Blaszczynski, and N. Turner (Eds.), *In the pursuit of winning*. New York: Springer.

Gupta, R., Derevensky, J., and Marget, N. (2004). Coping strategies employed by adolescents with gambling problems. *Child and Adolescent Mental Health, 9*(3), 115–20.

Hodgins, D. (2001). Processes of changing gambling behavior. *Addictive Behaviors, 26*(1), 121–28.

Hodgins, D. (2004). Workbooks for individuals with gambling problems: Promoting the natural recovery process through brief intervention. In L. Abate (Ed.), *Using workbooks in mental health: resources in prevention, psychotherapy, and rehabilitation for clinicians and researchers*. Binghamton, NY: The Haworth Reference Press.

Hodgins, D. (2005). Implications of a brief intervention trial for problem gambling for future outcome research. *Journal of Gambling Studies, 21*(1), 13–19.

Hodgins, D., Currie, S., and El-Guebaly, N. (2001). Motivational enhancement and self-help treatments for problem gambling. *Journal of Consulting and Clinical Psychology, 69*(1), 50–57.

Hodgins, D., Currie, S., el-Guebaly, N., and Diskin, K. (2007). Does providing extended relapse prevention bibliotherapy to problem gamblers improve outcome? *Journal of Gambling Studies, 23*, 41–54.

Hodgins, D., and Diskin, K. (2008). Motivational interviewing in the treatment of problem and pathological gambling. In H. Arkowitz, W. Westra and S. Rollnick (Eds). *Motivational interviewing in the treatment of psychological problems*. New York: Guilford Press.

Hodgins, D., and el-Guebaly, N. (2000). Natural and treatment-assisted recovery from gambling problems: a comparison of resolved and active gamblers. *Addiction, 95*, 777–89.

Hodgins, D., Currie, S. and el-Guebaly, N. (2001). Motivational enhancement and self-help treatments for problem gambling. *Journal of Consulting and Clinical Psychology, 69*, 50–57.

Hodgins, D. and Holub, A. (2007). Treatment of problem gambling. In G. Smith, D. Hodgins and R.J. Williams (Eds). *Research and measurement issues in gambling studies*. New York: Academic Press.

Hodgins, D., and Makarchuk, K. (2003). Trusting problem gamblers: Reliability and validity of self-reported gambling behavior. *Psychology of Addictive Behaviors, 17*(3), 244–48.

Hodgins, D. and Petry, N. (2004). Cognitive and behavioral treatments. In J. Grant and M. Potenza (Eds). *Pathological gambling: A clinical guide to treatment*. New York: American Psychiatric Association Press.

Hodgins, D., Stea, J. and Grant, J. (2011). Gambling disorders. *The Lancet, 378*, 1874–84.

Hollander, E., Buchalter, A. J., and DeCario, C. (2000). Pathological gambling. *Psychiatric Clinics of North America, 23*, 629–42.

Hollander, E., DeCaria, C., Mari, E., Wong, C., Mosovich, S., Grossman, R., and Begaz, T. (1998). Short-term single-blind Fluvoxamine treatment of pathological gambling. *American Journal of Psychiatry, 155*(12), 1781–83.

Hollander, E., Frenkel, M., DeCaria, C., Trungold, S., and Stein, D. J. (1992). Treatment of pathological gambling with clomipramine. *American Journal of Psychiatry, 149*, 710–11.

Hollander, E., Sood, E., Pallanti, S., Baldini-Rossi, N., and Baker, B. (2005). Pharmacological treatments of pathological gambling. *Journal of Gambling Studies, 21*(1), 101–10.

Jacobs, D. F. (1986). A general theory of addictions: A new theoretical model. *Journal of Gambling Behavior, 2*(1), 15–31.

Ladouceur, R., Boisvert, J. M., and Dumont, J. (1994). Cognitive-behavioral treatment for adolescent pathological gamblers. *Behavior Modification, 18*, 230–42.

Lesieur, H. R. (1990). Working with and understanding Gamblers Anonymous. *Working with self help*. Homewood, IL: Dorsey.

Lesieur, H. (1998). Costs and treatment of pathological gambling. *Annals of the American Academy of Social Science, 556*, 153–71.

McCown, W.G. and Howatt, W.A. (2007). *Treating gambling problems*. New York: John Wiley and Sons.

National Research Council. (1999). *Pathological gambling: A critical review*. Washington, DC: National Academy Press.

Pallesen, S., Molde, H., Arnestad, H., et al. (2007). Outcome of pharmacological treatments of pathological gambling: A review and meta-analysis. *Journal of Clinical Psychopharmacology, 27*, 357–64.

Petry, N. (2005). *Pathological gambling: Etiology, comorbidity, and treatment*. Washington, DC: American Psychological Association.

Petry, N. (2006). Stages of change in treatment-seeking pathological gamblers. *Journal of Consulting Psychology, 73*, 312–22.

Prochaska, J., and DiClemente, C. (1983). Stages and processes of self-change of smoking: Toward an integrative model of change. *Journal of Consulting and Clinical Psychology, 51*(3), 390–95.

Rosenthal, R. J. (1987). The psychodynamics of pathological gambling: A review of the literature. In T. Galski (Ed), *The handbook of pathological gambling*. Springfield, IL: Charles C Thomas.

Rosenthal, R.J. and Rugle, L.J. (1994). A psychodynamic approach to treatment of pathological gambling: Part I, Achieving abstinence. *Journal of Gambling Studies*, 10, 21–42.

Rugle, L., Derevensky, J., Gupta, R., Winters, K., and Stinchfield, R. (2001). The treatment of problem and pathological gamblers. Report prepared for the National Council for Problem Gambling, Center for Mental Health Services (CMHS) and the Substance Abuse Mental Health Services.

Salzmann, M. (1982). Treatment of compulsive gambling. *British Journal of Psychiatry*, 66, 28–33.

Shaffer, H.J. and Martin, R. (2011). Disordered gambling: Etiology, trajectory, and clinical considerations. *Annual Review of Clinical Psychology*, 7, 483–510.

Slutske, W. (2006). Natural recovery and treatment-seeking in pathological gambling: Results of two U.S. national surveys. *American Journal of Psychiatry*, 163, 297–302.

Toneatto, T. (2002). Cognitive therapy for problem gambling. *Cognitive and Behavioral Practice*, 9, 191–99.

Toneatto, T. (1999). Cognitive psychopathology of problem gambling. *Substance Use and Misuse*, 34, 1593–604.

Toneatto, T., and Ladouceur, R. (2003). Treatment of pathological gambling: A critical review of the literature. *Psychology of Addictive Behaviors*, 17, 284–92.

Vachon, D., and Bagby, R. (2009). Pathological gambling subtypes. *Psychological Assessment*, 21, 608–15.

Walker, M. B. (1993). Treatment strategies for problem gambling: A review of effectiveness. In W. Eadington and J. Cornelius (Eds.), *Gambling behavior and problem gambling*. Reno, NV: Institute for the Study of Gambling and Commercial Gaming.

World Health Organization. (1990). *International classification of diseases (ICD)*. Geneva: World Health Organization.

7

GAMBLING AS A PUBLIC HEALTH ISSUE

Throughout this book, ample evidence suggests that adolescents are gambling in greater numbers and view gambling as an enjoyable and socially acceptable recreational activity. Whether playing poker among friends in their basement, purchasing lottery tickets, playing on electronic gambling machines, or engaging in online gambling, there is little doubt about its widespread popularity around the globe. For some, what begins as a recreational form of entertainment all too quickly escalates into serious problems. The multitude of problems and issues facing pathological gamblers has been discussed throughout this book. The fact that adolescent and young adult problem gamblers are experiencing both severe short-term and long-term negative personal, social, economic, and legal consequences, at rates higher than their adult counterparts, remains quite troublesome. In summary, the potential negative consequences associated with problem gambling can be seen in figure 7.1.

The expansion of traditional forms of gambling, new gambling opportunities, and alternative ways of gambling is continuing at an unprecedented rate. Many states and countries are developing and expanding a growing diversity of regulated forms of land-based and online gambling (while still contentious in the United States pending legislation, the American Gaming Association on behalf of its members has accepted the importance of this form of gambling

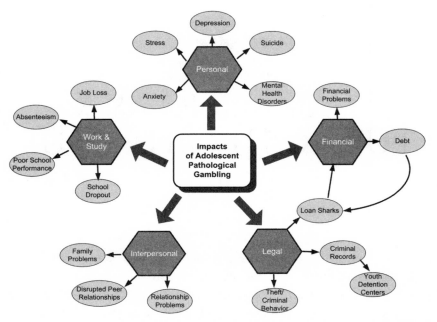

Figure 7.1. Consequences associated with adolescent pathological gambling. Adapted from the Productivity Commission (1999, p. 73).

and now supports the introduction of online gambling legislation for poker). Gambling has become synonymous with entertainment. For example, the Resorts World Sentosa casino in Singapore has partnered with Universal Studios, and another joint venture in Manila is being planned to host a theme park with gambling opportunities for adults on the same site. Other casinos with huge entertainment complexes are being proposed in multiple American states, Japan, Vietnam, Taiwan, and possibly Thailand. This love of gambling is indicative of its widespread cross-cultural social appeal. Internationally, we are seeing a relaxation by governments of their long-standing opposition to expanded gambling in spite of our growing knowledge of the resulting social costs. As more states elect to increase their gambling, neighboring states do so similarly for fear of lost revenues. This domino effect has resulted in the widespread proliferation of gambling opportunities.

With the expansion of gambling and ease of accessibility, some policy experts have predicted that the prevalence of problem gambling is likely to rise. Others have argued that adolescents and adults alike will ultimately adapt to the increasing opportunities to gamble. Proponents of this argument suggest that individuals over time become resistant to the influences of gambling so that the attractiveness of gambling eventually dissipates. While there may be some credence to this argument, land-based casinos in particular have employed marketing experts to keep their level of attractiveness high. Through the development of multipurpose facilities, gambling only being one component of a much larger entertainment complex, their appeal continues to grow. The gambling industry has executives and board rooms filled with ingenious, intelligent, creative, and energetic individuals who are investing billions of dollars to ensure their casinos are filled with "happy" gamblers. The same is true for most technically based online providers. In many land-based casinos and gambling venues, one can find outstanding Broadway productions, concerts, movie theatres, and a wide range of dining facilities to help attract individuals. The marketing divisions of gambling corporations have increased their corporate presence and have become an essential and integral part of their operation. Their marketing strategies are creative and show no limits.

With strong encouragement and endorsements for the gambling industry by our governments we have created an entire generation of youth, most of whom are attracted to the glitz, glamour, and excitement surrounding gambling. The incentives given to patrons (often referred to as "perks") by land-based operators appear endless. In addition to free or low-cost meals and entertainment, free trips, car giveaways, and accommodations for "high rollers" who gamble large sums of money, advertising gurus continue to come up with ingenious ideas to attract new patrons and to keep existing players gambling within their casinos. In addition to the traditional poker tournaments where large sums of money can be won, the opportunity to win automobiles and the use of player loyalty cards to redeem cash or gifts are just some ways to retain players. Most recently, Trump's Taj Mahal casino in Atlantic City, as part of its latest marketing campaign, appears to have taken promotional giveaways to a new level. Inspired by the FX television series *Nip/Tuck*, the marketing team, in what some gambling analysts have remarked is one of the quirkiest giveaways ever, embarked on a novel giveaway. The casino is awarding $25,000 worth of plastic surgery to one lucky winner in the "Nip, Tuck, and Lift Sweepstakes." The promotion, according to a casino senior vice president, allows the lucky winner to mix and match the types of plastic surgery desired—reconstructed nose, breast augmentation, facelift, liposuction, or whatever the winner desires (a total of 13 medical procedures are listed)—as long as the procedures fall within the $25,000 limit. The promotion is open to anyone gambling at the casino using a loyalty card. These cards are typically inserted into a slot machine and are often attached to the individual's clothes by a stretch cord. Some have commented that it looks as if the individual is hooked up to an intravenous line. For the lucky individual who wins and thinks he looks just fine as is, he can take the $25,000 in cash.

While the perceived risks associated with gambling are outweighed by the positive benefits of gambling, adolescents like their adult counterparts want to try to capture the dream of either becoming the next World Series of Poker champion or winning the "big one" in the lottery. The capability to win large amounts of money without working is indeed tempting for many, especially for those craving instant gratification.

The fact that most adolescents fail to view teen gambling as a concern is not surprising, given that parents and teachers hold similar views. Parents ultimately provide tacit approval of adolescents' gambling behaviors by purchasing lottery tickets, allowing them to gamble within the home, and frequently gambling with their children. Some schools have actually held gambling and casino nights as fundraisers, although alcohol-drinking nights as school fundraisers appear to be nonexistent. This tacit approval has certainly encouraged adolescents to continue their gambling without fear of repercussions or punishments.

The question repeatedly asked is why are adolescents such a highly vulnerable population for gambling problems? This is a simple question that is often difficult to answer. Yet what we know about adolescent development in general is that (a) they perceive themselves to be invincible and invulnerable, (b) they believe they are smarter than adults, (c) they are at a stage in their life where they have few financial or social responsibilities, (d) they typically engage in multiple risk-taking behaviors and view gambling as the least problematic of them all, and (e) they are notorious for externalizing negative consequences (losses are attributed to bad luck, poor dealer, someone else received "their" card, etc.). The removal of the negative associations of mobsters and seedy characters with gambling venues and the adulation afforded to the young poker stars has legitimized this activity. Never before in our history has gambling become so widely available, advertised, and socially acceptable as a legitimate form of entertainment.

We have witnessed a significant change in the gambling patterns and game preferences of today's youth. The largest increases tend to be related to both increased poker playing (in particular Texas Hold'em) and technological forms of gambling (e.g., Internet gambling, mobile gambling, poker playing via the Internet). This change is particularly noteworthy and may ultimately result in more adolescents beginning to gamble for money at an earlier age than ever before and subsequently experiencing multiple gambling-related problems. In spite of the American government's efforts to prohibit online wagering, many individuals continue successfully to circumvent the regulations.

While land-based poker playing may have reached a plateau, its popularity has not waned. Interestingly, the same structural characteristics found in electronic gambling machines that make them potentially addictive are also present in many forms of Internet gambling. However, while there are stringent controls prohibiting minors from gambling in many land-based activities, they are absent to a large degree in Internet gambling. The increasing numbers of American gamblers on Internet gambling websites have become a significant concern to legislators and gambling regulators. Most recently, the United States Department of Justice closed three of the largest offshore gambling websites, Full Tilt Poker, PokerStars, and Absolute Poker, which had made fortunes catering to American gamblers. PokerStars, based on the Isle of Man, became the largest online gambling site in the world, with estimated revenues exceeding $1.4 billion and reporting annual profits of $500 million. Citing the U. S. 2006 Unlawful Internet Gambling Enforcement Act (UIGEA), which bans online gambling websites and prohibits bank transfers of funds for the purpose of gambling, the U. S. Department of Justice charged these companies with bank fraud, money laundering, and illegal gambling. Since the closures (only for American bettors), Full Tilt Poker has subsequently been charged with defrauding customers of more than $300 million and the Department of Justice contends that the poker site was merely a global Ponzi scheme to bilk players out of their money. This has certainly raised serious concerns among online gamblers and has eroded confidence in many of the existing gambling websites. At the same time, there is pending legislation in a growing number of states and countries to legalize and regulate online gambling.

A recent study conducted by our research group at McGill University revealed that the reasons youth engaged in Internet gambling were slightly different from those cited for traditional forms of gambling. While most youth continue to report gambling for excitement, enjoyment, and to make money, a significant concern was that a large and growing percentage of these individuals reported gambling to relieve boredom. Individuals readily reported engaging in online gambling in the comfort of their home. The information provided in figure 7.2 typifies youth perceptions and their reasons for online gambling.

During the past year, almost one in twenty (4.6%) participants reported gambling online with their own money, with more than three times the number of males (7.8%) gambling compared to females (2.3%). The two most popular forms of Internet gambling for youth were card playing (online poker) and sports betting, with many reporting doing so with a family member (i.e., parent or older sibling). Among Internet gamblers, the prevalence rate of problem gambling was almost 19%. Although exceedingly high, similar rates of problem gambling prevalence among self-selected samples have been reported in Canada, Europe, and Australia.

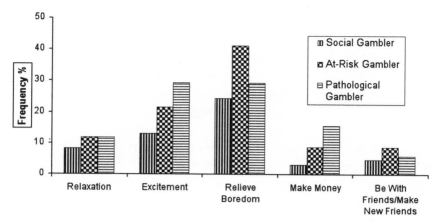

Figure 7.2.   Reported reasons why adolescents gamble on the Internet.

There is little doubt that individuals who gamble online exhibit greater gambling problems. The question one has to ask is: Does Internet gambling result in more problems or do people with gambling problems merely seek out Internet gambling sites? Within the research and clinical community, there currently is no consensus or answer to this question. Will new technologies evolve to enable even greater access to gambling?

There are other concerns with respect to Internet gambling for adolescents. In a number of studies, more individuals under the age of 18 years than 18- to 24-year-olds were reported to be playing "free" gambling-simulation games on Internet gambling sites. Most Internet gambling sites typically have a free site (often referred to as their .net site) in order that future players learn the rules of the various games and have an opportunity to "practice" and play for fun without risking losing money. In a number of adolescent studies, the most popular forms of "free play" activities were found to be card playing (poker and blackjack).

In a recent Canadian national study, it was found that 33% of underage minors (15- to 18-year-olds) reportedly had "gambled" online using the free play modes and/or via online social networking sites. Reasons for playing online free (gambling) games were to relieve boredom (59%), fun/entertainment (49%), excitement (15%), their friends play (14%), and as a good way to improve one's skills before playing with actual money (10%). A considerable number of these individuals (22%) indicated they played these games because it was found on a social networking site (e.g., Facebook). Are these sites only a breeding ground for future gamblers?

As the number of Internet gambling sites increases without strict monitoring and the inclusion of harm-minimization strategies, the ease of access represents a significant concern. Some clinical researchers have raised early concerns that Internet wagering may be problematic because (a) it is easily accessible, (b) it offers visually exciting effects and sounds similar to electronic gambling machines, (c) it incorporates highly attractive videogame technology with which adolescents are quite familiar (some even include avatars), and (d) the event frequency can be extremely rapid, especially if the individual is playing on multiple sites or multiple games simultaneously. Many Internet poker players report having multiple computer screens open and play on several tables simultaneously. This might be particularly problematic to a generation of individuals who have spent their childhood playing videogames. Parents need to be aware of the similarities between videogames and Internet gambling and carefully monitor their children's behavior and playing patterns.

Will Internet gambling among youth be the new "game changer" and ultimately result in increasing prevalence rates of problem gambling? What will be the impact of youth gambling when mass marketing through social media networks is realized? Will this have an impact on the gambling behaviors of today's youth? Unfortunately, we currently don't have the definitive answer to these important social policy and public health questions.

MOBILE GAMBLING: A SERIOUS CONCERN

Of even greater concern than Internet wagering for young people will likely be mobile gambling. Such technologies currently exist and their platforms are similar to Internet gambling. Rather than operating from a laptop or desktop computer, data connections are readily provided by a telecom provider that can use a multitude of data layer technologies. While still relatively underdeveloped in North America (the Nevada Gaming Control Board recently approved mobile phone use within Nevada for sports wagering), there are estimates that the mobile gaming market could reach between $7.5 billion and $48 billion worldwide by 2015. While these estimates vary widely, there is an overall general consensus that this platform will become a significant player in the gambling market. This platform, readily accessible and already accepted and embraced by adolescents, could easily incorporate traditional gambling opportunities including lottery purchases, casino-style games, slot machines, sports betting, poker, and virtually any game of chance in a totally unsupervised environment via smart phones. With the growing popularity and reduced prices of smart phones and Tablets (iPads, Playbooks, etc.) individuals will have their own casino in their pocket, backpack, or briefcase, readily accessible 24 hours a day, seven days per week, wherever they go. A recent study revealed that 73% of smart phone subscribers played mobile casino games within a three-month timeframe.

Imagine gambling on your cell phone while on a bus or train, at McDonald's or your favorite restaurant, or from the schoolyard while playing with your friends. While unheard of a couple of years ago, the reality is becoming much closer. MGM Resorts and others are already offering free applications for cell phones using multiple platforms to inform clients of room specials, new incentive packages, shows, etc. Will it be long before they offer mobile gambling? While state officials in Nevada have only recently begun to allow gamblers to wager on sports events using their smart phones, the potential for increasing gambling revenues through this technology is endless. This would nevertheless be a huge policy shift for state legislators, and there will be major legal and legislative hurdles to overcome before being permitted. However, like Internet gambling, it is likely that lost government revenues resulting from poor economic conditions will help drive and influence policy changes around the globe to accept this new form of gambling. Yet, there is little doubt that the issue of underage access to such gambling sites will be of significant concern given the widespread adoption of smart phones by youth. As many of these cell phones are registered in their parents' names, how we can be assured that such sites will be blocked for underage youth while allowing access for those of legal age?

Technological advances already permit access to Internet gambling websites via one's cell phone. In light of the findings that many parents are either unaware or are unconcerned about their children's gambling, will this new venue become even more problematic? While special filters and screens can be installed these will likely not be 100% effective. The difficulty of enforcing national or state laws on an international level in reality means there are few legal consequences to operators who provide minors with access to their websites. Given the technological limitations now faced by gambling operators in identifying which individuals are of legal age, in addition to potential revenue loss, operators have little incentive (other than a moral compass) to place greater restrictions on their sites in an effort to prohibit underage minors from gambling. The number of cell phone users among children and adolescents is in the millions and growing daily. As mobile gambling reaches its peak, its distribution network will be in the hundreds of millions of individuals.

NEW GAMBLING VENUES

Airline executives have thought about installing small casinos on board transatlantic flights, and land-based casinos can currently be found in hotels, shopping malls, and even some airports. It is difficult to turn on a television set in the evening without seeing some championship or celebrity poker tournament. No longer does one need to wait for the outcome of a sports event in order to gamble; there are dozens of bets one can make during each game. Betting on the outcome of a reality television show, the length of time for the national anthem to be sung by a celebrity, which college team will win the next game, who the next mayor of a city will be, or who will likely become the next Pope—we can gamble on virtually anything and everything. Our appetite to gamble seems insatiable.

Technological advances continue to develop at an unbelievably rapid pace and gaming operators have wholeheartedly embraced these new forms of technology. Alliances between land-based gambling operators and Internet gambling providers will likely continue. The land-based casino industry, once vehemently opposed to Internet gambling, has succumbed to its tremendous popularity and potential revenues. Caesar's Interactive Entertainment, a subsidiary of Caesar's and Harrah's land-based casinos, already operates an Internet-based casino currently based in Gibraltar available to residents of the United Kingdom and some other European countries. Like other Internet companies, they are anxiously awaiting legislative changes in the United States. Other strategic alliances, including those between Wynn Casinos and PokerStars, have been temporarily put on hold until legal and legislative issues can be resolved.

There are currently about 85 countries that have chosen to legalize and regulate online gambling, with the numbers growing daily. The industry as a whole has agreed that strict regulation can provide consumer protection for individuals while also generating employment, economic opportunity, and government revenue. The Internet gaming industry has argued that with existing technologies they can effectively ensure that (a) games are played fairly, according to their rules; (b) payments to consumers are made promptly as promised; (c) underage gamblers can be effectively prohibited from playing; (d) individuals who have difficulty in controlling their gambling can have access to a variety of harm-minimization techniques and strategies (e.g., tools to limit their deposits, bets, excessive playing, and self-exclusion); (e) they can effectively exclude gamblers from jurisdictions for which they do not have a legitimate license; and (f) measures are currently available to preclude money laundering and illegal transfers of funds to terrorist organizations.

STRATEGIES FOR MINIMIZING RISK

There are a number of broad strategies that may be used to help minimize the risks of gambling problems among adolescents. Such strategies include (a) ensuring that laws prohibiting underage adolescents from gambling are enforced, (b) monitoring the advertisements for gambling by enforcing a strict code of conduct and practice, (c) making the games safer and less potentially addictive, (d) changing the attitudes of parents and teachers to ultimately encourage safer, more responsible gambling, (e) delaying the age at which gambling begins, (f) providing greater oversight of Internet use (some groups have now developed Internet gambling blocking software), (g) introducing more prevention programs in schools, and (h) informing legislators and government policy makers about responsible gambling practices.

In an ideal world, there would be no temptations or triggers prompting gambling for our youth. However, the reality remains that new, more attractive and exciting gambling opportunities and venues will increase. Educating parents and youth about the risk signs associated with excessive gambling has a long way to go. Youth gambling has often been referred to as a "hidden addiction"—one can't smell it on the breath, see it in the eyes, or assess excessive gambling through blood or urine samples. For many adolescents, what starts off as a fun, enjoyable social activity can quickly escalate into a serious problem.

As has been noted elsewhere, the impact that the social media revolution has had in the way our children communicate and interact is unprecedented and the use of social media networks to advertise gambling will continue to grow exponentially. A global technological revolution has taken place with advancements so rapid that industries can barely keep up the pace. The importance placed on social media sites by the general population has dramatically changed how we receive information. The increase in use of websites such as Facebook has been remarkable, with reports suggesting in excess of 700 million worldwide account holders and these numbers are increasing daily. Not to be outdone, the gambling industry has sought to capitalize on such social media sites. The number one fan site as of August 2010 on Facebook was Texas Hold'em with an excess of 24 million members.

Our current social policies concerning problem gambling have generally been reactive to specific problems rather than proactive. For example, considerable attention has been focused on electronic gambling machines in certain jurisdictions. These machines (EGMs, pokies, VLTs) often referred to as the "crack cocaine of gambling," have resulted in a number of different policy initiatives, including limiting the number of machines per location, modifying hours of availability, and enforcement of smart card technology to help individuals establish and maintain preset limits. Today's hot topic of concern is over Internet gambling. The American Gaming Association recently released a proposed code of conduct for Internet gambling companies that ultimately will seek licensure once the UIGEA is repealed. Their code is predicated on six guiding principles:

- Extensive background checks to ensure that individuals with criminal records are kept out of the business.
- Appropriate identification procedures must be in place to assist law enforcement to keep minors, consumers from other jurisdictions, and cheaters from playing.
- Internet providers must permit and undergo regular periodic testing and auditing of their software to ensure that the games are fair and honest.
- The implementation of rigorous player exclusion processes to prevent minors, those from outside jurisdictions, and cheaters from accessing their online site must be in place
- The development and implementation of effective responsible gambling protections on all Internet gambling sites to help educate individuals and provide problem gamblers with easy access to tools to help monitor and control their behavior.
- Maintain stringent anti-money-laundering procedures that will assist the government in its law enforcement efforts.

In a more comprehensive analysis, Sally Monaghan and I recommended several initiatives to help protect players and to promote responsible gambling procedures for Internet gambling. These can be viewed in terms of the necessity for age verifications, the establishment of preset limits after which gambling is terminated for a specified period of time, the opportunity for self-exclusion from the website, and the inclusion of appropriate referral agencies and help-line support. We further contend that all pertinent documentation and information necessary for the individual to make informed choices concerning the probabilities of winning on all games, payout ratios, and prize structures should be provided. Players should have easy access to their account information from any part of the site and their account information should include a record of all wagers, outcomes, and records of deposits, time spent, and money transfers. A time reminder indicating both actual playing time and reminders when the player has been gambling for long periods of time as well as built-in pauses and pop-up messages indicating time and money wagered should be mandatory. We further recommended that no encouragement be provided to reinvest winnings or chase one's losses and that the "practice mode" must have the identical appropriate messages regarding responsible gambling and that player protection measures be identical to those for actual gamblers. It is imperative that payout rates used in the "free play" mode be identical to those used in the real game mode. Any sites verified to be adhering to regulatory processes, training, and oversight should receive accreditation and be identified with an approval stamp or logo endorsed by the regulator. Finally, we argued that advertising standards must be accurate, fair, and responsible and should avoid targeting underage minors or other high-risk groups.

A growing number of international jurisdictions have introduced responsible gambling programs in light of the number of individuals negatively impacted. Such programs are intended to minimize the harms and negative consequences associated with excessive, problematic gambling.

While gambling from an individual's perspective may be viewed as a freedom of choice, the vast array of negative consequences associated with gambling places it in a public health framework. Within such a framework, we all have a responsibility to help protect and minimize problems for highly vulnerable people.

Pathological gambling problems are not a result of what psychologists refer to as "single trial learning." One does not become a pathological gambler after gambling once. Rather, it is a progressive disorder that occurs over time. The long-term social impact and consequences for young people will likely take years to fully comprehend. Today's youth will spend their entire lives in an environment where gambling is not only normalized, prolific, and readily accessible, but where it is government supported, owned, and/or regulated.

A considerable number of other more highly visible adolescent mental health problems have prompted proactive social policy development (e.g., tobacco use, alcohol and substance use/abuse, increased rates of suicide, teenage pregnancy, unprotected sex, and bullying). Unfortunately, issues surrounding youth gambling problems have traditionally been largely ignored. While the incidence of severe gambling problems among youth still remains relatively low, the growing incidence of adolescent gambling is beginning to attract attention. Problem gambling during adolescence remains an important, growing social and public health issue that will not disappear soon. The negative consequences for the individual, family, and society are adding to our collective social costs.

While in several chapters the various warning signs associated with pathological gambling have been discussed, unless youth, educators, and parents become aware of these signs little can be done to help protect our children. Will these new and evolving technological forms of gambling eventually result in an increase in problems? Will mobile gambling outpace Internet gambling? Only time will tell. In the meantime, greater emphasis on outreach, awareness, and prevention programs remains essential. Our continued search for the best and most efficient strategies to help our youth is imperative.

Rather than confronting and acknowledging their problems, problem gamblers frequently deny their existence, claiming "I can stop gambling when I want to," or "in spite of what others think or say, I don't have a problem." Differences among problem gamblers with respect to their coping styles and adaptive behaviors are of critical importance. How to develop more resilient adolescents is equally challenging. Whether gambling in order to escape daily problems or the need for that adrenaline rush, alternative strategies must be sought. While gambling may temporarily relieve some anxiety and/or depression or induce a physiological high, the need to continue gambling for longer periods with more and more money eventually spins out of control.

Only recently have health professionals, educators, and governmental officials acknowledged the need for prevention of problem gambling in light of the vast expansion of gambling. While not necessarily viewed by parents or adolescents themselves as a problem, this hidden addiction, similar to other addictions, comes with a long list of negative consequences and problems. As gambling continues to be normalized in our society, the number of youth gambling continues to increase. As a result, the potential for increased adolescent problems is growing. Gambling, once thought to be only an adult activity, is now mainstream and popular among our youth. Technological forms of gambling continue to place our children at even greater risk for gambling problems. Efforts to better educate our youth, to delay the onset of gambling, and help to minimize problems are needed. President John F. Kennedy once said: "Children are the world's most valuable resource and its best hope for the future." Let's help protect our children.

REFERENCES

American Gaming Association. (September 2011). AGA Releases Online Poker Code of Conduct, Unveils Online Video. http://www.american-gaming.org/newsroom/press-releases/aga-releases-online-poker-code-of-conduct-unveils-online-video.

Blaszczynski, A., Ladouceur, R., Nower, L., and Shaffer, H.J. (2005). Informed choice and gambling: Principles for consumer protection. Report prepared for the Australian Gaming Council.

Blaszczynski, A. P., Ladouceur, R., and Shaffer, H. J. (2004). A science-based framework for responsible gambling: The Reno model. *Journal of Gambling Studies, 20*(3), 301–17.

comScore Inc. (2010). *Smartphone adoption shifting dynamics of U.S. mobile gaming market.* http://www.comscore.com/Press_Events/Press _Releases/2010/4/Smartphone_Adoption_Shifting_Dynamics_of_U.S. _Mobile_Gaming_Market.

Derevensky, J., Gupta, R., Messerlian, C., and Gillespie, M. (2004). Youth gambling problems: A need for responsible social policy. In J. Derevensky and R. Gupta (Eds.), *Gambling problems in youth: Theoretical and applied perspectives.* New York: Kluwer Academic.

Derevensky, J., and Gupta, R. (2007). Internet gambling amongst adolescents: A growing concern. *International Journal of Mental Health and Addictions, 5,* 93–101.

Griffiths, M. (2007). Mobile phone gambling. In D. Taniar (Ed.), *Encyclopedia of mobile computing and commerce.* Pennsylvania: Information Science Reference.

Griffiths, M., and Barnes, A. (2008). Internet gambling: An online empirical study among student gamblers. *International Mental Health Addiction, 6,* 194–204.

Griffiths, M., and Parke, J. (2010). Adolescent gambling on the Internet: A review. *International Journal of Adolescent Medicine and Health, 22,* 59–75.

H2 Gambling Capital. (2011). *Report on the Mobile Gambling Market.*

Hanman, N. (2005). Placing a bet on the mobile. *The Guardian* (London). http://www.guardian.co.uk/technology/2005/feb/10/mobilephones .onlinesupplement.

iGaming Business. (2011). Mobile and online growth at Paddy Power. Retrieved from: http://www.igamingbusiness.com/content/mobile-and-online-growth-paddy-power.

Johnson, L. (2011) Mobile gambling doubles to $65.8M in 2010: Study. *Mobile Commerce Daily.* http://mobilecommercedaily.com/2011/06/30.

Kennedy, J.F. (July 25, 1963). Speech concerning America's appeal for UNICEF.

Korn, D., and Shaffer, H. J. (1999). Gambling and the health of the public: Adopting a public health perspective. *Journal of Gambling Studies, 15*(4), 289–365.

McBride, J., and Derevensky, J. (2009). Internet gambling behaviour in a sample of online gamblers. *International Journal of Mental Health and Addiction, 7,* 149–67.

Meerkamper, E. (2010). Youth gambling 2.0. Understanding youth gambling, emerging technologies, and social platforms. Paper presented at the Nova Scotia Gaming Corporation 6th Annual Responsible Gambling Conference, Halifax, Nova Scotia.

Messerlian, C., Byrne, A. and Derevensky, J. (2004). Gambling, youth and the Internet: Should we be concerned? *Canadian Child and Adolescent Psychiatry Review, 13*(1), 3–6.

Monaghan, S., and Derevensky, J. (2008). A critical review of the Internet gambling literature: some policy recommendations. Report submitted to Nova Scotia Gaming Corporation.

Romer, D. (2010). Internet gambling among male and female youth ages 18 to 24. Report from the Annenberg Public Policy Center, University of Pennsylvania.

Sevigny, S., Cloutier, M., Pelletier, M., and Ladouceur, R. (2005). Internet gambling: Misleading payout rates during the "demo" period. *Computers in Human Behavior, 21*, 153–58.

Shaffer, H. J., Hall, M. N., and Vander Bilt, J. (1997). Estimating the prevalence of disordered gambling in the United States and Canada: A meta-analysis. *American Journal of Public Health, 89*, 1369-76.

Shaffer, H. J., LaBrie, R. A., LaPlante, D. A., Nelson, S. E., and Stanton, M. V. (2004). The road less travelled: moving from distribution to determinants in the study of gambling epidemiology. *Canadian Journal of Psychiatry, 49*, 504–16.

Welte, J., Barnes, G., Tidwell, M., and Hoffman, J. (2009). The association of form of gambling with problem gambling among American youth. *Psychology of Addictive Behaviors, 23*, 105–12.

Wittkowski, D. (2011). Trump Taj Mahal is giving away $25,000 worth of plastic surgery. http://www.pressofatlanticcity.com/news/breaking/trump-taj-mahal-is-giving-away-worth-of-plastic-surgery/article_d7a03018-eab3-11e0-960a-001cc4c03286.html.

Wood, R., and Williams, R. (2009). *Internet gambling: Prevalence, patterns, problems, and policy options.* Guelph, Ontario: Ontario Problem Gambling Research Center.

BIBLIOGRAPHY

Abbott, M., Volberg, R., Bellringer, M., and Reith, G. (2004). A Review of Research on Aspects of Problem Gambling. Report prepared for the Responsibility in Gambling Trust, U.K.

American Gaming Association. (2010). State of the states: The AGA survey of casino entertainment. Washington, DC: American Gaming Association.

American Gaming Association. (2011). State of the states: The AGA survey of casino entertainment. Washington, DC: American Gaming Association.

American Gaming Association. (September 2011). AGA Releases Online Poker Code of Conduct, Unveils Online Video. http://www.american-gaming.org/newsroom/press-releases/aga-releases-online-poker-code-of-conduct-unveils-online-video.

American Psychiatric Association. (1980). *Diagnostic and statistical manual of mental disorders (DSM-III), Third edition.* Washington, DC.

American Psychiatric Association. (1994). *Diagnostic and statistical manual of mental disorders (DSM-IV), Fourth edition.* Washington, DC: American Psychiatric Association.

American Psychiatric Association. (2000). *Diagnostic and statistical manual of mental disorders (DSM-IV-TR), Text revision.* Washington, DC: American Psychiatric Association.

Australian Government Productivity Commission. (2010). Gambling Inquiry.

Barnes, G. M., Welte, J. W., Hoffman, J. H., and Dintcheff, B. A. (1999). Gambling and alcohol use among youth: influences of demographic, socialization, and individual factors. *Addictive Behaviors, 24*(6), 749–67.

Beck, A., Wright, F., Newman, C., and Liese, B. (Eds.). (2001). *Cognitive therapy of substance abuse*. New York: Guilford Press.

Bergevin, T., Derevensky, J., Gupta, R., and Kaufman, F. (2006). Adolescent gambling: Understanding the role of stress and coping. *Journal of Gambling Studies, 22*(2), 195–208.

Black, D. (2004). An open-label trial of Bupropion in the treatment of pathologic gambling. *Journal of Clinical Psychopharmacology, 24*(1), 108–10.

Black, D. W., and Moyer, T. (1998). Clinical features and psychiatric co-morbidity of subjects with pathological gambling behavior. *Psychiatric Services, 49*, 1434–39.

Black, D. W., Moyer, T., and Schlosser, S. (2003). Quality of life and family history in pathological gambling. *Journal of Nervous and Mental Disease, 191*, 124–26.

Blaszczynski, A. P. (1985). A winning bet: Treatment for compulsive gambling. *Psychology Today, 38*, 42–44, 46.

Blaszczynski, A. P. (Ed.). (1998). *Overcoming compulsive gambling: A self help guide using cognitive behavioural techniques*. London: Robinson Publishing Ltd.

Blaszczynski, A. P. (2005). Pathological gambling: A clinical guide to treatment. *Addiction, 100*(4), 565–66.

Blaszczynski, A., Ladouceur, R., Nower, L., and Shaffer, H. (2005). Informed choice and gambling: Principles for consumer protection. Report prepared for the Australian Gaming Council gambling. *Addiction, 97*(5), 487–99.

Blaszczynski, A. P., Ladouceur, R., and Shaffer, H. J. (2004). A science-based framework for responsible gambling: The Reno model. *Journal of Gambling Studies, 20*(3), 301–17.

Blaszczynski, A. P., and McConaghy, N. (1989). The medical model of gambling: Current short-comings. *Journal of Gambling Behavior, 5*, 42–52.

Blaszczynski, A. P., McConaghy, N., and Frankova, A. (1991). Control versus abstinence in the treatment of pathological gambling: A two to nine year follow-up. *British Journal of Addiction, 86*, 299–306.

Blaszczynski, A. P., and Nower, L. (2002). A pathways model of problem and pathological gambling. *Addiction, 97*(5), 487–99.

Blaszczynski, A. P., and Silove, D. (1995). Cognitive and behavioral therapies for pathological gambling. *Journal of Gambling Studies, 11*, 195–220.

Blaszczynski, A., and Steel, Z. (1998). Personality disorders among pathological gamblers. *Journal of Gambling Studies, 14*, 51–71.

Boudreau, B., and Poulin, C. (2007). The South Oaks Gambling Screen-Revised Adolescent (SOGS-RA) revisited: A cut-point analysis. *Journal of Gambling Studies, 23*, 299–308.

Breen, R., and Zuckerman, M. (1999). "Chasing" in gambling behavior: Personality and cognitive determinants. *Personality and Individual Differences, 27*, 1097–111.

Brounstein, P. J., Zweig, J. M., and Gardner, S. E. (1999). *Understanding substance abuse prevention: Toward the 21st century-A primer on effective programs.* Substance Abuse and Mental Health Services Administration, Center for Substance Abuse Prevention, Division of Knowledge Development and Evaluation.

Bujold, A., Ladouceur, R., Sylvain, C., and Boisvert, J. M. (1994). Treatment of pathological gamblers: An experimental study. *Journal of Behavioral Therapy and Experimental Psychiatry, 25*, 275–82.

Byrne, A., Dickson, L., Derevensky, J., Gupta, R., and Lussier, I. (2005). An examination of social marketing campaigns for the prevention of youth problem gambling. *Journal of Health Communication, 10*, 681–700.

Campbell, C., Derevensky, J., Meerkamper, E. and Cutajar, J. (in press). The influence of cultural background on parental perceptions of adolescent gambling behaviour: A Canadian study. *International Journal of Mental Health and Addictions.*

Campbell, C., Derevensky, J., Meerkamper, E. and Cutajar, J. (2011). Parents' perceptions of adolescent gambling: A Canadian national study. *Journal of Gambling Issues, 25*, 36–53.

Carlton, P. L., and Goldstein, L. (1987). Physiological determinants of pathological gambling. In T. Galski (Ed.), *Handbook on pathological gambling.* Springfield, IL: Charles C Thomas.

Comings, D. E. (1998). The molecular genetics of pathological gambling. *CNS Spectrum, 3*(2), 20–37.

Comings, D. E., and Blum, K. (2000). Reward deficiency syndrome: Genetic aspects of behavioral disorders. *Progress in Brain Research, 126*, 325–41.

Comings, D. E., Gade-Andavolu, R., Gonzalez, N., Wu, S., Muhleman, D., Chen, C., et al. (2001). The additive effect of neurotransmitter genes in pathological gambling. *Clinical Genetics, 60*(2), 107–16.

Comings, D. E., Rosenthal, R. J., Lesieur, H. R., et al. (1996). A study of the dopamine D2 receptor gene in pathological gambling. *Pharmacogenetics, 6*, 223–34.

comScore Inc. (2010). *Smartphone adoption shifting dynamics of U.S. mobile gaming market.* http://www.comscore.com/Press_Events/Press_Releases/

2010/4/Smartphone_Adoption_Shifting_Dynamics_of_U.S._Mobile_Gaming_Market.

Cunningham, J. (2005). Little use of treatment among problem gamblers. *Psychiatric Services, 56,* 1024–25.

Curriculum Services Canada (CSC). (2008). Don't Bet on It–A Youth Problem ˙Gambling Prevention Program. http://curriculum.org/resources/dont-bet-on-it-8211-a-youth-problem-gambling-prevention-program.

Custer, R., and Milt, H. (1985). *When luck runs out: Help for compulsive gamblers and their families.* New York: Facts on File.

DeCaria, C. M., Hollander, E., Grossman, R., Wong, C. M., Mosovich, S. A., and Cherkasky, S. (1996). Diagnosis, neurobiology, and treatment of pathological gambling. *Journal of Clinical Psychiatry, 57*(suppl 8), 80–84.

Delfabbro, P. (2007). *Australasian Gambling Review Third Edition (1992–2007).* Adelaide: Independent Gambling Authority.

Delfabbro, P. (2009). *Australasian gambling review, Fourth Edition (1992-2008).* Adelaide: Independent Gambling Authority.

Derevensky, J. (2008). Gambling behaviors and adolescent substance use disorders. In Y. Kaminer and O. G.Buckstein (Eds.). *Adolescent substance abuse: Psychiatric comorbidity and high risk behaviors.* New York: Haworth Press, 403–33.

Derevensky, J., and Gillespie, M. (2005). Gambling in Canada. *International Journal of Mental Health and Addiction, 3*(1), 3–14.

Derevensky, J., and Gupta, R. (2000). Prevalence estimates of adolescent gambling: A comparison of the SOGS-RA, DSM-IV-J, and the G.A. 20 Questions. *Journal of Gambling Studies, 16* (2/3), 227–51.

Derevensky, J., and Gupta, R. (2004). The measurement of youth gambling problems: Current instruments, methodological issues and future directions. In J. Derevensky and R. Gupta (Eds.), *Gambling problems in youth: Theoretical and applied perspectives.* New York: Kluwer Academic/Plenum Publishers, 121–44.

Derevensky, J., and Gupta, R. (Eds.). (2004). *Gambling problems in youth: Theoretical and applied perspectives.* New York: Kluwer Academic/Plenum Publishers.

Derevensky, J., and Gupta, R. (2006). Measuring gambling problems amongst adolescents: Current status and future directions. *International Gambling Studies, 6*(2), 201–15.

Derevensky, J., and Gupta, R. (2007). Internet gambling amongst adolescents: A growing concern. *International Journal of Mental Health and Addictions, 5*(2), 93–101.

Derevensky, J., and Gupta, R. (2007). Adolescent gambling: Current knowledge, myths, assessment strategies and public policy implications. In G. Smith, D. Hodgins, and R. Williams (Eds.), *Research and measurement issues in gambling.* New York: Elsevier, 437–63.

Derevensky, J., Gupta, R., and Baboushkin, H. (2007). Underlying cognitions in children's gambling behaviour: Can they be modified? *International Gambling Studies, 7*(3), 281–98.

Derevensky, J., Gupta, R., and Della-Cioppa, G. (1996). A developmental perspective of gambling behaviour in children and adolescents. *Journal of Gambling Studies, 12*(1), 49–66.

Derevensky, J., Gupta, R., and Della-Cioppa, G. (2002). A developmental perspective on gambling behavior in children and adolescents. In J. Moratta, J. Cornelieus, and W. Eadington (Eds.), *The downside: Problem and pathological gambling.* Nevada: University of Nevada Press, 411–28.

Derevensky, J., Gupta, R., and Dickson, L. (2004). Adolescent gambling problems: Prevention and treatment implications. In J. E. Grant and M. N. Potenza (Eds.), *Understanding and treating pathological gambling.* Washington, DC: APPI Press, 159–68.

Derevensky, J., Gupta, R., Dickson, L., and Deguire, A-E. (2004). Prevention efforts toward reducing gambling problems. In J. Derevensky and R. Gupta (Eds.), *Gambling problems in youth: Theoretical and applied perspectives.* New York: Kluwer Academic/Plenum Publishers, 211–30.

Derevensky, J., Gupta, R., Dickson, L., Hardoon, K., and Deguire, A-E. (2003). Understanding youth gambling problems: A conceptual framework. In D. Romer (Ed.), *Reducing adolescent risk: Toward an integrated approach.* California: Sage Publications, 239–46.

Derevensky, J., Gupta, R., Messerlian, C. and Gillespie, M. (2004). Youth gambling problems: A need for responsible social policy. In J. Derevensky and R. Gupta (Eds.) *Gambling problems in youth: Theoretical and applied perspectives.* New York: Kluwer Academic.

Derevensky, J., Gupta, R., and Winters, K. (2003). Prevalence rates of youth gambling problems: Are the current rates inflated? *Journal of Gambling Studies, 19*(4), 405–25.

Derevensky, J., Pratt, L., Hardoon, K., and Gupta, R. (2007). The relationship between gambling problems and impulsivity among adolescents: Some preliminary data and thoughts. *Journal of Addiction Medicine, 1*(3), 165–72.

Derevensky, J., Shek,, D. T., and Merrick, J. (Eds.) (2011). *Youth gambling: the hidden addiction.* Berlin: de Gruyter.

Derevensky, J., Sklar, A., Gupta, R., and Messerlian, C. (2010). An empirical study examining the impact of gambling advertisements on adolescent gambling attitudes and behaviors. *International Journal of Mental Health and Addiction, 8,* 21–34.

Derevensky, J., Sklar, A., Gupta, R., and Messerlian, C., Laroche, M., and Mansour, S. (2007). *The effects of gambling advertisements on child and adolescent gambling attitudes and behaviors (Les effets de la publicité sur les attitudes et les comportements de jeu des enfants et des adolescents).* Fonds de recherché en santé du Québec (FRSQ), Quebec, 68 pp.

Derevensky, J., St-Pierre, R., Temcheff, C., and Gupta, R. (2011). Beliefs and attitudes of teachers with respect to youth gambling. Poster presented at the Canadian Psychological Association annual conference, Toronto, June.

Dickson, L., and Derevensky, J. (2006). Preventing adolescent problem gambling: Implications for school psychology. *Canadian Journal of School Psychology, 21*(1/2), 59–72.

Dickson, L., Derevensky, J., and Gupta, R. (2002). The prevention of youth gambling problems: A conceptual model. *Journal of Gambling Studies, 18*(2), 97–160.

Dickson, L., Derevensky, J., and Gupta, R. (2004). Youth gambling problems: A harm reduction prevention model. *Addiction Research and Theory, 12*(4), 305–16.

Dickson, L., Derevensky, J., and Gupta, R. (2004). Harm reduction for the prevention of youth gambling problems: Lessons learned from adolescent high-risk prevention programs. *Journal of Adolescent Research, 19*(2), 233–63.

Dickson, L., Derevensky, J., and Gupta, R. (2008). Youth gambling problems: An examination of risk and protective factors. *International Gambling Studies, 8*(1), 25–47.

DiClemente, C. C., and Prochaska, J. O. (1982). Self-change and therapy change of smoking behavior: A comparison of processes of change in cessation and maintenance. *Addictive Behaviors, 7*(2), 133–42.

DiClemente, C. C., Story, M., and Murray, K. (2000). On a roll: The process of initiation and cessation of problem gambling among adolescents. *Journal of Gambling Studies, 16,* 289–313.

Durham, S., and Hashimoto, K. (2010). *The history of gambling in America.* New Jersey: Prentice Hall.

Durlak, J. A. (1997). Primary prevention programs in schools. *Advances in Clinical Child Psychology, 19,* 283–318.

Ellenbogen, S., Derevensky, J., and Gupta, R. (2007). Gender differences among adolescents with gambling related problems. *Journal of Gambling Studies, 23,* 133–43.

Ellenbogen, S., Jacobs, D., Derevensky, J., Gupta, R., and Paskus, T. (2008). Gambling behavior among college athletes. *Journal of Applied Sports Psychology, 20,* 349–62.

Engel, G. L. (1977). The need for a new medical model: A challenge for biomedicine. *Science, 196*(4286), 129–36.

Faregh, N., and Derevensky, J. (2011). Prevention of impulse control disorders. In J. E. Grant and M. N. Potenza (Eds.), *Understanding impulse control disorders.* New York: Oxford University Press, 499–515.

Faregh, N., and Derevensky, J. (2011). Gambling behavior among adolescents with Attention Deficit Hyperactivity Disorder. *Journal of Gambling Studies, 27,* 243–56.

Felsher, J., Derevensky, J. and Gupta, R. (2003). Parental influences and social modeling of youth lottery participation. *Journal of Community and Applied Social Psychology, 13,* 361–77.

Felsher, J., Derevensky, J. and Gupta, R. (2004). Lottery participation by youth with gambling problems: Are lottery tickets a gateway to other gambling venues? *International Gambling Studies, 4*(2), 109–26.

Felsher, J., Derevensky, J. and Gupta, R. (2004). Lottery playing amongst youth: Implications for prevention and social policy. *Journal of Gambling Studies, 20*(2), 127–53.

Felsher, J., Derevensky, J., and Gupta, R. (2010). Young adults with gambling problems: The impact of childhood maltreatment. *International Journal of Mental Health and Addiction, 8,* 545–56.

Ferland, F., Ladouceur, R., and Vitaro, F. (2001). Prevention of problem gambling: modifying misconception and increasing knowledge. *Journal of Gambling Studies, 18,* 19–30.

Fisher, S. E. (1992). Measuring pathological gambling in children: The case of fruit machines in the UK. *Journal of Gambling Studies, 8,* 263–85.

Fisher, S. (1993). Gambling and pathological gambling in adolescents. *Journal of Gambling Studies, 9,* 277–88.

Fisher S. (2000). Developing the DSM-IV-MR-J criteria to identify adolescent problem gambling in non-clinical populations. *Journal of Gambling Studies, 16,* 253–73.

Fleming, A. (1978). *Something for nothing: A history of gambling.* New York: Delacorte Press.

Gaboury, A., and Ladouceur, R. (1993). Evaluation of a prevention program for pathological gambling among adolescents. *The Journal of Primary Prevention, 14,* 21–28.

Galambos, N. L., and Tilton-Weaver, L.C. (1998). Multiple risk behavior in adolescents and young adults. *Health Review, 10,* 9–20.

GAM-GaRD. http://www.gamgard.com.

Garboury, A., and Ladouceur, R. (1989). Erroneous perceptions and gambling. *Journal of Social Behavior and Personality, 4,* 411–20.

Gillespie, M., Derevensky, J., and Gupta, R. (2007). The utility of outcome expectancies in the prediction of adolescent gambling behavior. *Journal of Gambling Issues, 19,* 69–85.

Gillespie, M., Gupta, R., Derevensky, J., Pratt, L., and Vallerand, R. (2005). Adolescent Problem Gambling: Evaluating Perceived Risks and Benefits (Le jeu problématique chez les adolescents: perceptions des risques et des bénéfices). Report prepared for the Fonds de recherché en santé du Québec (FRSQ), Québec.

Goorney, A. B. (1968). Treatment of compulsive gambling by aversion therapy. *British Journal of Psychiatry, 114,* 329–82.

Govoni, R., Rupcich, N., and Frisch, G. R.(1996). Gambling behavior of adolescent gamblers. *Journal of Gambling Studies, 12,* 305–17.

Grant, J. E., and Kim, S. W. (2002). Effectiveness of pharmacotherapy for pathological gambling: A chart review. *Annals of Clinical Psychiatry, 14*(3), 155–61.

Grant, J. E., and Kim, S. (2002). Pharmacotherapy of pathological gambling. *Psychiatric Annals, 32,* 186–91.

Grant, J. E., Kim, S. W., and Potenza, M. N. (2003). Advances in the pharmacological treatment of pathological gambling. *Journal of Gambling Studies, 19,* 85–109.

Grant, J., Kim, S., Potenza, M., Blanco, C., Ibanez, A., Stevens, L., et al. (2003). Paroxetine treatment of pathological gambling: A multi-centre randomized controlled trial. *International Clinical Psychopharmacology, 18*(4), 243–49.

Grant, J. E., and Potenza, M. N. (2004). *Pathological gambling: A clinical guide to treatment.* Washington, DC: American Psychiatric Publishing Inc.

Grant, J. E., Potenza, J. D., Marc, N., Hollander, E., Cunningham-Williams, R., Nurminen, T., and Kallio, A. (2006). Multicenter investigation of the opioid antagonist nalmefene in the treatment of pathological gambling. *American Journal of Psychiatry, 163*(2), 303–12.

Griffiths, M. (1989). Gambling in children and adolescents. *Journal of Gambling Behavior, 5*, 66–83.

Griffiths, M. (1990). Addiction to fruit machines: A preliminary study among young males. *Journal of Gambling Studies, 6*, 113–26.

Griffiths, M. (1990). The cognitive psychology of gambling. *Journal of Gambling Studies, 6*, 31–42.

Griffiths, M. (1993). Pathological gambling: Possible treatment using an audio feedback technique. *Journal of Gambling Studies, 9*, 295–97.

Griffiths, M. (1994). An exploratory study of gambling cross addictions. *Journal of Gambling Studies, 10*, 371–84.

Griffiths, M. (1995). *Adolescent gambling*. London, UK: Routledge.

Griffiths, M. (1995). Technological addictions. *Clinical Psychology Forum, 76*, 14–19.

Griffiths, M. (1996). Pathological gambling and treatment. *British Journal of Clinical Psychology, 35*, 477–79.

Griffiths, M. (2007). Mobile phone gambling. In D. Taniar (Ed.), *Encyclopedia of mobile computing and commerce*. Pennsylvania: Information Science Reference.

Griffiths, M. (2008). Convergence of gambling and computer game playing: Implications. *E-Commerce, Law and Policy, 10*(2), 12–13.

Griffiths, M., and Barnes, A. (2008). Internet gambling: An online empirical study among student gamblers. *International Mental Health Addiction, 6*, 194–204.

Griffiths, M., and Macdonald, H. (1999). Counselling in the treatment of pathological gambling: An overview. *British Journal of Guidance and Counselling, 27*(2), 179–90.

Griffiths, M., King, D., and Delfabbro, P. (2009). Adolescent gambling-like experiences: Are they a cause for concern? *Education and Health, 27*, 27–30.

Griffiths, M., and Parke, J. (2010). Adolescent gambling on the Internet: A review. *International Journal of Adolescent Medicine and Health, 22*, 59–75.

Griffiths, M., and Sutherland, I. (1998). Adolescent gambling and drug use. *Journal of Community and Applied Social Psychology, 8*, 423–27.

Gupta, R., and Derevensky, J. (1996). The relationship between gambling and video game playing behavior in children and adolescents. *Journal of Gambling Studies, 12*(4), 375–94.

Gupta, R., and Derevensky, J. (1997). Familial and social influences on juvenile gambling. *Journal of Gambling Studies, 13*, 179–92.

Gupta, R., and Derevensky, J. (1998). Adolescent gambling behavior: A prevalence study and examination of the correlates associated with problem gambling. *Journal of Gambling Studies, 14*, 319–45.

Gupta, R., and Derevensky, J. (1998). An empirical examination of Jacobs' General Theory of Addictions: Do adolescent gamblers fit the theory? *Journal of Gambling Studies, 14*(1), 17–49.

Gupta, R., and Derevensky, J. (2000). Adolescents with gambling problems: From research to treatment. *Journal of Gambling Studies, 16*, 315–42.

Gupta, R., and Derevensky, J. (2008). A treatment approach for adolescents with gambling problems. In M. Zangeneh, A. Blaszczynski, and N. Turner (Eds.), *In the pursuit of winning*. New York: Springer.

Gupta, R., and Derevensky, J. (2008). Gambling practices among youth: Etiology, prevention and treatment. In C. A. Essau (Ed.), *Adolescent addiction: Epidemiology, assessment and treatment*. London, UK: Elsevier, 207–30.

Gupta, R., and Derevensky, J. (2011). Understanding the etiology of youth problem gambling . In J. Derevensky, D. Shek, and J. Merrick (Eds.), *Youth gambling problems: The hidden addiction*. Berlin: De Gruyter.

Gupta, R., Derevensky, J., and Ellenbogen, S. (2006). Personality characteristics and risk-taking tendencies among adolescent gamblers. *Canadian Journal of Behavioural Science, 38*(2), 201–13.

Gupta, R., Derevensky, J., and Marget, N. (2004). Coping strategies employed by adolescents with gambling problems. *Child and Adolescent Mental Health, 9*(3), 115–20.

H2 Gambling Capital. (April 2010). United States: Regulated Internet Gambling Economic Impact Reports.

H2 Gambling Capital. (April 2011). National Summary Sheet Report.

H2 Gambling Capital (2011). Report on the Mobile Gambling Market.

H2 Gambling Capital. (August 2011). Mobile Gambling Report.

Hanman, N. (2005). Placing a bet on the mobile. *The Guardian* (London). http://www.guardian.co.uk/technology/2005/feb/10/mobilephones.onlinesupplement.

Hardoon, K., Derevensky, J., and Gupta, R. (2001). Social influences involved in children's gambling behavior. *Journal of Gambling Studies, 17*(3), 191–215.

Hardoon, K., Derevensky, J., and Gupta, R. (2003). Empirical vs. perceived measures of gambling severity: Why adolescents don't present themselves for treatment. *Addictive Behaviors, 28*, 933–46.

Hardoon, K., Gupta, R., and Derevensky, J. (2004). Psychosocial variables associated with adolescent gambling: A model for problem gambling. *Psychology of Addictive Behaviors, 18*(2), 170–79.

Hodgins, D. (2001). Processes of changing gambling behavior. *Addictive Behaviors, 26*(1), 121–28.

Hodgins, D. (2004). Workbooks for individuals with gambling problems: Promoting the natural recovery process through brief intervention. In L. Abate (Ed). *Using workbooks in mental health: resources in prevention, psychotherapy, and rehabilitation for clinicians and researchers.* Binghamton, NY: The Haworth Reference Press.

Hodgins, D. (2005). Implications of a brief intervention trial for problem gambling for future outcome research. *Journal of Gambling Studies, 21*(1), 13–19.

Hodgins, D., and Diskin, K. (2008). Motivational interviewing in the treatment of problem and pathological gambling. In H. Arkowitz, W. Westra and S. Rollnick (Eds.), *Motivational interviewing in the treatment of psychological problems.* New York: Guilford Press.

Hodgins, D., and el-Guebaly, N. (2000). Natural and treatment-assisted recovery from gambling problems: a comparison of resolved and active gamblers. *Addiction, 95,* 777–89.

Hodgins, D. and Holub, A. (2007). Treatment of problem gambling. In G. Smith, D. Hodgins, and R. J. Williams (Eds). *Research and measurement issues in gambling studies.* New York: Academic Press.

Hodgins, D., and Makarchuk, K. (2003). Trusting problem gamblers: Reliability and validity of self-reported gambling behavior. *Psychology of Addictive Behaviors, 17*(3), 244–48.

Hodgins, D., and Petry, N. (2004). Cognitive and behavioral treatments. In J. Grant and M. Potenza (Eds.), *Pathological gambling: A clinical guide to treatment.* New York: American Psychiatric Association Press.

Hodgins, D., Currie, S. and el-Guebaly, N. (2001). Motivational enhancement and self-help treatments for problem gambling. *Journal of Consulting and Clinical Psychology, 69,* 50–57.

Hodgins, D., Currie, S., el-Guebaly, N., and Diskin, K. (2007). Does providing extended relapse prevention bibliotherapy to problem gamblers improve outcome? *Journal of Gambling Studies, 23,* 41–54.

Hodgins, D, Stea, J., and Grant, J. (2011). Gambling disorders. *The Lancet, 378,* 1874–84.

Hollander, E., Buchalter, A. J., and DeCaria, C. (2000). Pathological gambling. *Psychiatric Clinics of North America, 23,* 629–42.

Hollander, E., DeCaria, C., Mari, E., Wong, C., Mosovich, S., Grossman, R., and Begaz, T. (1998). Short-term single-blind Fluvoxamine treatment of pathological gambling. *American Journal of Psychiatry, 155*(12), 1781–83.

Hollander, E., Frenkel, M., DeCaria, C., Trungold, S., and Stein, D. J. (1992). Treatment of pathological gambling with clomipramine. *American Journal of Psychiatry, 149*, 710–11.

Hollander, E., Sood, E., Pallanti, S., Baldini-Rossi, N., and Baker, B. (2005). Pharmacological treatments of pathological gambling. *Journal of Gambling Studies, 21*(1), 101-110.

Huang, J-H., Jacobs, D., and Derevensky, J. (2011). DSM-based problem gambling: Increasing the odds of heavy drinking in a national sample of U.S. athletes. *Journal of Psychiatric Research, 45*, 302–8.

Huang, J-H., Jacobs, D., Derevensky, J., Gupta, R., and Paskus, T. (2007). Gambling and health risk behaviors among U.S. college student athletes: Findings from a national study. *Journal of Adolescent Health, 40*(5), 390–97.

Huang, J-H., Jacobs, D., Derevensky, J., Gupta, R., Paskus, T., and Petr, T. (2007). Pathological gambling amongst college athletes. *Journal of American College Health, 56*(2), 93–99.

iGaming Business. (2011). Mobile and online growth at Paddy Power. http://www.igamingbusiness.com/content/mobile-and-online-growth-paddy-power.

Jacobs, D. F. (1986). A general theory of addictions: A new theoretical model. *Journal of Gambling Behavior, 2*(1), 15–31.

Jacobs, D. F. (2004). Youth gambling in North America: Long-term trends and future prospects. In J. Derevensky and R. Gupta (Eds.), *Gambling problems in youth: Theoretical and applied perspectives.* New York: Kluwer Academic/Plenum Publishers.

Jacobs, D. R., Marston, A. R., Singer, R. D., Widaman, K., Little, T., and Veizades, J. (1989). Children of problem gamblers. *Journal of Gambling Behavior, 5*, 261–67.

Jacques, C., and Ladouceur, R. (2003). DSM-IV-J criteria: A scoring error that may be modifying the estimates of pathological gambling among youths. *Journal of Gambling Studies, 19*(4), 427–31.

Jessor, R. (Ed.). (1998). *New perspectives on adolescent risk behavior.* Cambridge, UK: Cambridge University Press.

Johnson, L. (2011) Mobile gambling doubles to $65.8M in 2010: Study. *Mobile Commerce Daily.* http://mobilecommercedaily.com/2011/06/30.

Kaminer, Y., Burleson, J., and Jadamec, A. (2002). Gambling behavior in adolescent substance abuse. *Substance Abuse, 23*, 191–98.

Kaminer, Y., and Haberek, R. (2004). Pathological gambling and substance abuse. *Journal of the American Academy of Child and Adolescent Psychiatry, 43*, 1326–27.

Kennedy, J. F. (July 25, 1963). Speech concerning America's appeal for UNICEF.

Korn, D., and Shaffer, H. J. (1999). Gambling and the health of the public: Adopting a public health perspective. *Journal of Gambling Studies, 15*(4), 289–365.

Ladouceur, R., Boisvert, J. M., and Dumont, J. (1994). Cognitive-behavioral treatment for adolescent pathological gamblers. *Behavior Modification, 18*, 230–42.

Ladouceur, R., and Mireault, C. (1988). Gambling behaviors amongst high school students in the Quebec area. *Journal of Gambling Studies, 4*, 3–12.

Langhinrichsen-Rohling, J., Rohling, M. L., Rohde, P., and Seeley, J. R. (2004). The SOGS-RA vs the MAGS-7: Prevalence estimates and classification congruence. *Journal of Gambling Studies, 20*(3), 259–81.

Lesieur, H. (1998). Costs and treatment of pathological gambling. *Annals of the American Academy of Social Science, 556*, 153–71.

Lesieur, H. R. (1990). *Working with and understanding Gamblers Anonymous: Working with self help.* Homewood, IL: Dorsey.

Lesieur, H. R., and Blume, S. B. (1987). The South Oaks Gambling Screen (SOGS): A new instrument for the identification of pathological gamblers. *American Journal of Psychiatry, 144*, 1184–88.

Lesieur, H. R., and Blume, S. B. (1993). Revising the South Oaks Gambling Screen in different settings. *Journal of Gambling Studies, 9*, 213–23.

Lesieur, H. R., and Klein, R. (1987). Pathological gambling among high school students. *Addictive Behaviors, 12*, 129–35.

Lussier, I., Derevensky, J., and Gupta, R. (2009). Youth gambling problems: An international perspective. In A. Browne-Miller (Ed.), *The Praeger International collection on addictions. Volume IV.* CT: Praeger, 259–80.

Lussier, I., Derevensky, J., and Gupta, R. (2009). Youth gambling prevention and resilience education: A harm reduction approach. In A. Browne-Miller (Ed.), *The Praeger International collection on addictions. Volume IV.* CT: Praeger, 339–50.

Lussier, I., Derevensky, J., Gupta, R., Bergevin, T., and Ellenbogen, S. (2007).Youth gambling behaviors: An examination of the role of resilience. *Psychology of Addictive Behaviors, 21*, 165–73.

Magoon, M., Gupta, R., and Derevensky, J. (2005). Juvenile delinquency and adolescent gambling: Implications for the juvenile justice system. *Criminal Justice and Behavior, 32(6)*, 690–713.

Magoon, M., Gupta, R., and Derevensky, J. (2007). Gambling among youth in detention centers. *Journal for Juvenile Justice and Detention Services, 21*, 17-30.

McBride, J., and Derevensky, J. (2009). Internet gambling behaviour in a sample of online gamblers. *International Journal of Mental Health and Addiction, 7*, 149–67.

McCormick, J., Delfabbro, P. and Denson, L. (2011). Pathological gambling: Understanding the role of early trauma and psychological vulnerability. Paper presented at the 8th conference on prevalence, prevention, treatment and responsible gambling, Reykjavik, Iceland.

McCown, W.G., and Howatt, W.A. (2007). *Treating gambling problems*. New York: John Wiley and Sons.

Meerkamper, E. (2010). *Youth gambling 2.0. Understanding youth gambling, emerging technologies, and social platforms*. Paper presented at the Nova Scotia Gaming Corporation 6th Annual Responsible Gambling Conference, Halifax, Nova Scotia.

Messerlian, C., Byrne, A., and Derevensky, J. (2004). Gambling, youth and the Internet: Should we be concerned? *Canadian Child and Adolescent Psychiatry Review, 13*(1), 3–6.

Messerlian, C., and Derevensky, J. (2005). Youth gambling: A public health perspective. *Journal of Gambling Issues, 14*, 97–116.

Messerlian, C., and Derevensky, J. (2006). Social marketing campaigns for youth gambling prevention: Lessons learned from youth. *International Journal of Mental Health, 4*, 294–306.

Messerlian, C., and Derevensky, J. (2007). Evaluating the role of social marketing campaigns to prevent youth gambling problems: A qualitative study. *Canadian Journal of Public Health, 98*, 101–4.

Messerlian, C., Derevensky, J., and Gupta, R. (2004). A public health perspective for youth gambling: A prevention and harm minimization framework. *International Gambling Studies, 4*(2), 147–60.

Messerlian, C., Gillespie, M., and Derevensky, J. (2007). Beyond drugs and alcohol: Including gambling in our high-risk behavior framework. *Paediatrics and Child Health, 12*(3), 199–204.

Meyer, G., Hayer, T. and Griffiths, M. (Eds.) (2009). *Problem gambling in Europe: Challenges, prevention and interventions*. New York: Springer.

Monaghan, S., and Derevensky, J. (2008). A Critical Review of the Internet Gambling Literature: Some Policy Recommendations. Report prepared for the Nova Scotia Gaming Corporation.

Monaghan, S., and Derevensky, J. (2008). An appraisal of the impact of the depiction of gambling in society on youth. *International Journal of Mental Health and Addiction, 6*, 1557–74.

Monaghan, S., Derevensky, J., and Sklar, A. (2008). Impact of gambling advertisements on children and adolescents: Policy recommendations to minimize harm. *International Gambling Studies, 22*, 252–74.

Mooss, A. (2009). *Gambling behaviors among youth involved in juvenile and family courts.* Psychology Dissertations. Paper 63. Georgia State University.

Najavits, L. M., Grymala, L. D., and George, B. (2003). Can advertising increase awareness of problem gambling: A statewide survey of impact. *Psychology of Addictive Behaviors, 17*, 324–27.

National Research Council. (1999). *Pathological gambling: A critical review.* Washington, DC: National Academy Press.

North American Training Institute. Kids Don't Gamble...Wanna Bet?–A curriculum for Grades 3-8. https://nati.org/products/index.aspx?mode =descandid=28.

Nower, L., and Blaszczynski, A. (2004). A pathways approach to treating youth gamblers. In J. Derevensky and R. Gupta (Eds.), *Gambling problems in youth: Theoretical and applied perspectives.* New York: Kluwer Academic/Plenum Publishers.

Nower, L., Gupta, R., Blaszczynski, A., and Derevensky, J. (2004). Suicidality ideation and depression among youth gamblers: A preliminary examination of three studies. *International Gambling Studies, 4*(1), 69–80.

Olason, D. T., Sigurdardottir, K. J. and Smari, J. (2006). Prevalence estimates of gambling participation and problem gambling among 16-18 year old students in Iceland: A comparison of the SOGS-RA and DSM-IV-MR-J. *Journal of Gambling Studies, 22*(1), 23–39.

Pagani, L., Derevensky, J., and Japel, C. (2009). Predicting gambling behavior in sixth grade from kindergarten. *Archives of Pediatric and Adolescent Medicine, 163*(3), 238–43.

Pagani, L., Derevensky, J., and Japel, C. (2010). Does early childhood emotional distress predict later gambling behavior? *Canadian Journal of Psychiatry, 55*, 159–65.

Pallesen, S., Molde, H., Arnestad, H., et al. (2007). Outcome of pharmacological treatments of pathological gambling: A review and meta-analysis. *Journal of Clinical Psychopharmacology, 27*, 357–64.

Partucci, C. (August 2009). *The True Statistics of Sports Gambling*. http://www.articlesbase.com/online-gambling-articles/the-true-statistics-of-sports-gambling-1097238.html.

Petry, N. (2005). *Pathological gambling: Etiology, comorbidity, and treatment*. Washington, DC: American Psychological Association.

Petry, N. (2006). Stages of change in treatment-seeking pathological gamblers. *Journal of Consulting Psychology, 73*, 312–22.

Pew Research Center. (May 2006). Gambling: As the Take Rises, So Does Public Concern. Pew Research Social Trends Reports.

Potenza, M. N. (2001). The neurobiology of pathological gambling. *Seminars in Clinical Neuropsychiatry, 6*, 217–26.

Potenza, M. (2006). Should addictive disorders include non-substance-related conditions? *Addiction, 101*(suppl 1), 142–51.

Potenza, M. N., Fiellin, D. A., Heninger, G. R., Rounsaville, C. M., and Mazure, C. M. (2002). Gambling: An addictive behavior with health and primary care implications. *Journal of General Internal Medicine, 17*, 721–32.

Potenza, M. N., Kosten, T. R., and Rounsaville, B. J. (2001). Pathological gambling. *Journal of the American Medical Association, 286*(2), 141–44.

Potenza, M. N., Steinberg, M. A., McLaughlin, S. D., Wu, R., Rounsaville, B. J., and O'Malley, S. S. (2000). Illegal behaviors in problem gambling: Analysis of data from a gambling helpline. *Journal of the American Academy of Psychiatry and the Law, 28*, 389–403.

Potenza, M. N., and Wexler, B. E. (2000). Magnetic resonance imaging used to study urges in pathological gamblers. *Report on Problem Gambling, 1*, 45–46.

Potenza, M., Xian, H., Shah, K., Scherrer, J., and Eisen, S. A. (2005). Shared genetic contributions to pathological gambling and major depression in men. *Archives of General Psychiatry, 62*(9), 1015–21.

Poulin, C. (2000). Problem gambling among adolescents in the Atlantic provinces of Canada. *Journal of Gambling Studies, 16*, 53–78.

Poulin, C., and Elliot, D. (2007). *Student Drug Use Survey in the Atlantic Provinces: Atlantic Technical Report*. Halifax: Dalhousie University, Community Health and Epidemiology.

Powell, G. J., Hardoon, K., Derevensky, J., and Gupta, R. (1999). Gambling and risk taking behavior of university students. *Substance Use and Misuse, 34*(8), 1167–84.

Prochaska, J., and DiClemente, C. (1983). Stages and processes of self-change of smoking: Toward an integrative model of change. *Journal of Consulting and Clinical Psychology, 51*(3), 390–95.

Productivity Commission. (1999). Australia's Gambling Industries. Report No. 10. Canberra: AusInfo.

Productivity Commission. (2010). Gambling, Report No. 50. Canberra: AusInfo.

Reith, G. (1999). *The age of chance in Western culture*. London: Routledge.

Romer, D. (2010). Internet gambling grows among male youth ages 18 to 22. Gambling also increases in high school age female youth. Unpublished report. Retrieved from http://www.annenbergpublicpolicycenter .org/Downloads/Releases/ACI/Card%20Playing%202010%20Release%20 final.pdf.

Rosenthal, R. J. (1987). The psychodynamics of pathological gambling: A review of the literature. In T. Galski (Ed.), *The handbook of pathological gambling*. Springfield, IL: Charles C Thomas.

Rosenthal, R. J., and Rugle, L. J. (1994). A psychodynamic approach to treatment of pathological gambling: Part I, Achieving abstinence. *Journal of Gambling Studies, 10*, 21-42.

Rugle, L., Derevensky, J., Gupta, R., Winters, K., and Stinchfield, R. (2001). The treatment of problem and pathological gamblers. Report prepared for the National Council for Problem Gambling, Center for Mental Health Services (CMHS) and the Substance Abuse Mental Health Services.

Salzmann, M. (1982). Treatment of compulsive gambling. *British Journal of Psychiatry, 66*, 28–33.

Schwartz, D. G. (2006). *Roll the bones: The history of gambling*. New York: Gotham Books.

Sevigny, S., Cloutier, M., Pelletier, M., and Ladouceur, R. (2005). Internet gambling: Misleading payout rates during the "demo" period. *Computers in Human Behavior, 21*, 153–58.

Shaffer, H. J., Hall, M. N., and Vander Bilt, J. (1997). Estimating the prevalence of disordered gambling in the United States and Canada: A meta-analysis. *American Journal of Public Health, 89*, 1369–76.

Shaffer, H. J., LaBrie, R., and LaPlante, D. (2004). Laying the foundation for quantifying regional exposure to social phenomena: Considering the case of legalized gambling as a public health toxin. *Psychology of Addictive Behaviors, 18*, 40–48.

Shaffer, H. J., LaBrie, R. A., LaPlante, D. A., Nelson, S. E., and Stanton, M. V. (2004). The road less travelled: Moving from distribution to determinants in the study of gambling epidemiology. *Canadian Journal of Psychiatry, 49*, 504–16.

Shaffer, H. J., LaBrie, R., Scanlon, K. M. and Cummings, T. N. (1994). Pathological gambling among adolescents: Massachusetts Gambling Screen (MAGS). *Journal of Gambling Studies, 10,* 339–62.

Shaffer, H. J., and Martin, R. (2011). Disordered gambling: Etiology, trajectory, and clinical considerations. *Annual Review of Clinical Psychology, 7,* 483–510.

Shead, N. W., Derevensky, J., and Meerkamper, E. (2011). Your mother should know: A comparison of maternal and paternal attitudes and behaviors related to gambling among their adolescent children. *International Journal of Mental Health and Addiction, 9,* 264–75.

Shead, N. W., Derevensky, J., and Gupta, R. (2010). Risk and protective factors associated with youth problem gambling. *International Journal of Adolescent Medicine and Health, 22*(1), 39–58.

Sklar, A., Gupta, R., and Derevensky, J. (2010). Binge gambling behaviors reported by youth in a residential drug treatment setting: A qualitative investigation. *International Journal of Adolescent Medicine and Health, 22*(1), 153–62.

Sklar, A., and Derevensky, J. (2010). Way to play: Analyzing gambling ads for their appeal to underage youth. *Canadian Journal of Communication, 35*(4), 533–54.

Slutske, W. (2006). Natural recovery and treatment-seeking in pathological gambling: Results of two U.S. national surveys. *American Journal of Psychiatry, 163,* 297–302.

Slutske, W., Caspi, A., Moffitt, T., and Poulton, R. (2005). Personality and problem gambling: A prospective study of a birth cohort of young adults. *Archives of General Psychiatry, 62*(7), 769–75.

Slutske, W. S., Eisen, S., True, W. R., Lyons, M. J., Goldberg, J., and Tsuang, M. (2000). Common genetic vulnerability for pathological gambling and alcohol dependence in men. *Archives of General Psychiatry, 57,* 666–73.

Slutske, W., Eisen, S., Xian, H., True, W., Lyons, M., Goldberg, J., and Tsuang, M. (2001). A twin study of the association between pathological gambling and antisocial personality disorder. *Journal of Abnormal Psychology, 110*(2), 297–308.

Slutske, W. S., Zhu, G., Meier, M. H., and Martin, N. G. (2010). Genetic and environmental influences on disordered gambling in men and women. *Archives of General Psychiatry, 67*(6), 624–30.

Steinberg, M. (1997). *Connecticut high school problem gambling surveys 1989 and 1996.* Guilford, CT: Connecticut Council on Problem Gambling.

Ste-Marie, C., Gupta, R., and Derevensky, J. (2002). Anxiety and social stress related to adolescent gambling behavior. *International Gambling Studies, 2*(1), 123–41.

Ste-Marie, C., Gupta, R., and Derevensky, J. (2006). Anxiety and social stress related to adolescent gambling behavior and substance use. *Journal of Child and Adolescent Substance Abuse, 16*(4), 55–74.

St-Pierre, R., Derevensky, J., Gupta, R., and Martin, I. (2011). Preventing lottery ticket sales to minors: Factors influencing retailers' compliance behavior. *International Gambling Studies, 11*, 173–92.

Stewart, D. O. (May 2011). Online Gambling Five Years After UIGEA. American Gaming Association White Paper.

Stewart, S. H, Kushner, M. G. (2003). Recent research on the comorbidity of alcoholism and pathological gambling. *Alcoholism Clinical and Experimental Research, 27*(2), 285–91.

Stinchfield, R. (2000). Gambling and correlates of gambling among Minnesota public school students. *Journal of Gambling Studies, 16*, 153–73.

Stinchfield R. (2001). A comparison of gambling among Minnesota public school students in 1992, 1995 and 1998. *Journal of Gambling Studies, 17*(4), 273–96.

Stinchfield, R. (2001). Reliability, validity, and classification accuracy of the South Oaks Gambling Screen (SOGS). *Addictive Behaviors, 27*, 1–19.

Stockwell, T., Gruenewald, P. J., Toumbourou, J. W. (2005). *Preventing harmful substance use: The evidence base for policy and practice.* New York: Wiley.

Temcheff, C., Derevensky, J., and Paskus, T. (2011). Pathological and disordered gambling: A comparison of the DSM-IV and DSM-V criteria. *International Gambling Studies, 11*, 213–20.

Thompson, W. (2001). *Gambling in America: An encyclopedia of history, issues and society.* California: ABC-CLIO.

Toneatto, T. (1999). Cognitive psychopathology of problem gambling. *Substance Use and Misuse, 34*, 1593–604.

Toneatto, T. (2002). Cognitive therapy for problem gambling. *Cognitive and Behavioral Practice, 9*, 191–99.

Toneatto, T., and Ladouceur, R. (2003). Treatment of pathological gambling: A critical review of the literature. *Psychology of Addictive Behaviors, 17*, 284–92.

Turchi, R. M., and Derevensky, J. (2006). Youth gambling: Not a safe bet. *Current Opinions in Pediatrics, 18*(4), 454–58.

Turner, N. E., Macdonald, J., and Somerset, M. (2008). Life skills, mathematical reasoning and critical thinking: A curriculum for the prevention of problem gambling. *Journal of Gambling Studies, 24*(3), 367–80.

Vachon, D., and Bagby, R. (2009). Pathological gambling subtypes. *Psychological Assessment, 21*, 608–15.

van Hamel, A., Derevensky, J., Dickson, L., and Gupta, R. (2007). Adolescent gambling and coping within a generalized high-risk behaviour framework. *Journal of Gambling Studies, 23*(4), 377–93.

Vitaro, F., Arseneault, L., and Tremblay, R. (1999). Impulsivity predicts problem gambling in low SES adolescent males. *Addiction, 94*(4), 565–75.

Vitaro, F., Brendgen, M., Ladouceur, R., and Tremblay, R. E. (2001). Gambling, delinquency, and drug use during adolescence: Mutual influences and common risk factors. *Journal of Gambling Studies, 17*(3), 171–90.

Vitaro, F., Ladouceur, R., and Bujold, A. (1996). Predictive and concurrent correlates of gambling in early adolescent boys. *Journal of Early Adolescence, 16*, 211–28.

Vitaro, F., Wanner, B., Ladouceur, R., Brendgen, M., and Trembay, R. E. (2004). Trajectories of gambling during adolescence. *Journal of Gambling Studies, 20*, 47-69.

Volberg, R. (2002). The epidemiology of pathological gambling. *Psychiatric Annals, 32*(3), 171–78.

Volberg, R., Gupta, R., Griffiths, M., Olason, D., and Delfabbro, P. (2010). An international perspective on youth gambling prevalence studies. *International Journal of Adolescent Medicine and Health, 22*, 3–38.

Walker, M. B. (1993). Treatment strategies for problem gambling: A review of effectiveness. In W. Eadington and J. Cornelius (Eds.), *Gambling behavior and problem gambling*. Reno, NV: Institute for the Study of Gambling and Commercial Gaming.

Welte J. W., Barnes, G. M., Tidwell, M. O., and Hoffman, J. H. (2008). The prevalence of problem gambling among U.S. adolescents and young adults: Results from a national survey. *Journal of Gambling Studies, 24*, 119–33.

Welte, J. W., Barnes, G. M., Tidwell, M. O., and Hoffman, J. H. (2009). The association of form of gambling with problem gambling among American youth. *Psychology of Addictive Behaviors, 23*, 105–12.

Welte, J. W., Barnes, G. M., Tidwell, M. O., and Hoffman, J. H. (2011). Gambling and problem gambling across the lifespan. *Journal of Gambling Studies, 27*, 49–61.

Welte J.W., Barnes, G.M., Wieczorek, W.F., Tidwell, M.C., and Parker, J. (2001). Alcohol and gambling pathology among U.S. adults: prevalence, demographic patterns and comorbidity. *Journal of Studies on Alcohol and Drugs, 62*(5), 706–12.

Welte, J W., Barnes, G. M., Wieczorek, W., Tidwell, M. C., and Parker, J. (2002). Gambling participation in the U.S. Results from a national survey. *Journal of Gambling Studies, 18*(4), 313–37.

Welte, J. W., Barnes, G. M., Wieczorek, W., Tidwell, M., and Parker, J. (2004). Risk factors for pathological gambling. *Addictive Behaviors, 29*(2), 323–35.

Wiebe J., Wynne, H., Stinchfield, R., and Tremblay, J. (2005). Measuring problem gambling in adolescent populations: Phase I report. Canadian Centre on Substance Abuse.

Wiebe J., Wynne, H., Stinchfield, R., and Tremblay, J. (2007). The Canadian Adolescent Gambling Inventory (CAGI): Phase II Final Report. Canadian Centre on Substance Abuse, Available at: http://www. gamblingresearch .org.

Williams, R. J., Connolly, D., Wood, R. T., Currie, S. and Davis, R. M. (2004). Program findings that inform curriculum development for the prevention of problem gambling. *Gambling Research, 16*, 47–69.

Williams, R.J., Simpson, R.I., and West, B. (2007). Prevention of problem gambling. In G. Smith, D.C. Hodgins and R.J. Williams (Eds.). *Research and measurement issues in gambling studies*. New York: Academic Press.

Williams, R.J., Wood, R.T., and Currie, S. (2010). *"Stacked Deck": An effective high school curriculum to prevent problem gambling*. Lethbridge: Authors.

Winters, K. C., and Anderson, N. (2000). Gambling involvement and drug use among adolescents. *Journal of Gambling Studies, 16*, 175–98.

Winters, K.C., Stinchfield, R., and Fulkerson, J. (1993). Patterns and characteristics of adolescent gambling. *Journal of Gambling Studies, 9*(4), 371–86.

Wittkowski, D. (2011). Trump Taj Mahal is giving away $25,000 worth of plastic surgery. Retrieved from: http://www.pressofatlanticcity.com/news/breaking/trump-taj-mahal-is-giving-away-worth-of-plastic-surgery/article_d7a03018-eab3-11e0-960a-001cc4c03286.html.

Wood, R., and Williams, R. (2009). *Internet gambling: Prevalence, patterns, problems, and policy options*. Guelph, Ontario: Ontario Problem Gambling Research Center.

World Health Organization. (1990). *International classification of diseases (ICD-10)*. Geneva: World Health Organization.

Wynne, H., Smith, G., and Jacobs, D. (1996). *Adolescent gambling and prob-lem gambling in Alberta*. Alberta Alcohol and Drug Abuse Commission.

Young, M., Tyler, B., and Lee, W. (2007). Destination-style gambling–A review of the literature concerning the reduction of problem gambling and related social harm through the consolidation of gambling supply structures. Report prepared for the Department of Justice, Victoria Government.

INDEX

ABOUT THE AUTHOR

Jeffrey L. Derevensky is professor and director of clinical training in the School/Applied Child Psychology Program, professor of Psychiatry, and co-director of the International Centre for Youth Gambling Problems and High-Risk Behaviors at McGill University in Montreal.